Lecture Notes in Artificial Intelligence   7471

Subseries of Lecture Notes in Computer Science

LNAI Series Editors

Randy Goebel
  University of Alberta, Edmonton, Canada
Yuzuru Tanaka
  Hokkaido University, Sapporo, Japan
Wolfgang Wahlster
  DFKI and Saarland University, Saarbrücken, Germany

LNAI Founding Series Editor

Joerg Siekmann
  DFKI and Saarland University, Saarbrücken, Germany

T0216178

Martin Beer   Cyril Brom   Frank Dignum
Von-Wun Soo (Eds.)

Agents for Educational Games and Simulations

International Workshop, AEGS 2011
Taipei, Taiwan, May 2, 2011
Revised Papers

 Springer

Series Editors

Randy Goebel, University of Alberta, Edmonton, Canada
Jörg Siekmann, University of Saarland, Saarbrücken, Germany
Wolfgang Wahlster, DFKI and University of Saarland, Saarbrücken, Germany

Volume Editors

Martin Beer
Sheffield Hallam University, UK
E-mail: m.beer@shu.ac.uk

Cyril Brom
Charles University in Prague, Czech Republic
E-mail: brom@ksvi.mff.cuni.cz

Frank Dignum
Utrecht University, The Netherlands
E-mail: f.p.m.dignum@uu.nl

Von-Wun Soo
National Tsing Hua University, Hsinchu, Taiwan
E-mail: soo@cs.nthu.edu.tw

ISSN 0302-9743   e-ISSN 1611-3349
ISBN 978-3-642-32325-6   e-ISBN 978-3-642-32326-3
DOI 10.1007/978-3-642-32326-3
Springer Heidelberg Dordrecht London New York

Library of Congress Control Number: 2012943170

CR Subject Classification (1998): I.2, H.5, H.4, D.2.8, D.2, H.3, C.2

LNCS Sublibrary: SL 7 – Artificial Intelligence

Typesetting: Camera-ready by author, data conversion by Scientific Publishing Services, Chennai, India

Printed on acid-free paper

Springer is part of Springer Science+Business Media (www.springer.com)

Preface

This book consists mainly of revised papers that were presented at the Agents for Educational Games and Simulations (AEGS) workshop held on May 2, 2011, as part of Autonomous Agents and MultiAgent Systems (AAMAS) conference in Taipei. This was the latest of a series of workshops that have been held at AAMAS conferences covering different aspects of how agents interact with humans in a variety of situations. Examples of these can be found in various human activities, such as in education, business transactions, military operations, medical care, and crisis management. Human–agent interaction is particularly important where training and support can be provided effectively using serious games and simulations. The role of agents to model and simulate naturally behaving characters becomes more and more important in these types of games and simulations. This is especially true where the games are not just meant to provide fun, but are used to support the learning process.

The workshop brought together various aspects of current work in this area. It was divided into four sessions:

– Middleware Applications
– Dialogues and Learning
– Adaption and Convergence
– Agent Applications

Three papers were presented in the first session, Middleware Applications. The first by Ranathunga et al. entitled "Interfacing a Cognitive Agent Platform with Second Life" describes how the authors developed a framework to facilitate agent-based interactions on the basis of the JASON BDI interpreter within the popular Second Life virtual world. In their paper "CIGA: A Middleware for Intelligent Agents in Virtual Environments," Van Oijen et al. present CIGA, a middleware to facilitate this coupling by tackling the design issues in a structured approach, not only for embodied agent design but also for the system as a whole. In "How to Compare Usability of Techniques for the Specification of Virtual Agents' Behavior? An Experimental Pilot Study with Human Subjects," Gemrot et al., investigate the effectiveness of using a high-level AI system, POSH, to program behaviors against using Java. While their results were inconclusive, in that POSH outperforms Java in one task but not the other, they discuss the lessons learnt from the evaluation process and propose possible improvements to the experimental design.

The second session considered Dialogues and Learning and again consisted of three papers. In "Dialog Designs in Virtual Drama: Balancing Agency and Scripted Dialogs," Kao and Von-Wun Soo present a speech-based dialogue generation framework to define the relationship between dialogues and story plots. In "Learning by Playing in Agent-Oriented Virtual Learning Environment," Cai and Shen propose an agent-oriented virtual learning environment to support a new learning by playing paradigm, in which each learning object is built up as a goal of a goal-oriented learning agent. In "Collection and Analysis of Multimodal Interaction in Direction Giving Dialogues: Toward an Automatic Gesture Selection Mechanism for Met-averse Avatars," Tsukamoto et al. report an empirical study designed to build a spatial gesture mechanism in Metaverse avatars (the avatars used in Second Life).

In the third session, entitled Adaption and Convergence, Westra et al. discussed "Organizing Scalable Adaptation in Serious Games" and show that using agent organizations to coordinate the agents is scalable, allowing adaptation in very complex scenarios while ensuring that the storyline is preserved at the right difficulty level for the trainee. Chien and Soo investigated how dialogical interactions affect the mental states of individual agents, and the relations between them in "Inferring Pragmatics from Dialogue Contexts in Simulated Virtual Agent Games." Alvarez-Napagao et al. propose an extension of their framework to support emergent narrative in games in "Socially Aware Emergent Narrative." An additional paper by Wißner et al., "Increasing Learners' Motivation Through Pedagogical Agents: The Cast of Virtual Characters in the DynaLearn ILE," describes different character roles; how their knowledge is generated and related to the pedagogical purpose at hand; how they interact with the learners; and finally how this interaction helps increase the learners' motivation.

The final session considered Agent Applications. Two papers were presented. Hadad and Rosenfeld in "ADAPT: Abstraction Hierarchies to Better Simulate Teamwork Under Dynamics" present a lightweight teamwork implementation by using abstraction hierarchies. The basis of this implementation is ADAPT, which supports **A**utonomous **D**ynamic **A**gent **P**lanning for **T**eamwork. ADAPT succinctly decomposes teamwork problems into two separate planners: a **task** network for the set of activities to be performed by a specific agent and a separate **group** network for addressing team organization factors. Finally Campano et al. in "An Architecture for Affective Behaviour Based on the Conservation of Resources" offer a model for autonomous virtual agents that enables them to adopt behaviors that can be perceived by human observers as emotional.

We would like to thank all the authors, the Program Committee and the referees, without whose help and hard work, we would not have been able to run a successful workshop.

May 2012

Frank Dignum
Martin Beer
Von-Wun Soo
Cyril Brom

Organization

Program Committee

Martin Beer	Sheffield Hallam University, UK
Cyril Brom	Charles University, Czech Republic
Frank Dignum	Utrecht University, The Netherlands
Von-Wun Soo	National Tsing Hua University, Taiwan

Table of Contents

Interfacing a Cognitive Agent Platform
with Second Life

Surangika Ranathunga, Stephen Cranefield, and Martin Purvis

Department of Information Science, University of Otago,
P.O. Box 56, Dunedin 9054, New Zealand
{surangika,scranefield,mpurvis}@infoscience.otago.ac.nz

Abstract. Second Life is a popular multi-purpose online virtual world that provides a rich platform for remote human interaction. It is increasingly being used as a simulation platform to model complex human interactions in diverse areas, as well as to simulate multi-agent systems. It would therefore be beneficial to provide techniques allowing high-level agent development tools, especially cognitive agent platforms such as belief-desire-intention (BDI) programming frameworks, to be interfaced to Second Life. This is not a trivial task as it involves mapping potentially unreliable sensor readings from complex Second Life simulations to a domain-specific abstract logical model of observed properties and/or events. This paper investigates this problem in the context of agent interactions in a multi-agent system simulated in Second Life. We present a framework that facilitates the connection of any multi-agent platform with Second Life, and demonstrate it in conjunction with an extension of the Jason BDI interpreter.

1   Introduction

Second Life [1] is a popular multi-purpose online virtual world that is increasingly being used as a simulation platform to model complex human interactions in diverse areas such as eduction, business, medical and entertainment. This is mainly because of the rich platform it provides for remote human interactions, including the possibility of enabling software-controlled agents to interact with human-controlled agents. Second Life is more sophisticated than conventional 2D simulation tools, and is more convenient than cumbersome robots, thus it has started to gain attention as a simulation platform for testing multi-agent systems and other AI concepts. Because of its provisions for creating simulations for a multitude of scenarios, Second Life is more suitable for agent-based simulations compared to simulations created in game-based virtual environments such as UnrealTournament. It would therefore be beneficial to provide techniques allowing high-level agent development tools, especially cognitive agent platforms such as belief-desire-intention (BDI) programming frameworks, to be interfaced with Second Life.

When interfacing agent platforms with Second Life, there are two important issues to be addressed: how the sensor readings from Second Life environments

M. Beer et al. (Eds.): AEGS 2011, LNAI 7471, pp. 1–21, 2012.

are mapped to a domain-specific abstract logical model of observed properties and/or events, and how the agent actions are performed in the Second Life virtual environment. The first aspect can be quite complex when considering the high volumes of potentially unreliable sensor readings an agent receives. This is essentially the problem of identifying a suitable abstraction level to present the low-level data received from a virtual world to the agent, as identified by research related to virtual worlds [2,3,4]. As for the second issue, it is important to identify ways of correctly interfacing the agents with their representation module inside Second Life (the Second Life avatar), because Second Life may have synchronisation issues with respect to carrying out the actions specified by the agent model.

With the use of the LIBOMV client library [5], we have developed a framework that facilitates the connection of any multi-agent framework with Second Life and addresses the above challenges. The main focus of this paper is to highlight the importance and difficulty of creating an abstract logical model of the sensory inputs of an agent deployed in Second Life, and to present the solution we developed in our connection framework to address this problem. We propose two mechanisms that lead to the creation of an abstract logical model of the low-level data received from Second Life, and note that these solutions are general enough to be used in the context of other virtual worlds.

Creating a high-level abstract logical model of agent sensory data involves two main steps: extracting sensory readings from Second Life accurately, and formulating a high-level domain-specific abstract logical model to be passed to an agent's cognitive module. The latter has not gained much attention in the research on deploying intelligent agents inside Second Life.

In our framework, an agent deployed in Second Life can sense the Second Life environment around it with the use of its LIBOMV client, and the framework records these sensor readings. There are some difficulties in obtaining accurate sensor readings from Second Life simulations. Therefore we have introduced a novel technique in our framework, which extracts sensor readings from Second Life more accurately than the commonly used data extraction methods.

The extracted sensory data result in a high volume of low-level information (avatar and object position information and avatar animation information), making it difficult to directly use these data in an agent's reasoning process. It may also result in generating a cognitive overload for an agent [4]. However, generating a complete picture of the environment around an agent is also important in identifying information at different abstraction levels.

We present a data amalgamation mechanism that generates snapshots of a given Second Life environment based on the individually received data items. In order to convert this low-level information into a suitable abstraction level that can be used by the multi-agent system, we first process it to identify 'contextual information' mainly based on the spatial relationships of avatars and objects. This contextual information is also included in the snapshot. We then employ a complex event processing mechanism on these snapshots, and identify the high-level temporally correlated complex events. To the best of our knowledge no previous research has attempted this approach to close the information representation gap between virtual worlds and agent systems.

The output of the framework is a snapshot of the Second Life environment that contains all the low-level and high-level events and other contextual information that took place in a given instant of time, encoded as propositions. This provides an agent a complete view of the environment around it, thus eliminating the possibility of having to base its reasoning on a partial set of data. At this level, it is also possible to remove low-level data received from Second Life, thus reducing the amount of data being sent to the agent.

We also note that our framework facilitates the co-existence of agents belonging to multiple agent platforms in the same Second Life simulation. In this paper, we demonstrate this framework in conjunction with an extension of the Jason BDI interpreter that allows agents to specify their expectations of future outcomes in the system and to respond to fulfilments and violations of these expectations [6]. An agent may base its practical reasoning on the assumption that one or more of its expectations will hold, while ensuring that it will receive notification events when these rules are fulfilled and/or violated.

With the extended functionality of the Jason platform, we demonstrate how a Jason agent deployed in Second Life using our framework can take part in complex simulations. We also demonstrate how the identification of high-level abstract information helps in making the agent more reactive to the important events taking place around it, and respond to the received percepts from Second Life, as well as to the identified fulfilments and violations of its expectations. The fulfilments and violations of an agent's expectations are detected by an expectation monitor [7] that is integrated with the framework through an interface, and the agent's expectations are defined as temporal logic formulae to be monitored by the expectation monitor. The framework forwards the processed sensory readings from Second Life to both the Jason environment and the expectation monitor. Therefore, in parallel to a Jason agent being able to respond to the observed changes in the environment, the expectation monitor matches these changes with the monitored formulae and identifies the fulfilment or violation of the defined expectations. The notifications of the identified fulfilments or violations are also passed to the Jason agent, and the agent can have plans that respond to these identified fulfilments and violations.

The rest of the paper is organised as follows. Section 2 describes the potential of Second Life as a simulation environment and the related implementation problems. Section 3 describes the developed framework and in Section 4, we demonstrate this developed system by means of an example. Section 5 discusses some related work. Section 6 concludes the paper.

2   Second Life as a Simulation Environment

Second Life provides a sophisticated and well developed virtual environment for creating simulations for different domains and to test AI theories, including agent-based modelling. With the average monthly repeated user logins at around

800000[1], and with the virtual presence of many organisations [8], Second Life contains many interaction possibilities, which inherently lead to the provision of new scenarios to be used in simulations. Second Life is not restricted to a specific gaming or training scenario. Developers can create a multitude of scenarios as they wish, using the basic building blocks that are provided. For example, in Second Life, these scenarios could be in the areas of education, business, entertainment, health or games. The significance of using Second Life scenarios lies in the fact that they can be carried out between software-controlled agents, and also between software-controlled agents and human-controlled agents.

Second Life has been identified as a good simulation platform for testing AI theories [9] and specifically multi-agent systems [10]. A detailed analysis on the benefits of using Second Life over traditional 2D simulations and physical robots has also been done [9], with the main advantage reported being the ability to create sophisticated test beds in comparison to 2D simulations, and more cost effective test beds compared to physical robots. The ability to create different simulations makes Second Life a better platform for agent-based simulations, compared to other game-based virtual environments. For example, researchers trying to adopt the UnrealTournament game environment for a non-game simulation have reported the difficulty in creating such general purpose agent simulations in UnrealTournament [11]. Using game engines such as UnrealTournament containing violent actions is identified to be limiting AI related research [12].

Despite this, still we do not see Second Life being used for complex simulations of AI theories or multi-agent systems modelling. The lack of use of Second Life as a simulation environment for AI research can be, to a certain extent, attributed to the previous lack of a convenient programming interface. Traditional programming in Second Life is done using in-world scripts created using the proprietary *Linden Scripting Language (LSL)*. These scripts are associated with objects, and in order to use them to control an agent inside Second Life, the objects should be attached to the agent. This approach has many limitations when used for AI simulations, for reasons such as the limited control over the agent wearing the scripted object. We discuss this in more detail in Section 2.1.

With the development of the third party library LibOpenMetaverse (LIBOMV), Second Life can now be accessed through a more sophisticated programming interface. LIBOMV is a ".Net based client/server library used for accessing and creating 3D virtual worlds" [5], and is compatible with the Second Life communication protocol. Using the LIBOMV client-side API, "bots" can be defined to control avatars in Second Life. With appropriate programming techniques, the LIBOMV library can be used to create avatars that have behavioural abilities similar to those controlled by humans. This includes moving abilities such as walking, running or flying, performing animations such as crying, or laughing, communication abilities using instant messaging or public chat channels, and the ability to sense the environment.

---

[1] http://community.secondlife.com/t5/Featured-News/
The-Second-Life-Economy-in-Q4-2010/ba-p/674618

2.1   Challenges in Monitoring Agent Interactions in Second Life

For Second Life simulations that contain a lot of agents and objects moving at speed, there is a challenge in retrieving accurate position information at a high frequency to make sure that important events are not missed out.

Although an in-world sensor created using an LSL script can retrieve accurate position information of avatars and objects, it has limitations when extracting position and animation information of a large number of moving objects and avatars. A sensor can detect only 16 avatars and/or objects in one sensor function call, and the maximum sensor range is 96 metres. One approach to overcoming this problem is to employ multiple sensors; however multiple scripts operating for long durations at high frequency introduce "lag" to the Second Life servers[2], i.e. they slow the rate of simulation. For the same reason, and because of the imposed memory limitations on scripts, an LSL script cannot undertake complex data processing, and since there is no provision to store the recorded data in-world at runtime, recorded data must be communicated outside the Second Life servers using HTTP requests, which are throttled to a maximum of only 25 requests per 20 seconds. Moreover, there is a possibility that avatar animations with a shorter duration (e.g. crying or blowing a kiss) may go undetected, because a sensor can record only animations that are played during the sensor operation.

With a LIBOMV client deployed in Second Life, all the aforementioned limitations can be avoided. Avatar and object movements and avatar animations inside a Second Life environment generate corresponding update events in the Second Life server, and the server passes this information to the LIBOMV client using the Second Life communication protocol. The processing of this information is done outside the Second Life servers, thus causing no server lag.

However, this approach does have its own limitations that affect the accuracy of recorded information. As with other viewer clients, the Second Life server sends information to the LIBOMV client only if there is any change in the environment perceived by the LIBOMV client. This means that the client has to "assume" its perceived environment. For objects and avatars that are moving, the client has to keep on extrapolating their position values based on the previously received velocity and position values until it receives an update from the server. Extrapolated position values may not be completely in tally with the server-sent values and this situation is evident when extrapolating position values for objects and avatars that move fast. Moreover, it was noted that there is an irregularity in the recorded position data for small objects that may easily go out of the viewing range of the LIBOMV client, which directly affects the recording of accurate position information for small objects.

In order to overcome these challenges, we introduce a combined approach (described in Section 3) based on attaching an object containing an LSL script to a LIBOMV client deployed in Second Life. These communicate with each other and produce near-accurate position information about avatars and objects that move at speed.

---

[2] http://lslwiki.net/lslwiki/wakka.php?wakka=lag

Both LSL-based and LIBOMV-based data extraction mechanisms only generate low-level position and animation information, making it difficult for a multi-agent system to directly utilise the retrieved data. Therefore the retrieved data should be further processed to identify the high-level domain-specific information embedded in the low-level data. In doing this, it is important that the data collected using the LIBOMV client and the LSL script are formed into one coherent snapshot that resembles the state of the Second Life environment. When deducing the high-level domain-specific information, it is important that these coherent snapshots are used, in order to make use of all the events and other related information that took place in a given instant of time. Otherwise an agent's decision may be based on partial information.

3   System Design

Figure 1 shows how different components of the system are interfaced with each other. The LIBOMV client creates and controls an avatar inside the Second Life server. It continuously senses the environment around it, and carries out movement, animation and communication acts as instructed and passes back the result notifications to the connected agent module whenever necessary (e.g. the result notification of the login attempt). We have used the Jason agent development platform [13], which is based on the BDI agent model, to demonstrate the integration of multi-agent platforms with Second Life using our framework. Here, a Jason agent acts as the coordinator component of this system. It instantiates the LIBOMV client to create the corresponding Second Life avatar, and commands the LIBOMV client to carry out actions inside Second Life on behalf of it.

3.1   The Extended Jason Platform

The Jason platform we have integrated with the framework is an extended version [6] of Jason. The Jason agent platform contains an environment interface that facilitates the easy integration of Jason agents with other simulations. With this interface, it is possible to execute agent actions in an external simulated environment and it is also possible to retrieve the sensory readings of the simulated environment to be presented as percepts for agents.

The extended version of the Jason architecture used in this work implements a tight integration of expectation monitoring with the Jason BDI agent model. With this Jason extension, domain-specific individual agents can directly react to the identified fulfilments and violations of their expectations, by specifying plans that are executed in response to those fulfilments and violations. The Jason interpreter is extended with built-in actions to initiate and terminate monitoring of expectations, and with these built in actions, any expectation monitoring tool can be "plugged in" to the Jason environment.

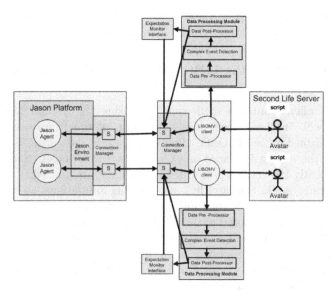

Fig. 1. Overall System Design

3.2   Interface between the LIBOMV Client and the Jason Agent

The interface between the LIBOMV client and the Jason agent is facilitated using a simple protocol we have developed (which we intend to develop further), and they communicate through sockets (denoted by 'S' in Figure 1). This decoupling makes it possible to connect any agent platform with the LIBOMV clients easily, and it could well be the case that different LIBOMV clients are connected with agents in different agent platforms. The protocol currently defines how an agent should pass commands to the LIBOMV client such as requesting the LIBOMV client to log into the Second Life server, uttering something in the public chat channels, sending instant messages to other avatars, moving to a given location and executing an animation. It also defines how an agent platform can interpret a message sent by the LIBOMV client. These messages mainly consist of the snapshots generated by our framework. The Jason environment class makes use of this protocol and converts the agent actions into the corresponding protocol constructs and passes them to the LIBOMV client. Similarly, it interprets the messages sent by LIBOMV clients to generate percepts for the Jason agents.

The module that contains LIBOMV clients is capable of handling multiple concurrent LIBOMV clients and socket connections. Therefore, if the corresponding multi-agent system is capable of creating concurrently operating agents, this can easily create a multi-agent simulation inside Second Life. Consequently, the module that contains the Jason platform is designed in such a way that it is capable of handling multiple concurrent instances of socket connections connected to the Jason agents. As shown in Figure 1, a Jason agent connects to its interface socket through the Jason Environment class, and the Jason Connection Manager interface. The Jason connection manager and the LIBOMV connection manager together ensure that all these individual Jason agents are connected to the correct LIBOMV client, through the interface sockets.

3.3   Interface between the LIBOMV Client and the Second Life Server

The LIBOMV client connects to Second Life using the Second Life communication protocol. In the current implementation of the framework, we have mainly focused on how a LIBOMV client can extract data from Second Life. Consequently, the emphasis placed on executing agent actions in Second Life is minimal. Currently the actions performed by an agent are limited to performing movements (stand, walk, run, and fly), and playing animations.

As an attempt to overcome the limitations of data extraction using LSL and LIBOMV, we have implemented a combined approach to extract data from Second Life. In this new approach, a scripted object is attached to the bot deployed in Second Life, as shown in Figure 1.

The LIBOMV client detects avatars and objects in its viewing range and records their UUIDs. It then sends this UUID list to the script. The LIBOMV client continuously checks for new avatars or objects that entered the Second Life environment or simulation, based on the movement and animation updates it receives. Whenever a new avatar or an object is detected, the UUID list is updated with the newly found UUID, and the list is sent to the script. This makes sure newly arrived avatars and objects are also detected. Since the script receives UUIDs of the avatars and objects, it can use the llGetObjectDetails LSL function to extract position and velocity information for the corresponding avatar and or object. llGetObjectDetails is a light-weight function and is much faster than the sensor operation because it is sensing a given set of avatars and objects. This function is repetitively called for the UUIDs in the received string. When trying to locate an avatar or an object, this function covers the entire Second Life "region". The llGetObjectDetails is executed by a timer and the collected data are sent back to the LIBOMV client. The timer interval can be decided according to the requirements of the simulation. If the llGetObjectDetails function cannot detect an avatar or an object specified by a given UUID, an empty string is returned instead of the recorded position and velocity information. In this case, the corresponding UUID is removed from the globally maintained UUID list and the list is re-sent to the script, in order to avoid searching for avatars or objects that are no longer there.

This function cannot detect the animation that an avatar is currently playing. Therefore we use the LIBOMV client to directly receive the animation changes of avatars. Communication taking place in the public chat channel is also captured directly by the LIBOMV client. In this combined approach, the accuracy of extracted movement data is high, because the position extraction is done on the server side. The extracted values are always server-generated, rather than extrapolated by the client to predict the positions of objects and avatars.

Because of the light-weight nature of the script, it does not introduce any noticeable lag on the Second Life servers [14].

3.4   Data Processing Module

The data processing module consists of three main components; the data pre-processor, the complex event detection module and the data post-processor. The responsibility of the data processing module is to map the received sensor readings from complex Second Life environments to a domain-specific abstract logical model. In essence, it creates snapshots of the system that include low-level movement and animation information of avatars and movement information of objects in the given Second Life environment in a given instant of time, along with the identified high-level domain-specific information and other contextual information, which are encoded as propositions.

Data Pre-processor: The responsibility of the data pre-processor is to amalgamate data received from the different sources (LSL script, animation and message updates) and create a coherent snapshot that represents the state of the Second Life environment at a given instant of time. It is also responsible for identifying the domain-specific 'contextual information' of a simulation.

As mentioned above, the LIBOMV client receives movement information of objects and avatars from the script, and updates corresponding to avatar animations and communication messages are directly captured by the LIBOMV client. This means that a received movement information update does not contain the information about the current animation of the avatars, and the received animation and message updates do not contain the information about the current position or velocity of the avatar. Moreover, these animation and communication updates do not contain the movement information of other avatars and objects in the environment, or animation information of avatars. However, whenever an update is received by the LIBOMV client (whether it be the movement updates from the script, or an animation or a communication update), it is important that we create a snapshot that contains movement and animation information of all the avatars and objects of interest, in order to make it a complete snapshot representing the Second Life environment.

Therefore the data pre-processor caches the latest received animation and movement information for all the avatars and objects of interest. When a new set of movement information is received from the script, for all the avatars that have a movement record in that received information set, their cached animation values are associated with the received movement information. The LIBOMV client receives an update corresponding to every avatar animation change (e.g. if an avatar is currently standing and suddenly starts running, the LIBOMV client receives an animation update 'run'). Therefore it is safe to assume that an avatar keeps on performing the animation already recorded in the cache. When an animation update is received for an avatar, it is associated with the extrapolated movement information of that avatar, based on the cached movement information. If the frequency of the position updates received from the script is high, the extrapolation error can be assumed to be very low. We also generate the movement and animation information of other avatars and objects in that Second Life environment, for the time instant represented by that received animation update.

This is because a received animation update does not contain any information related to other avatars and objects in that simulation, as mentioned earlier. Whenever, a communication message is received by the LIBOMV client, the movement and animation information of avatars and objects are generated for the time instant corresponding to that communication update, using the cached information. Thus, for every set of movement information sent by the script and every animation and communication message update sent by the Second Life server, the data pre-processor generates a complete snapshot of the environment that contains the avatar and object movement information and avatar animation information. These snapshots can be easily distinguished from each other with the use of the associated timestamp.

The low-level data included in a snapshot are used to deduce basic high-level information about avatars and objects, which are termed 'contextual information'. Contextual information is the first level of abstraction identified on the data received from Second Life. Contextual information depends on the avatar and object relations that are identified at a given instant of time (i.e. in a single snapshot), and makes the complex event identification easy. Some of the contextual information that can be identified are whether an avatar is moving, and if so, in which direction and the movement type (e.g. walking, running or flying), and whether an avatar is in close proximity to another avatar or an object of interest. Other contextual information such as the location of the avatar or the role it is playing can also be attached to this retrieved information as needed. As the nature of contextual information that should be identified depends on a given simulation, the related logic is included in a script that is dynamically linked with the data pre-processor. It is also possible to make use of pre-recorded static information such as regional locations and land marks when identifying contextual information. Vosinakis and Panayiotopoulos have proposed the identification of 'geometric information' from virtual environments [15], which closely relates to our approach in identifying contextual information.

The processed data are then sent to another sub-component of the data pre-processor that prepares data to be sent to the complex event detection module. We specifically extracted this sub-component from the main data pre-processing logic in order to make it possible to easily customise the data preparation logic according to the selected complex event detection module. For example, for the complex event detection module we have employed currently, this sub-component decomposes the generated snapshot into the constituent data structures corresponding to individual avatars and objects, and sends the information related to objects to the complex event detection module before those corresponding to avatars.

Complex Event Detection Module: The responsibility of the complex event detection module is to identify information at different abstraction levels, by identifying the temporal relations between the data items in the snapshots generated by the data pre-processor.

An event stream processing engine called Esper [16] is used to identify the complex high-level domain-specific events embedded in the data streams generated by the data pre-processor. The Esper engine allows applications to store queries and send the low-level data streams through them in order to identify the high-level aggregated information. Esper keeps the data received in these data streams for time periods specified in these queries, thus acting as an in-memory database. Esper also has the ability to process multiple parallel data streams.

Esper provides two principal methods to process events: event patterns and event stream queries. We make use of both these methods when identifying the high-level domain-specific events. The received data streams are sent through the event stream queries first, to filter out the needed data. Then these filtered data are sent through a set of defined patterns corresponding to the high-level events that should be identified. Event identification using patterns is done in several layers to facilitate the detection of events with a duration. The output of each layer is subsequently passed on to the layer that follows, thus building up hierarchical patterns. The ability to define hierarchical patterns helps in identifying information at different abstraction levels, using the same set of basic data.

The output of the complex event detection module is sent to the data post-processor.

Data Post-processor: The responsibility of the data post-processor is to recreate the snapshot that was decomposed into its constituent data structures while being input to the complex event detection module. In addition to the low-level data, the snapshot now includes the high-level information identified by the complex event detection module.

The data post-processor converts the data included in the snapshot into a proposition string that can be sent to the agent module. At this stage, it is possible to remove the low-level data received from Second Life, as these have a very low abstraction level to be used by an agent depending on declarative information.

When looking at these different components in the data processing module, it can be seen that only the snapshot generation part of the data pre-processor is dependent on Second Life. Identification of contextual information and complex temporal events are concepts that can be readily used to bridge the information representation gap between agent systems and any virtual world. In fact, by introducing data structures general enough to capture avatar and object information received from different virtual worlds, the framework can be easily extended to be used with other virtual worlds.

Expectation Monitor Interface: The expectation monitor interface shown in Figure 1 is an optional sub-component that processes the output of the data post-processor a step further by adding a reference to the dependent state for those events that depend on previous other high-level events. It sends these data to an expectation monitor attached to it, and in this work we use an expectation monitor that was developed in previous research [7]. The responsibility of the expectation monitor is to identify the fulfilments and violations of agent expectations that are defined using the extended version of the Jason platform explained in Section 3.1.

When an expectation monitor is initially started, it receives a rule to start monitoring (a condition and an expectation) and expectation monitoring mode (fulfilment or violation) through the expectation monitor interface. The rule's condition and resulting expectation are provided as separate arguments using a specific form of temporal logic, with the expectation expressing a constraint on the future sequence of states [7]. When the monitor starts receiving the output of the data post-processor as a sequence of states, it matches these against the rule's condition to determine if the expectation has become active. It also evaluates any active expectations (created by a condition evaluating to true), progressively simplifies the monitored expectation and finally deduces fulfilment or violation of the expectation[3].

The fulfilments and violations of agent expectations add a new level of abstraction above the state descriptions generated by the data post-processor, where the expectations are introduced by the agent dynamically and the fulfilments and violations of those expectations are detected based on the already identified information in the snapshots. Therefore, in addition to the continuous stream of domain-specific high-level events and state information that our framework supplies to the agent from Second Life, an agent developed using this extended version of the Jason platform can dynamically subscribe to fulfilment and violation events for specific rules of expectation that are appropriate to its personal or social context.

4   Example - A Jason Agent Engaged in the Football Team Play Scenario "Give and Go"

In this section we demonstrate how a Jason agent can engage in a SecondFootball [17] virtual football training scenario with a human controlled player[4], and how it can reason based on received percepts and the detected fulfilments and violations of its expectations.

SecondFootball is a simulation in Second Life that enables playing virtual football. It is a multi-avatar, fast-moving scenario that promises to be a hard test case to test our framework when compared with most of the publicly accessible environments in Second Life. The simulation provides scripted stadium and ball objects that can be deployed inside Second Life, as well as a "head-up display" object that an avatar can wear to allow the user to initiate kick and tackle actions.

---

[3] The system employs multiple expectation monitor instances in parallel in order to monitor multiple concurrently active expectations an agent may have. This is due to a limitation in the expectation monitor we have employed that it cannot monitor for concurrently active individual expectations.

[4] One of our agents is currently controlled by a human as our Jason agents are still not capable of handling complex reasoning involved with playing football.

In this example, we implement a simplified version of the football team play scenario "give and go". Here, the Jason agent Ras_Ruby is engaged in the team play scenario with the player Su_Monday, who is controlled by a human. When Ras_Ruby receives the ball, she adopts the expectation that Su_Monday will run until she reaches the PenaltyB area, so that she can pass the ball back to Su_Monday, to attempt to score a goal.

In order to implement this team-play scenario, the high-level complex events of the SecondFootball domain we wanted to detect were whether the ball was in the possession of a particular player, whether the ball is being advanced towards a goal, and successful passing of the ball among players by means of up-kicks and down-kicks. Though not used in the example, the framework is also capable of detecting goal scoring by up-kicks and down-kicks, dribbling the ball over the goal line, and successful or unsuccessful tackles.

4.1   Esper Patterns to Identify "successful_pass_by_up_kick "

The identification of the high-level event related to successful passing of the ball between two players using an up kick is done using three Esper patterns, as shown below.

Level One — Identifying the "up_kick" Event
The incoming data stream is analysed to find out whether a player performed the up-kick animation when he has got the possession of the ball. The following complex event pattern identifies this "up_kick" event, where a and b are aliases for two data item inputs to the Esper engine. Here, EntitySnapshot is the data structure corresponding to an avatar or an object.

```
SELECT * FROM PATTERN [
  EVERY a = EntitySnapshot(Name = 'ball'
                          AND Possession LIKE '%in possession%')
      ->
      (b = EntitySnapshot(AnimationName = 'up shot'
                          AND Timestamp = a.Timestamp
                          AND Name = GetPlayer(a.Possession)))
  WHERE timer:within(0.5 sec)]
```

This complex event pattern searches for a sequence of basic data items where an EntitySnapshot corresponding to the soccer ball is followed by (identified by the sequence operator '− >') an EntitySnapshot corresponding to a player, in which the player has the possession of the ball when he performed the animation up-kick. The check for the equality of timestamps makes sure that we consider basic data items belonging to the same snapshot. The method GetPlayer in the connected programme is used to extract the name of the player in possession of the ball. Using a timer avoids the necessity of keeping the basic data items related to the ball in memory for unnecessarily long periods. The wild card option in the select clause specifies that all the attributes of both 'a' and 'b' should be selected.

Level Two — Identifying the "ball_land" Event: Depending on the strength of the up kick, the ball may travel an arbitrary distance above the ground before landing on the ground. This is captured by the "ball_land" event described below.

If a is the "up_kick" event identified in level one and b and c are EntitySnapshots, a "ball_land" event is identified by the following pattern:

```
SELECT * FROM PATTERN [
 EVERY a = up_kick
      ->
      ( b = EntitySnapshot(Name = 'ball'
                           AND PositionZ > region_height)
      UNTIL ([2]c = EntitySnapshot(Name = 'ball'
                           AND PositionZ = region_height)
          )
      )
]
```

Here, after an "up_kick" event is detected, we look for one basic data item that records the ball being above the ground level and two basic data items that record the ball at the ground level immediately following it. We use two basic data items recording the ball at the ground level to cater for the uncertainty in the accuracy of the received data values.

There is a third level pattern called "successful_pass_by_up_kick" (which is not shown here) that identifies the ball in the possession of another player.

As can be seen, complex events identified in earlier levels are used in the levels that follow. Identification of higher level contextual information such as the player in possession of the ball and the location of the ball makes it much easier to implement the Esper patterns.

4.2   Jason Agent Program for the "Give and Go Scenario"

When the system starts, the Jason agent corresponding to Ras_Ruby is initialised. When the Jason agent starts executing, it first tries to log itself in to Second Life. The following Jason plan initiates the login process.

```
// The '+!' prefix resembles a new goal addition
+!start
   <-
   connect_to_SL("xxxx", "Manchester United, 88, 118, 2500");
   !check_connected.
```

The parameters specify the login password and the login location, respectively.

After sending this login request to the LIBOMV client, the agent has to wait until it gets the confirmation of the successful login from the LIBOMV client, as shown in the following plan:

```
+!check_connected: not connected
    <-
    .wait(2000);
    // '!!' means tail-recursion optimised posting of a goal
    !!check_connected.
```

When it finally receives the successful login notification, the agent instructs the LIBOMV client to run the avatar to the area MidfieldB2 using the plan shown below.

```
+!check_connected: connected
    <-
    action("run","MidfieldB2").
```

Once in the area MidfieldB2, the agent Ras_Ruby waits for Su_Monday to kick and pass the ball to it. Once it successfully receives the ball the agent gets the "successful_kick(su_monday, ras_ruby)" percept (which is generated by the framework and states that Su_Monday successfully passed the ball to Ras_Ruby through a kick), and this generates a new belief addition event ('+successful_kick') that triggers the corresponding plan given below. Note that the agent would not be able to easily react to such a high-level event if it only had to rely on the low-level data received from Second Life.

In this plan, we have used the internal action *start_monitoring* defined in the extended version of the Jason platform [6], and initiate monitoring for the fulfilment and violation of the expectation. Here, in the first parameter we define the type of expectation; whether it is a fulfilment or a violation. The second parameter assigns a name for the expectation. The third parameter is the name of the expectation monitor used. The fourth parameter is the triggering condition for the expectation, and in this example, it is a keyword with a special meaning (#once). For this scenario the initiating agent wants the rule to fire precisely once, as soon as possible, and this can be achieved in our current expectation monitor by using a 'nominal' (a proposition that is true in exactly one state) for the current state as the rule's condition. However, the BDI execution cycle only executes a single step of a plan at each iteration, and any knowledge of the current state of the world retrieved by the plan may be out of date by the time the monitor is invoked. The #once keyword instructs the monitor to insert a nominal for the current state of the world just before the rule begins to be monitored. Here, the actual expectation formula is given by the fifth parameter, and the sixth parameter is a list of optional context information, which we do not utilise in this example.

The fulfilment of this expectation occurs when Su_Monday advances towards GoalB ('advanceToGoalB(su_monday)'), until ('U') she reaches PenaltyB, denoted by 'penaltyB(su_monday)'. Similarly, the violation of this expectation occurs if Su_Monday stopped somewhere before reaching penaltyB, or she moves in the opposite direction before reaching the PenaltyB area[5].

```
//The '+' prefix resembles an event relating to belief addition
+successful_kick(su_monday,ras_ruby)
    <-
    //internal actions
    .start_monitoring("fulf",
        "move_to_target",
        "expectation_monitor",
        "#once",
        "('U',
            'advanceToGoalB(su_monday)',
            'penaltyB(su_monday)')",
        []);

    .start_monitoring("viol",
        "move_to_target",
        "expectation_monitor",
        "#once",
        "('U',
            'advanceToGoalB(su_monday)',
            'penaltyB(su_monday)')",
        []).
```

If Su_Monday fulfilled Ras_Ruby's expectation, the expectation monitor detects this and reports back to the Jason agent. The following plan handles this detected fulfilment and instructs the avatar to carry out the kick action.

```
+fulf("move_to_target", X)
    <-
    //Calculate kick direction and force, turn, then ...
    action("animation", "kick").
```

If Su_Monday violated the expectation, the expectation monitor reports the violation to the Jason agent, and the agent uses the first plan below to decide the agent's reaction to the detected violation, which creates a goal to choose a new tactic for execution. The second plan (responding to this new choose_and_enact_new_tactic) is then triggered, and the agent adopts the tactic of attempting to score a goal on its own by running towards the PenaltyB area with the ball[6] .

---

[5] The conditions and expectations are defined in temporal logic and we do not wish to elaborate on them in the scope of this paper. These are written as nested Python tuples, as this is the input format for the expectation monitor written in Python.

[6] When an avatar is in possession of the ball and the avatar starts moving, the ball moves in front of the avatar.

```
+viol("move_to_target",X)
   <-
   !choose_and_enact_new_tactic.

+!choose_and_enact_new_tactic : .my_name(Me)
   <-
   action("run", "penaltyB").
```

5   Related Work

Research on programming with Second Life has focused either on extracting sensory readings from Second Life, or controlling avatar movement and conversational behaviours to create Intelligent Virtual Agents (IVAs). Not much research has attempted to model reactive agents that generate behavioural responses to their observations on the Second Life environment, or addressed the issue of mapping low-level sensory data to high-level domain-specific information.

Most of the research on extracting sensory readings from Second Life has utilised this retrieved information for statistical purposes. Both LSL scripts and LIBOMV clients have been used for sensory data extraction from Second Life servers, but the latter has been more effective in collecting large amounts of data. LIBOMV clients have been successfully used to create crawler applications that collected large amounts of data about avatars and user-created content, in order to statistically analyse the number of avatars and objects present in various Second Life regions over periods of time [18,19]. LSL scripts and LIBOMV clients have been used in combination to produce a data gathering tool that collected more than 200 million records over a period of time [20]. There have also been several investigations into the collection of data from Second Life to examine social norms related to gender, interpersonal distance, interaction proximities and spatio-temporal dynamics of user mobility in a virtual environment [21,22,23].

Cranefield and Li presented an LSL script-based framework that sensed the Second Life environment and tried to identify the fulfilments and violations of rules defined in structured virtual communities [24]. However, this research was conducted in a narrow scope that addressed only animations of human-controlled avatars.

Burden provided a theoretical proposal for creating IVAs inside Second Life with the sophisticated abilities of concurrent perception, rational reasoning and deliberation, emotion and action, and also pointed out the complexities of a practical implementation [25]. A theoretical framework has also been proposed to integrate different modules that handle these different capabilities [10]. However, the practical implementation of both of these approaches is still limited to simple sensory, movement and conversational abilities.

There have been several approaches for creating IVAs inside Second Life using LIBOMV clients, but their main focus has been on improving the conversational and animation abilities of virtual agents [26,27].

Research has been carried out by Bogdanovych et al. [28] on connecting agents to Second Life in specially designed environments that are instrumented to connect to "electronic institution" middleware. As part of this work they have developed a number of useful libraries, including their own BDI interpreter for controlling agents inside Second Life. In contrast, our research focused on developing a framework that supports connecting multi-agent systems with existing Second Life environments. Moreover, they have not much focused on how to create coherent snapshots that provide a complete view of a given Second Life environment at a given instant of time to be presented to the multi-agent system, or how the extracted low-level data can be used to identify much complex high-level information, which was the main focus of our work.

Although research related to Second Life-based agent simulations is still in its infancy, there is a considerable amount of research that has used virtual environments for agent-based simulations. Such research not only helps to test agent systems better, but virtual agents created using these agent systems help to improve the usability of the virtual worlds as well.

A virtual environment that has been extensively used for AI research is the UnrealTournament. The Gamebots project was the first attempt to extend the UnrealTournament environment to be used for multi-agent systems related research [29]. The Pogamut project later extended the Gamebots system to be compatible with the later versions of UnrealTournament [12]. The Pogamut framework also contains different cognitive modules such as an episodic memory component and an emotion handling component that can be used to improve the cognitive ability of an agent. There have also been other uses of this framework in agent-related research (e.g. [4]). Currently the Pogamut framework is tightly coupled with the UnrealTournament environment, however there are proposals to generalise the framework to be used in the context of other virtual environments, including Second Life [12].

CIGA is middleware that is designed to facilitate the coupling between agent technology and game engine technology in a generic manner [30]. Similar to our framework, this middleware contains a component that is dependent on the selected virtual world, and currently it has been only tested with a game engine developed by the authors. In order to fill the representational gap between agent systems and virtual worlds, CIGA presents the concept of a 'social world model'. This is based on semantic data generated using a given domain ontology, and is only concerned with static information.

In our opinion, our framework will not replace any of these frameworks. Rather, it will complement them when trying to integrate them with Second Life, because the potential of Second Life for agent-based virtual simulations is enormous. Firstly, our Second Life related implementation techniques are useful for these aforementioned frameworks to be integrated with Second Life. Secondly, the concepts of 'contextual information' based on relations between avatars and objects, and the identification of complex events based on the temporal correlations of information in different states can be readily integrated with these frameworks. In particular, the ability to identify dynamic high-level information is very useful in creating more rational agents, as so far the attention has been only on identifying relatively static high-level information [31,32,15,30].

6 Conclusion

In this paper we presented a framework that can be used to deploy multiple concurrent agents in complex Second Life simulations, and focused on how the potentially unreliable data received by an agent deployed in a Second Life simulation should be processed to create a domain-specific high-level abstract model to be used by the agent's cognitive modules. This problem has not gained much attention from the past research on Second Life. We hope the implementation details we provided will be a valuable road map for future researchers hoping to use Second Life for multi-agent simulations in different paradigms, apart from the developed framework being a potential starting point for further research in integrating multi-agent systems with Second Life. The solutions we proposed for identifying high-level abstract information are generic enough to be used in the context of any other virtual world.

We note that any multi-agent platform can be connected with Second Life using our framework, and demonstrated this with an extended version of the Jason BDI interpreter. With the use of an example, we showed how a Jason agent can execute actions inside Second Life and how it can respond to the observed changes in the environment. We also integrated an expectation monitor with our framework and demonstrated how Jason agents can use the sensory data to identify higher level events associated with fulfiled and violated personal expectations, based on the complex interactions that they take part in.

Most of the simulation-specific logic in our framework is required by the contextual information generation and by the Esper module. Therefore by changing the logic in these two components, the framework can be easily customised to be used for different simulations. In future, we plan to identify a generic data representation that is suitable for many of the virtual worlds that are commonly used for agent-based simulations. There is also a possibility to experiment with our framework in various simulations such as medical training scenarios. Moreover, the framework requires a data filtering mechanism to send only the information that is of interest to the agent, in order to further reduce the cognitive overload of an agent.

References

1. Linden Lab. Second Life Home Page, http://secondlife.com
2. Gemrot, J., Brom, C., Plch, T.: A Periphery of Pogamut: From Bots to Agents and Back Again. In: Dignum, F. (ed.) Agents for Games and Simulations II. LNCS, vol. 6525, pp. 19–37. Springer, Heidelberg (2011)
3. Dignum, F., Westra, J., van Doesburg, W.A., Harbers, M.: Games and agents: Designing intelligent gameplay. International Journal of Computer Games Technology 2009, 1–18 (2009), doi: 10.1155/2009/837095

4. Hindriks, K.V., van Riemsdijk, B., Behrens, T., Korstanje, R., Kraayenbrink, N., Pasman, W., de Rijk, L.: UNREAL GOAL Bots: Conceptual Design of a Reusable Interface. In: Dignum, F. (ed.) Agents for Games and Simulations II. LNCS, vol. 6525, pp. 1–18. Springer, Heidelberg (2011)
5. OpenMetaverse Organization. LibOpenMetaverse developer wiki, http://lib.openmetaverse.org/wiki/Main_Page
6. Ranathunga, S., Cranefield, S., Purvis, M.: Integrating Expectation Monitoring into BDI Agents. In: Dennis, L.A., Boissier, O., Bordini, R.H. (eds.) ProMAS 2011. LNCS, vol. 7217, pp. 74–91. Springer, Heidelberg (2012)
7. Cranefield, S., Winikoff, M.: Verifying social expectations by model checking truncated paths. Journal of Logic and Computation 21(6), 1217–1256 (2011)
8. Jennings, N., Collins, C.: Virtual or virtually U: Educational institutions in Second Life. International Journal of Social Sciences 2, 180–187 (2007)
9. Veksler, V.D.: Second Life as a simulation environment: Rich, high-fidelity world, minus the hassles. In: Proceedings of the 9th International Conference on Cognitive Modeling (2009)
10. Weitnauer, E., Thomas, N.M., Rabe, F., Kopp, S.: Intelligent Agents Living in Social Virtual Environments – Bringing Max into Second Life. In: Prendinger, H., Lester, J., Ishizuka, M. (eds.) IVA 2008. LNCS (LNAI), vol. 5208, pp. 552–553. Springer, Heidelberg (2008)
11. Richards, D., Porte, J.: Developing an agent-based training simulation using game and virtual reality software: experience report. In: Proceedings of the Sixth Australasian Conference on Interactive Entertainment, pp. 9:1–9:9. ACM (2009)
12. Gemrot, J., Brom, C., Kadlec, R., Bída, M., Burkert, O., Zemčák, M., Píbil, R., Plch, T.: Pogamut 3 — virtual humans made simple. In: Gray, J. (ed.) Advances in Cognitive Science, pp. 211–243. The Institution Of Engineering And Technology (2010)
13. Bordini, R.H., Hubner, J.F., Wooldridge, M.: Programming multi-agent systems in AgentSpeak using Jason. John Wiley & Sons Ltd., England (2007)
14. Ranathunga, S., Cranefield, S., Purvis, M.: Extracting Data from Second Life. Discussion Paper 2011/07, Department of Information Science, University of Otago (2011), http://otago.ourarchive.ac.nz/handle/10523/1802
15. Vosinakis, S., Panayiotopoulos, T.: Programmable Agent Perception in Intelligent Virtual Environments. In: Rist, T., Aylett, R.S., Ballin, D., Rickel, J. (eds.) IVA 2003. LNCS (LNAI), vol. 2792, pp. 202–206. Springer, Heidelberg (2003)
16. EsperTech. Esper Tutorial, http://esper.codehaus.org/tutorials/tutorial/tutorial.html
17. Vstex Company. SecondFootball Home Page, http://www.secondfootball.com
18. Varvello, M., Picconi, F., Diot, C., Biersack, E.: Is there life in Second Life? In: Proceedings of the ACM CoNEXT Conference, pp. 1:1–1:12. ACM (2008)
19. Eno, J., Gauch, S., Thompson, C.: Intelligent crawling in virtual worlds. In: Proceedings of the IEEE/WIC/ACM International Joint Conference on Web Intelligence and Intelligent Agent Technology, vol. 3, pp. 555–558. IEEE Computer Society (2009)
20. Kappe, F., Zaka, B., Steurer, M.: Automatically detecting points of interest and social networks from tracking positions of avatars in a virtual world. In: Proceedings of the International Conference on Advances in Social Network Analysis and Mining, pp. 89–94. IEEE Computer Society (2009)
21. Friedman, D., Steed, A., Slater, M.: Spatial Social Behavior in Second Life. In: Pelachaud, C., Martin, J.-C., André, E., Chollet, G., Karpouzis, K., Pelé, D. (eds.) IVA 2007. LNCS (LNAI), vol. 4722, pp. 252–263. Springer, Heidelberg (2007)

22. Yee, N., Bailenson, J.N., Urbanek, M., Chang, F., Merget, D.: The unbearable likeness of being digital; the persistence of nonverbal social norms in online virtual environments. Cyberpsychology and Behavior 10, 115–121 (2007)
23. La, C.-A., Michiardi, P.: Characterizing user mobility in Second Life. In: Proceedings of the First Workshop on Online Social Networks, pp. 79–84. ACM (2008)
24. Cranefield, S., Li, G.: Monitoring Social Expectations in Second Life. In: Padget, J., Artikis, A., Vasconcelos, W., Stathis, K., da Silva, V.T., Matson, E., Polleres, A. (eds.) COIN 2009. LNCS (LNAI), vol. 6069, pp. 133–146. Springer, Heidelberg (2010)
25. Burden, D.J.H.: Deploying embodied AI into virtual worlds. Knowledge-Based Systems 22, 540–544 (2009)
26. Ullrich, S., Bruegmann, K., Prendinger, H., Ishizuka, M.: Extending MPML3D to Second Life. In: Prendinger, H., Lester, J., Ishizuka, M. (eds.) IVA 2008. LNCS (LNAI), vol. 5208, pp. 281–288. Springer, Heidelberg (2008)
27. Jan, D., Roque, A., Leuski, A., Morie, J., Traum, D.: A Virtual Tour Guide for Virtual Worlds. In: Ruttkay, Z., Kipp, M., Nijholt, A., Vilhjálmsson, H.H. (eds.) IVA 2009. LNCS, vol. 5773, pp. 372–378. Springer, Heidelberg (2009)
28. Bogdanovych, A., Rodriguez-Aguilar, J.A., Simoff, S., Cohen, A.: Authentic interactive reenactment of cultural heritage with 3D virtual worlds and artificial intelligence. Applied Artificial Intelligence 24(6), 617–647 (2010)
29. Adobbati, R., Marshall, A.N., Scholer, A., Tejada, S., Kaminka, G., Schaffer, S., Sollitto, C.: Gamebots: A 3D virtual world test-bed for multi-agent research. In: Proceedings of the Second International Workshop on Infrastructure for Agents, MAS, and Scalable MAS (2001)
30. van Oijen, J., Vanhée, L., Dignum, F.: CIGA: A middleware for intelligent agents in virtual environments. In: Proceedings of the International Workshop on the Uses of Agents for Education, Games and Simulations (AEGS 2011), pp. 17–32 (2011)
31. Chang, P.H.-M., Chen, K.-T., Chien, Y.-H., Kao, E., Soo, V.-W.: From Reality to Mind: A Cognitive Middle Layer of Environment Concepts for Believable Agents. In: Weyns, D., Van Dyke Parunak, H., Michel, F. (eds.) E4MAS 2004. LNCS (LNAI), vol. 3374, pp. 57–73. Springer, Heidelberg (2005)
32. Zhang, W., Hill Jr., R.W.: A template-based and pattern-driven approach to situation awareness and assessment in virtual humans. In: Proceedings of the Fourth International Conference on Autonomous Agents, pp. 116–123. ACM (2000)

CIGA: A Middleware for Intelligent Agents in Virtual Environments

Joost van Oijen[1,2], Loïs Vanhée[3,1], and Frank Dignum[1]

[1] Utrecht University,
P.O. Box 80.089, 3508 TB Utrecht, The Netherlands
{oijen,lois,dignum}@cs.uu.nl
[2] VSTEP
Weena 598, 3012 CN Rotterdam, The Netherlands
joost@vstep.nl
[3] ENS de Cachan - Antenne de Bretagne

Abstract. Building intelligent behavior in (educational) games and simulations can greatly benefit from the use of agent technology. Intelligent agents within a multi-agent system can be developed for controlling virtual characters in a simulation environment within a game engine. Coupling a multi-agent system to a game engine is not a trivial task and introduces several conceptual design issues concerning embodied agent design. In this paper we present CIGA, a middleware to facilitate this coupling tackling the design issues in a structured approach, not only for embodied agent design but also for the system as a whole.

Keywords: Middleware, Multi-Agent Systems, Virtual Environments, Intelligent Agents, Simulation.

1 Introduction

As the technology to create more realistic, complex and dynamic virtual environments advances, there is an increasing interest to create intelligent virtual agents (IVAs) to populate these environments for the purpose of games, simulations or training. Designing an IVA, game engine technology can be employed to simulate its physical embodiment, equipped with sensors and actuators interacting with the virtual environment. The use of agent technology in the form of multi-agent systems (MASs) is a good fit to realize the cognitive and decision-making aspects of an IVA.

Combining these technologies is not a trivial task and introduces conceptual and technical design issues. First of all, both technologies often work at different abstraction levels. Games engines work with low-level data representations for virtual environments and the characters populating it. MASs work with more high-level semantic concepts designed to form a suitable abstraction from the physical environment representing an agent's perceptive view on the environment and the actions for influencing it. Second, agent actions in a typical MAS

M. Beer et al. (Eds.): AEGS 2011, LNAI 7471, pp. 22–37, 2012.

environment are non-durative. When embodied in a real-time environment, actions become durative and low-level reasoning over their execution is required. MASs are generally not designed to handle this aspect. Third, the designs of an agent's embodiment in a game engine and its cognitive counterpart in the MAS are highly depend on each other. An agent's view on the environment is dependent on his sensory capabilities provided by its embodiment whereas its ability to influence the environment through its embodiment is bounded by the possible control over an avatar in the game engine. This, in turn, has implications on an agent's deliberation on possible goals, plans and actions. Last, the required connection between the two specialized software systems introduces some technical issues concerning software engineering.

Current attempts in combining these technologies often use a pragmatic approach when tackling these design issues. A direct connection between a game engine and a MAS is created either with or without the help of standard technologies or interfaces that may provide access to a specific game engine [1] or range of MASs [3]. Although such an approach can be a productive solution, design decisions are often influenced and bounded by the individual capabilities of the employed technologies. There is often no structured approach in bridging the conceptual gap between the two systems. There are systems that focus more on the conceptual issues attempting to employ agent technology by translating the physical world model to a social world model suitable for cognitive reasoning [5,16]. Though, these systems don't pretend to give a structured approach for tackling the technical issues when using their system with alternative MASs or game engines.

In this paper we present CIGA[1], a middleware to facilitate the coupling between agent technology and game engine technology, tackling the inherent design issues in a structured way. An architecture for using this middleware is presented to solve technical issues when connecting agents in a MAS to their embodiments in a game engine. Additionally we show the need for using ontologies to provide a design contract between not only an agent's mind and body connection but also for the system as a whole. This can lead to a new methodology for game design using agent technology. An initial fully functional version of CIGA has been implemented and currently undergoes evaluation.

The paper is organized as follows. In the following section we outline the motivation for introducing CIGA. Section 3 describes the architectural design of the proposed middleware. In section 4 we compare the middleware with related technologies. Finally, section 5 we conclude and discuss results.

2 Bridging the Conceptual Gap

Designing an embodied agent with current game engine and agent technology, one must overcome several inherent conceptual design issues. In this section, we provide a description of each issue and present the functional role CIGA plays to overcome these issues.

---

[1] Creating Intelligent Games with Agents.

2.1 Social World Model

In a MAS, an agent's interpretation of the environment is based on semantic concepts forming an abstraction of the virtual physical world. The data representations of these concepts in a game engine often are at a different abstraction level than what is suitable for agents in a MAS to work with. For example, an agent's concept of "a person sitting on a chair" may be represented in the game engine by a character's location in the vicinity of a chair in combination with the positions of each skeletal bone, forming a sitting posture. Instead of the physical world state representations in a game engine, agents work with (high-level) semantics concepts. The use of rich semantic concepts is particularly important for the more socially-oriented simulations with communicating agents like in serious games. Though, the demand for rich semantics in the more action-oriented games is getting increasingly important [17].

CIGA overcomes the difference of data representation by translating the *physical simulation* to a *social simulation* for agents. To accomplish this, semantic data is generated during agent sensing which is translated from raw data of game objects or events. This semantic information forms the basis for an agent's view and interpretation of the environment. Inferences can be made to provide agents with semantic concepts relevant for the social simulation. For example, the meaning of a certain gesture performed by an embodied agent can be inferred from an animation in the game engine. Making higher-level information directly available for agents is efficient as agents don't have to infer these themselves. CIGA employs *domain ontologies* to specify a formal representation of the semantic concepts. The ontologies are accessible in both the game engine to perform the required translations and in the MAS representing the agent's *social world model*.

The risk of translating raw data to semantic data is the problem of *over-inference*. As implemented inferences are the same for all agents we might make an inference we don't want a certain agent to be able to make. Further, we might loose the ability for an agent to interpret perceived information in his own way. For example, how an agent interprets the meaning of a perceived gesture can be dependent on an agent's cultural identity. This makes it important to design the semantic concepts in the domain ontology at the right abstraction level such that agents don't have to perform too much low-level inferences on their own, but can still make different interpretations based on their individual context. CIGA doesn't enforce the use of any abstraction level as this is dependent on the application domain.

2.2 Perception

Agents in a MAS get information from their environment through percepts. If an agent becomes embodied in a virtual environment, these percepts are based on sensory information retrieved from one or more sensors attached to the embodiment in a game engine. When creating percepts directly from sensory information, we do not only face the problem of information representation as described above, but there's also the risk for an agent to become flooded with percepts that are irrelevant with respect to his current state of mind. An agent should have the ability to direct his attention to selected information from the environment such that irrelevant information can be filtered, though still allowing an agent to be susceptible to unexpected events. Filtering sensory information should not be performed in the game engine as this process is dependent on the agent's mind in a MAS. On the other hand, delegating this process to the MAS is not ideal as the cost of communicating the unfiltered information can have a negative performance impact on the system as a whole. Additionally, MASs generally don't provide standard facilities implementing perception filtering.

CIGA tackles this problem by introducing a *filtering mechanism* located closely to an agent's sensors in the game engine. Agents in a MAS can show their *interest* in the environment in the form of subscriptions that define how sensory information has to be filtered. Using the environment semantics defined in the domain ontology introduced before, powerful subscriptions can be made to give an agent full control over the range of percepts to receive. A description of this mechanism can be found in [20] and falls out of the scope of this paper.

2.3   Action

In a MAS, an agent's capability to influence the environment is defined by a set of actions designed to change the state of an environment. The success or failure of an action denotes that the desired state of the environment was reached or could not be reached respectively. In a typical MAS environment, actions are instantaneous and the result is known immediately. When an agent becomes embodied in a virtual environment, its capability to influence the environment becomes bounded by the available actuators of the embodiment. Since these actuators work in real-time, actions become durative and the environment may change during the execution, possibly preventing the action from finishing successfully. For example, an action like *open door* can fail during execution if the door is opened from the other side by another agent. Further, this raises questions about the meaning of the success or failure of an action performed by an embodied agent. Is an action said to be successfully executed if the body performed the action or if the desired state of the environment was reached?

To deal with this different view on *actions*, CIGA provides a generic *action monitoring* facility to deliver action requests from an agent to its embodiment and communicate feedback about the realization of the action, allowing an agent to follow the progress and intervene if necessary. The meaning of the success or failure of an action is left to the designer where he can use the feedback mechanism to specify the state of the action and how it was reached (E.g. the agent didn't fully perform the action in the environment, but we still consider the action to be succeeded as the desired environment state defined by the semantics for the action was reached). A more elaborate overview is given in section 3.2.

A well known design issue is the need for finding a suitable abstraction level for behavior control. Choosing an abstraction level has implications on both agent design and system performance. The use of more low-level, physically-oriented actions gives an agent more control over its body but increases the communication cost of delivering the instructions to the game engine. Using more high-level, cognitive-oriented actions delegates more control to the game engine, but the ability is lost to take an agent's individuality into account. For example, it becomes harder to reflect an agent's own personality or mental state on his behavior if this information is defined in the MAS (E.g. drunk and sober agents will walk in the same way). Although the communication cost for sending instructions is decreased, agents are more dependent on perception to see if the intents of their actions have been achieved. The aim is to find the right *balance of intelligence* distributed between the mind and body of an agent in the MAS and game engine respectively. CIGA doesn't enforce the use of any abstraction level for actions as this is dependent on the specific application domain.

2.4   Communication

MASs often provide an inter-agent communication mechanism for agents to communicate. The messages being communicated usually adhere to standards like FIPA ACL where content can be represented using formal semantics understood by both agents. Simulating human-like communication requires agents to perform (non)verbal communicative behavior and perception through their body's actuators and sensors in the environment. Like actions, communication becomes durative. Further, the desired effect of the communication cannot easily be determined as this is dependent on mental processes within the receiving agent. Successful reception of a communicative act is not trivial as this depends on the available medium from sender to receiver, bounded by the simulated laws of physics in the environment. For example, two agents may not be able to hear each other in a noisy bar when they are at different sides of the room.

CIGA facilitates in the communication process between embodied agents by introducing its own communication mechanism taking into account both the durative nature of communication and environmental factors. For example, the delivery of a communication message is only performed when the corresponding action realizing the communicative act in the environment is successfully achieved and the receiving agent is physically able to perceive this act. This mechanism is briefly mentioned later in this section but an elaborate functional overview falls outside the scope of this paper.

3   CIGA Framework

In this section we present an architectural framework for integrating the CIGA middleware with both game engine and agent technology. An illustration of the main framework is given in figure 1.

Since the proposed middleware must connect to two specialized software systems, the common design approach was taken to internally divide the middleware into two functional components. The *Physical Interface* layer connects to a game

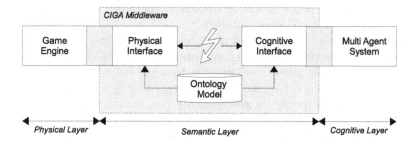

Fig. 1. Middleware Framework

engine whereas the *Cognitive Interface* layer connects to a MAS. Both components are internally connected using a communication mechanism. The *Ontology Model* provides access to domain ontologies specified for a specific application domain containing formal representations of the communicated content between an agent's mind and body.

This internal distributed design several advantages. First, it helps to bridge the conceptual gap between a game engine and a MAS by dedicating separate components for the integration with the technologies. Second, from a technical point of view, it allows both components to be implemented in different programming languages. It is often the case that the used game engine and MAS are written in different languages. For the middleware as a whole to be able to interface with both technologies while matching the language of that technology results in an easy integration process and an efficient, tight connection. Last, the design introduces connection transparency since the game engine and MAS can run in different processes or distributed over different computers or platforms, depending on the used internal connection mechanism.

Next we'll first describe the role of ontologies within the middleware after which we'll look at the individual components connecting to game engine and MAS respectively.

3.1   The Role of Ontologies

The *Ontology Model* represents a storage facility for semantic concepts. It consists of domain ontologies designed for a specific application domain to capture an agent's perceptual and interactional capabilities within an environment. The use of ontologies forces an agreement between a game engine and a MAS on the required domain concepts. This is known as a *design by contract* [14], increasing robustness and reusability within the system.

Building a domain ontology for the simulation environment encompasses defining object and event classes with their attributes. Attributes for objects represent their physical or functional properties whereas attributes for events represent parameters specifying event details. Classes can be organized in a hierarchical fashion where attributes are inherited from parent classes. To form an agreement on the actions agents can perform in an environment, (parameterized) action classes should be specified in the domain ontology.

Domain ontologies can be created using an ontology editor like Protégé. An interesting feature is the ability to change and extend meta-classes for objects, events or actions. This allows the ontology to support custom data fields for specific types of concepts. For example, a *perceptibility type* can be assigned to an object property to specify its perceivability (e.g. visual, auditory or tactile) which use will be described later. Additionally, *affordances* can be specified for object classes which can facilitate agents in understanding their world in terms of interactions they can have with it. The use of Affordance Theory has been previously explored in [6,4]. Related to affordances, information associated with *smart objects* can be stored [11,15]. A small example showing the possibilities of a simple domain ontology is illustrated in figure 2.

Objects	Properties
PhysicalObject	location,size
– Human	gender,age
– Fire	type,heat
– FireExtinguisher	type
– Bucket	content,amount
Actions	**Parameters**
AttackFire	fire,equipment
Pickup	target
Communicate	target,message

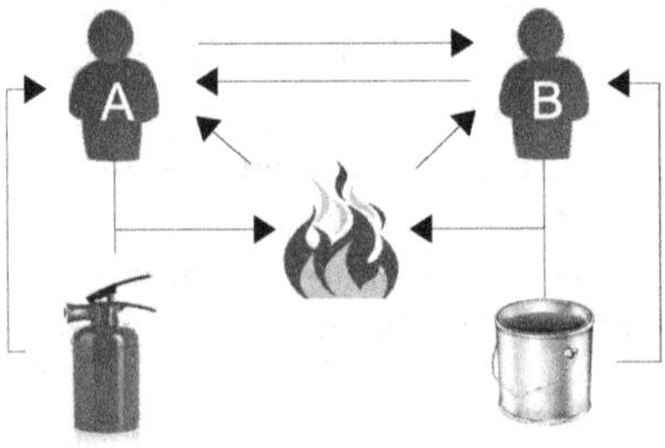

Fig. 2. Domain Ontology Example

The left side of the illustration shows a domain ontology consisting of several object classes and actions for human actors. The right side of the example shows a simple scene with two human agents (A and B), a fire and two objects which can be used to attack a fire. Now assume *agent A* notices a small fire starting near *agent B* who is unaware of this. *Agent A* would like to resolve the situation and has several options. He can pick up the fire extinguisher and use it to put out the fire or he can use the bucket of water positioned near *agent B*. This choice may depend on the size and type of the fire and the type fire extinguisher. For example, an electrical fire should not be extinguished using water which makes the first option preferable if it concerns a chemical fire extinguisher. Further, *agent A* can communicate with *agent B* to advise him to deal with the fire, although this choice may not be suitable if *agent B* is a small child.

Agent A is able to perform this line of reasoning based on the given domain ontology. Here, object properties provide information about the objects (E.g. object positions, the type of fire extinguisher or the age of *Agent B*). Object classes can be annotated with *conditional affordances* helping an agent to understand how he can interact with objects being perceived. For example, physical objects of a certain size can be picked up or a bucket filled with water can be used to attack a fire. The concepts in the domain ontology are also interesting for use as content in communication languages between agents [21].

These domain ontologies cover concepts relevant to both an agent's embodiment and his mind. In CIGA they are fully accessible at runtime to both the game engine and MAS as will become clear in the next parts of this section.

3.2   Connecting the Game Engine

As shown in Figure 1, the *Physical Interface* layer of CIGA connects to a game engine. Its main task is the administration of agent embodiments participating in the middleware and individually control their sensors and actuators. Abstraction from the game engine is achieved using an intermediate layer, hereafter called the *GE Interface* layer, connecting a specific game engine. Figure 3 illustrates the design focusing on the functional interfaces and data flows.

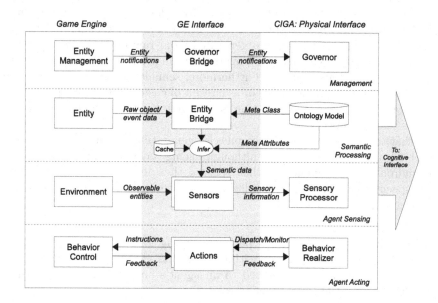

Fig. 3. Integration Middleware in Game Engine

A prerequisite for using CIGA is the ability to modify the game engine allowing implementation of the *GE Interface* layer. This layer is responsible for integrating CIGA's *Physical Interface* component as an external game engine component to be included in the engine's update loop which allows it to run processes on its own. For example, agent sensing can be controlled to run at a configurable frequency or the MAS can be provided with regular time updates. This approach makes CIGA less dependent on specific features that may or may not be available in a specific game engine. Next we describe each horizontal layer from figure 3 in more detail.

Management. The role of the *Governor* in the *Physical Interface* is to provide a connection mechanism for synchronizing the simulation between the game engine and the MAS. It monitors the creation and destruction of entities in the environment that are candidates for agent embodiment and notifies the MAS about their existence. Additionally, simulation time is synchronized by sending regular time updates to the MAS, who often don't have an internal clock explicitly defined.

Semantic Processing. The goal of semantic processing is to translate raw object and event data available in the game engine to semantic data. Semantic data is used as sensory information which allows an agent to build a social model of the environment based on meaningful concepts. The *Ontology Model* can be accessed to retrieve the formal representation of those concepts.

Creating semantic data from raw data at runtime is a process performed in the *GE Interface* layer. Here, at design time, entity bridges are created associating object classes from a domain ontology to entities defined in the game engine (E.g. associating the *fire* concept to a fire class in the game engine). During runtime, the object's attributes are generated from raw entity data (E.g. an object's *size* property is calculated). This translation process is performed when agents sense environment entities. Furthermore, semantic event classes can be generated based on raw game events or as a result of custom inferences. Inference based on previously sensed information is achieved using a cache belonging to an agent's sensory processor.

Note that translation and inference rules for generating semantic data are the same for all agents. At this stage, although agents have their individual view of the environment determined by their sensors, their interpretation of it is the same as specified by the domain ontology. This fact must be taken into account when designing the ontology.

Agent Sensing. Agent sensing is performed using a *Sensory Processor* provided for each participating agent within CIGA. Its goal is to collect sensory information from all sensors assigned to an agent's embodiment and prepare them as *percepts* for the MAS agent to receive.

Sensors obtain sensory information from the environment. The processing logic for a sensor is implemented in the *Physical Interface* using a sensor base class. Specific sensors must be created in the *GE Interface* layer and are required to assign a *perceptibility type* (e.g. visual, auditory, tactile) to the sensor and provide an implementation of the abstract method **GetObservableEntities()**. This method is responsible for building a list of entities from the environment the sensor is currently able to observe. Access to game engine queries can support this process (E.g. to determine if an agent can observe another agent standing behind a wall or if a sound can still be heard at a certain distance from its origin). We assume the game engine offers us the functionality to achieve the required queries. With this approach, one can easily build a sensor library in the *GE Interface* layer to store different sensors with more or less advanced algorithms.

Since sensors can be dynamically replaced, one can support different level of details (LODs) for sensors.

Based on the list of *observable entities*, sensing in the base class continues by extracting sensory information from these entities using the *Semantic Processing* described before. The sensor's *perceptability type* is used to filter the object properties and events that can be sensed. E.g., In the example from figure 2, the *heat* property of the *fire* entity can only be sensed by a *tactile* sensor.

After all sensors have been processed, the *Sensory Processor* filters the collected data as further described in [20].

Agent Acting. Agent behavior is performed using a *Behavior Realizer* provided for each agent participating within CIGA. Its goal is to realize semantic actions instructed by a MAS by managing an action's life cycle and communicating feedback about its state back to the MAS agent. Actions are executed in parallel in an interleaved fashion driven by the game engine loop.

Actions themselves are implemented in the *GE Interface* layer. They are responsible for realizing the intended action semantics by accessing game engine instructions. The *Physical Interface* layer provides an abstract base class for actions. Creating specific actions involves implementing the following methods:

- **CheckPreconditions():** This method is called before the action is executed. Here any preconditions can be checked which must pass before the realization of the action can be started. If the preconditions are not met the action will not continue further and the agent is notified.
- **Body():** This is the main execution loop. Here game engine functionality can be addressed to realize the intent of the action. This includes controlling the actuators of the agent's embodiment and monitoring its progress. For virtual characters, this often involves interacting with an *Animation System* in the game engine. The action can end prematurely when problems arise during realization after which the agent is notified about the cause.
- **CheckEffects():** This method is called after the action was successfully realized. Here the intended effects of the action on the game state can be validated. If the effects are not met the action will end with a corresponding notification.
- **OnAborted():** A MAS agent has the ability to abort any scheduled action. This method is called when it decides to do so. Here logic can be implemented to properly interrupt and clean up the action's realization in the game engine.

Note that it is up to the MAS agent to infer success or type of failure of an action based on the received action feedback notifications. Further, CIGA doesn't impose any rules for the implementation technique or data formats used for actions. It merely provides a generic facility to deliver instructions from a MAS agent to its embodiment and to communicate feedback about the realization of these instructions. For example, a common technique for behavior control is the use of *parameterized actions* representing an API for agents to control their embodiment [1,22,2]. In CIGA, *parameterized actions* can be defined in the domain ontology to form an agreement on the used API.

This does not restrict the use of more specialized techniques. For example, upcoming language standards such as *BML* can still be used [12], which is an XML-based language for communicative behavior realization. Here, a single action can be defined for communicative behavior sending BML data and feedback information between the MAS and the game engine.

3.3   Connecting the MAS

The *Cognitive Interface* layer of CIGA connects to a MAS, providing a generic interface for agents in a MAS with their embodiment in a real-time environment. This interface should allow for the communication of percept data and action instructions whose data is associated with semantic concepts from the domain ontology. Similar to the interface with the game engine, abstraction from the MAS is achieved using an intermediate layer, hereafter called the *MAS Interface* layer. Figure 4 illustrates the connection framework.

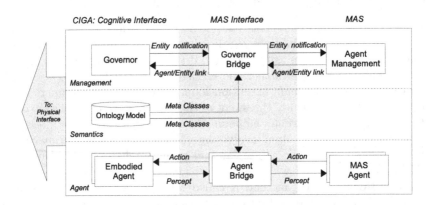

Fig. 4. Integration Middleware in MAS

Unlike the *Physical Interface*, the *Cognitive Interface* is a pure event-based component passing information to and from the MAS. An *MAS Interface* layer must be implemented for a specific MAS to comply with the provided interfaces by the *Cognitive Interface* layer. This layer is less complex than the *GE Interface* layer since it's a simple message-passing connection for data that is already rooted in semantics (no conceptual translation is required).

Management Interface. As described previously, the *Governor* notifies the MAS about the creation and destruction of candidate embodiments in the simulation. Based on this information, the MAS can create and destroy agents. To link an agent with an embodiment, the MAS must notify the *Governor* about the entity it wants to embody. The *Governor Bridge* in the *MAS Interface* can achieve this functionality for a specific MAS to be used. The *Ontology Model* can be accessed to retrieve semantic data about the embodiments. This information can support the MAS in deciding what type of agent to associate with an entity.

Agent Interface. The agent interface between CIGA and a MAS consists of the common act and sense interfaces required for MAS agents. The *Agent Bridge* in the *MAS Interface* is responsible for converting the different message formats used between the CIGA middleware and a specific MAS. Here, the *Ontology Model* can play several roles. The model can be accessed to retrieve semantic meta-data associated with incoming percepts. For example, agents can retrieve the *affordances* associated with perceived objects. Also type hierarchies of objects in the ontology can be inspected, allowing agents to make generalizations about objects they perceive. In addition, the model can be used to validate the semantics of action instructions performed by a MAS agent. Being able to validate actions can greatly support the development of agents whose code for action-selection cannot be type-checked at design time (E.g. in 2APL).

Three types of percepts have been defined in CIGA's *Cognitive Interface* layer:

- *Object percepts* contain semantic data about objects perceived from the environment. A unique object identifier is provided giving agents the ability to relate subsequent percepts with the same object.
- *Event percepts* contain semantic data about events from the environment. An object's identifier provides the source where the event originated from.
- *Action percepts* contain feedback information about ongoing actions. The MAS agent can associate this feedback with a dispatched action using the included unique action identifier. Feedback information includes the progress status of the action and possible failure conditions.

Two types of actions have been defined in CIGA's *Cognitive Interface* layer:

- *Action instructions* are used for the physical (durative) actions agents perform. They correspond to the actions implemented in the *GE Interface* layer described previously and are executed by the *Behavior Realizer*.
- *Communication instructions* are used for physical communication between agents. These are *special* actions consisting of two parts. The first part contains the physical action the agent performs to realize the communication, corresponding to the previous type of instruction. The second part includes the communicative intent which may be represented in an agent communication language. This part cannot be send directly to the receiving agent if the physical communication action has not started yet. The *Cognitive Interface* layer is responsible for orchestrating this process.

For the implementation of the *MAS Interface* layer, interface standards like EIS [3] can be employed which has been explored to interface with multi-agent platforms like 2APL, GOAL, Jadex and Jason. Though, such platforms focus on high-level decision-making and deliberation aspects of agents and lack other aspects of behavior that may be required to form a fully cognitive architecture (E.g. the modeling of physiology, emotion or reflexive behaviors). These aspects can play an important role in simulating virtual humans for example. This issue has been addressed before as seen in CoJACK [8] which extends the JACK platform by combining its symbolic decision-making module with what is called a moderator layer for emotional and physiological factors. The *MAS Interface* layer can easily be used to connect such an additional MAS layer with its environment.

4   Related Technologies

In this section, we compare CIGA with related research and technologies with similar functionalities. First we'll look at technologies providing an interface to an environment in a game engine for external access. Gamebots [1] is a modification of the UT game engine and provides fixed sense-act interfaces for in-game avatars accessible using socket communication. It is often used in research on embodied agents mainly because of the lack of good alternatives for accessing virtual environments [7,9]. Gamebots can be compared to CIGA's *GE Interface* layer (see Figure 3). Though, in Gamebots, there is no methodology for using domain ontologies as the interface messages are fixed and geared specifically towards the UT engine. Further, *action monitoring* is not supported since Gamebots doesn't offer explicit execution and monitoring of actions.

The High Level Architecture (HLA) is an architecture for distributed simulations. Its goal is to synchronize environments running in separate simulations. There have been attempts to connect external agents to simulation environments using HLA [13]. We consider HLA not suitable for connecting MASs since it was not designed for this purpose and therefore lacks facilities for agent-centric sensing and acting. Similarities between CIGA and HLA are the use of *ontologies* as a design contract and the use of a subscription mechanism to control the flow of information sent between components. For CIGA, this is described in [20].

Next we'll compare the system of *Pogamut* which has a goal similar to CIGA. *Pogamut* is designed as a mediation-layer between a game engine (GE) and a decision-making system (DMS) to bridge the "representational gap" [10]. It is based on a general abstract framework for connecting a DMS to a GE [9]. The architecture of a Pogamut agent consists of a *WorldView* component for GE facts, augmented with optional components like a *Working Memory*, an *Inference Engine*, a *Reactive Layer* and a *DMS*. The main conceptual difference between Pogamut and CIGA is that where Pogamut presents an agent architecture connected to a game engine, the CIGA middleware offers facilities to connect an agent in a MAS directly to an avatar in the game engine. It doesn't enforce any agent architecture as we consider this to be contained in the MAS. Providing a tight connection with an avatar in the game engine requires CIGA to enforce modifying the game engine. Although this is a strong requirement, we think it is a necessity to better aid in the connection design of an agent's mind and body, allowing us to perform *perception filtering* and *action monitoring* in the game engine's native programming language. Although Pogamut is more flexible in connecting to different game engines (using Gamebots or HLA), it is highly dependent on the specific game engine. Here, the game engine not only dictates the mechanisms for sensing and acting, but also the use of fixed data representations for actions and sensory information. Although ontologies can be implicitly defined as Java classes, there is no explicit formal agreement between the GE and a Pogamut agent.

Facilitating the connection between MAS agents and MAS environments, the *Environment Interface Standard* (EIS) has been proposed. It provides a general purpose interface for associating environment entities with MAS agents and their sense-act interface [3]. The proposed interface is not primarily geared towards connecting agents directly to a real-time virtual environment. Although EIS can be used for real-time environments, little is said on how to deal with the design issues presented in section 2. EIS has been used in connecting agents to an environment using Pogamut [18].

Last, there are systems which have addressed a subset of the design issues presented in the paper. For example, in [22,16], Mimesis is presented as an architecture to integrate special-purpose intelligent components with a game engine. The architecture addresses both the gap of information representation and action execution, though its design is less geared towards an agent-body connection such that issues in perception and communication are not addressed. In [5], a cognitive middleware layer is introduced which has a similar goal to the semantic processing in CIGA, providing agents with a *social world model*. Unlike CIGA, this system doesn't discuss the technological issues in creating embodied agents. In [19], the *ION Framework* is said to separate the simulation environment from a realization engine. Although it recognizes similar issues, it is unclear about the methods for implementing these guidelines.

5   Conclusion and Future Work

In this paper we presented CIGA, a middleware for facilitating the coupling of MASs to game engines providing a connection between a MAS agent and its embodiment in a virtual environment. It is designed as a general-purpose middleware employable in a wide range of applications with different requirements for agents. For example, in one simulation, believable embodied conversational agents (ECAs) are required where detailed (non)verbal communicative behavior and perception is important. In another simulation an agent's interaction and understanding of the environment may be more important requiring a more extended model of the environment and the actions for influencing it. A combination of such qualitative and quantitative aspects may also be desired. Here, CIGA facilitates the development of such simulations by supporting developers to bridge the conceptual gap between a MAS and a game engine without enforcing agent design decisions.

CIGA employs domain ontologies to form an agreement between the game engine and the MAS on the semantics of an agent's perceptual and behavioral interfaces. This allows designers to formally specify the concepts used within a specific application domain and reference them directly from within the game engine or the MAS. A sensory processing mechanism allows an agent to perceive its environment and build a *social world model* based on formal semantics. Designers are able to choose the required realism for sensors and control the way sensory information is filtered [20]. An action monitoring mechanism enables agents to be synchronized with the realization of their actions performed by their embodiments. Designers are left to provide an implementation of the actions specified for the application domain.

CIGA has been implemented connecting several MASs to an in-house developed game engine[1]. The *Physical Interface* of CIGA has been developed in C++ and the *Cognitive Interface* in Java. The internal connection mechanism employs TCP/IP sockets. MASs that have been tested include *2APL*, *Jadex* and a custom developed MAS testing industry-standard techniques. On top of the middleware platform a graphical user interface has been developed to provide logging and debugging facilities during the development process.

Future work involves validating the principled approach taken by CIGA by exploring different application settings where agents have different requirements. This also involves creating an interface with an alternate game engine. On the conceptual side, further research will be performed concerning the topic of agent communication within CIGA, dealing with formal agent communication in MASs on one side and believable human-like interactions in real-time environments on the other side.

References

1. Adobbati, R., Marshall, A.N., Scholer, A., Tejada, S.: Gamebots: A 3d virtual world test-bed for multi-agent research. In: Proceedings of the Second International Workshop on Infrastructure for Agents, MAS, and Scalable MAS (2001)
2. Badler, N.I., Bindiganavale, R., Allbeck, J., Schuler, W., Zhao, L., Palmer, M.: Parameterized action representation for virtual human agents. In: Embodied Conversational Agents, pp. 256–284. MIT Press, Cambridge (2000)
3. Behrens, T., Hindriks, K., Dix, J.: Towards an environment interface standard for agent platforms. Annals of Mathematics and Artificial Intelligence, pp. 1–35 (2010)
4. Brom, C., Lukavskỳ, J., Šerỳ, O., Poch, T., Šafrata, P.: Affordances and level-of-detail AI for virtual humans. In: Proceedings of Game Set and Match 2 (2006)
5. Chang, P.H.-M., Chen, K.-T., Chien, Y.-H., Kao, E., Soo, V.-W.: From Reality to Mind: A Cognitive Middle Layer of Environment Concepts for Believable Agents. In: Weyns, D., Van Dyke Parunak, H., Michel, F. (eds.) E4MAS 2004. LNCS (LNAI), vol. 3374, pp. 57–73. Springer, Heidelberg (2005)
6. Cornwell, J., O'Brien, K., Silverman, B., Toth, J.: Affordance theory for improving the rapid generation, composability, and reusability of synthetic agents and objects. In: Proceedings of the Twelfth Conference on Behavior Representation in Modeling and Simulation (2003)

---

[1] www.vstep.nl

7. Davies, N.P., Mehdi, Q., Gough, N.: A framework for implementing deliberative agents in computer games. In: Proceedings of the 20th European Conference on Modeling and Simulation, ECMS 2006 (2006)
8. Evertsz, R., Ritter, F.E., Busetta, P., Pedrotti, M., Bittner, J.L.: CoJACK - Achieving Principled Behaviour Variation in a Moderated Cognitive Architecture. In: Proceedings of the 17th Conference on Behavior Representation in Modeling and Simulation (2008)
9. Gemrot, J., Brom, C., Plch, T.: A Periphery of Pogamut: From Bots to Agents and Back Again. In: Dignum, F. (ed.) Agents for Games and Simulations II. LNCS, vol. 6525, pp. 19–37. Springer, Heidelberg (2011)
10. Gemrot, J., Kadlec, R., Bída, M., Burkert, O., Píbil, R., Havlíček, J., Zemčák, L., Šimlovič, J., Vansa, R., Štolba, M., Plch, T., Brom, C.: Pogamut 3 Can Assist Developers in Building AI (Not Only) for Their Videogame Agents. In: Dignum, F., Bradshaw, J., Silverman, B., van Doesburg, W. (eds.) Agents for Games and Simulations. LNCS, vol. 5920, pp. 1–15. Springer, Heidelberg (2009)
11. Kallmann, M., Thalmann, D.: Modeling objects for interaction tasks. In: Proc. Eurographics Workshop on Animation and Simulation, pp. 73–86 (1998)
12. Kopp, S., Krenn, B., Marsella, S., Marshall, A.N., Pelachaud, C., Pirker, H., Thórisson, K.R., Vilhjálmsson, H.: Towards a Common Framework for Multimodal Generation: The Behavior Markup Language. In: Gratch, J., Young, M., Aylett, R.S., Ballin, D., Olivier, P. (eds.) IVA 2006. LNCS (LNAI), vol. 4133, pp. 205–217. Springer, Heidelberg (2006)
13. Lees, M., Logan, B., Theodoropoulos, G.: Agents, games and hla. Simulation Modelling Practice and Theory 14(6), 752–767 (2006)
14. Meyer, B.: Applying "design by contract". Computer 25, 40–51 (1992)
15. Peters, C., Dobbyn, S., MacNamee, B., O'Sullivan, C.: Smart objects for attentive agents. In: WSCG (2003)
16. Riedl, M.O.: Towards Integrating AI Story Controllers and Game Engines: Reconciling World State Representations. In: Proceedings of the 2005 IJCAI Workshop on Reasoning, Representation and Learning in Computer Games (2005)
17. Tutenel, T., Bidarra, R., Smelik, R.M., Kraker, K.J.D.: The role of semantics in games and simulations. Computers in Entertainment 6, 57:1–57:35 (2008)
18. Hindriks, K.V., van Riemsdijk, B., Behrens, T., Korstanje, R., Kraayenbrink, N., Pasman, W., de Rijk, L.: UNREAL GOAL Bots. In: Dignum, F. (ed.) Agents for Games and Simulations II. LNCS, vol. 6525, pp. 1–18. Springer, Heidelberg (2011)
19. Vala, M., Raimundo, G., Sequeira, P., Cuba, P., Prada, R., Martinho, C., Paiva, A.: ION Framework – A Simulation Environment for Worlds with Virtual Agents. In: Ruttkay, Z., Kipp, M., Nijholt, A., Vilhjálmsson, H.H. (eds.) IVA 2009. LNCS, vol. 5773, pp. 418–424. Springer, Heidelberg (2009)
20. van Oijen, J., Dignum, F.: Scalable Perception for BDI-Agents Embodied in Virtual Environments. In: Proceedings of the 2011 IEEE/WIC/ACM International Conference on Intelligent Agent Technology (2011)
21. van Oijen, J., van Doesburg, W., Dignum, F.: Goal-Based Communication Using BDI Agents as Virtual Humans in Training: An Ontology Driven Dialogue System. In: Dignum, F. (ed.) Agents for Games and Simulations II. LNCS, vol. 6525, pp. 38–52. Springer, Heidelberg (2011)
22. Young, R., Riedl, M., Branly, M., Jhala, A., Martin, R., Saretto, C.J.: An architecture for integrating plan-based behavior generation with interactive game environments. Journal of Game Development 1(1) (2004)

How to Compare Usability of Techniques for the Specification of Virtual Agents' Behavior? An Experimental Pilot Study with Human Subjects

Jakub Gemrot[1], Cyril Brom[1], Joanna Bryson[2], and Michal Bída[1]

[1] Faculty of Mathematics and Physics, Charles University in Prague,
Malostranske namesti 25,
118 00, Prague 1, Czech Republic
[2] University of Bath,
Bath, BA2 7AY, United Kingdoms

Abstract. Reactive or dynamic planning is currently the dominant paradigm for controlling virtual agents in 3D videogames. Various reactive planning techniques are employed in the videogame industry while many reactive planning systems and languages are being developed in the academia. Claims about benefits of different approaches are supported by the experience of videogame programmers and the arguments of researchers, but rigorous empirical data corroborating alleged advantages of different methods are lacking. Here, we present results of a pilot study in which we compare the usability of an academic technique designed for programming intelligent agents' behavior with the usability of an unaltered classical programming language. Our study seeks to replicate the situation of professional game programmers considering using an unfamiliar academic system for programming in-game agents. We engaged 30 computer science students attending a university course on virtual agents in two programming assignments. For each, the students had to code high-level behavior of a 3D virtual agent solving a game-like task in the Unreal Tournament 2004 environment. Each student had to use Java for one task and the POSH reactive planner with a graphical editor for the other. We collected quantitative and qualitative usability data. The results indicate that POSH outperforms Java in terms of usability for one of the assigned tasks but not the other. This implies that the suitability of an AI systems-engineering approach is task sensitive. We also discuss lessons learnt about the evaluation process itself, proposing possible improvements in the experimental design. We conclude that comparative studies are a useful method for analyzing benefits of different approaches to controlling virtual agents.

1   Introduction

Reactive planning is currently the dominant paradigm for controlling virtual agents in 3D videogames and simulations. Prominent reactive planning techniques used in the industry are derivations of finite state machines (FSMs) [1], and more recently, behavior trees [2]. Technically, these are implemented in a scripting language, be it a

M. Beer et al. (Eds.): AEGS 2011, LNAI 7471, pp. 38–62, 2012.

general-purpose language such as Lua [3] or a special-purpose language tailored at a particular game, such as UnrealScript [4], or hard-coded in a game's native language, typically C++ [5]. Advantages and drawbacks of different approaches used by the industry have been commented on widely [6,7,8].

At the same time, academic action-selection systems for AI planning are becoming increasingly mature, and the question arises whether they have advantages over the solutions employed presently by the industry. These systems include decision making modules of several cognitive architectures, e.g., Soar and ACT-R [9, 10], stand-alone BDI-based programming languages, e.g. GOAL [11], and stand-alone reactive planners such as POSH [12]. It has been already demonstrated that some of these systems, for instance Soar [9], POSH [13], GOAL [11] and Jazzyk [14], can be used for controlling virtual agents acting in game-like environments. From the perspective of efficacy of code execution, these systems are sluggish and can be considered as prototypes only at the present stage of maturity; however, they could potentially outperform some industry solutions in terms of usability (from the programmers' perspective), re-usability (of parts of code) and agent's cognitive performance, as assumed, for instance, by part of the academic community studying BDI-based languages [15].

Sound empirical data demonstrating the alleged advantages of different reactive planning technique, both industrial and academic, are generally lacking. Tyrell analyzed various robotics and ethology-based action selection mechanisms in terms of agent performance given approximately equal amounts of time devoted by a programmer [16]. This work was extended by Bryson in an effort to provide an evaluation for her own POSH action selection. [17]. Tyrrell's system was to test a single action-selection mechanism over a large number of "lifespans" by agents inhabiting an extremely rich and varied environment. The complexity of the environment lead to enormous variation in the results, so statistical significance was determined by running enough trials to compare the standard error rather than the standard deviation.

Bryson also provided a more theoretically formal but less rigorous comparison of POSH action selection to FSMs, showing that POSH plans were able to express action an intelligence was likely to choose to do in a more efficient way than an FSM [18]. However, none of these studies engaged programmers other than the authors themselves in the mechanisms' evaluation. In contrast, Hindriks et al [19] conducted an extensive qualitative analysis of the code of 60 first year computer science students developing (in teams of five students) three Capture The Flag agents for the videogame Unreal Tournament 2004 (UT 2004) using GOAL agent programming language. Hindriks's team aimed at "providing insight into more practical aspects of agent development" and "better understanding problems that programmers face when using (an agent programming) language" and identified a number of structural code patterns, information useful for improvements to the language. However, that study was not comparative and did not report the programmers' feedback.

Here, we are interested in a complementary approach, namely feasibility of quantitative comparative quasi-experimental studies (as used in psychology and social sciences) for investigating usability of action selection systems from the users' (programmers') perspective. We specifically address the usability issue as opposed to the efficiency or performance issue. This perspective encompasses various objective and subjective measures, such as steepness of the learning curve, time spent by development, programming vs. testing time ratio, number of bugs made by the programmer, subjective attitude towards the technique etc. We designed and conducted a pilot study with the following objectives:

a) to investigate the subjectively-perceived usability of an academic action selection system designed to be useful for programming agents' behavior, when compared to perceived usability of an unenhanced classical programming language; this mimics the situation of game programmers considering using an academic system they are not familiar with for programming in-game artificial intelligence;

b) to compare the quality of solutions implemented in the academic action selection system and in the classical programming language; this measure plays an important role in the adoption of new systems in general;

c) to consider whether the experimental method *per se* is useful and whether (and under which conditions) it can produce helpful results.

We have been running a course on virtual agents development for computer science students at Prague University since 2005. Students are taught various techniques for controlling virtual agents [20] and trained to program their behavior in the virtual environment UT 2004 (similarly to Hindriks et al.). For that task, our integrated development environment Pogamut [21] is used by the students. In the academic year 2009/10, we turned the final exam for the course into a scientific experiment engaging 30 computer science students in two programming assignments lasting 3 hours each. Each student had to code the high-level behavior of a 3D virtual agent solving a game-like task in the UT 2004. The conventional language and the language underlying the academic system were both Java. We use Java because its learning curve is less steep than that of C++ (a more usual game development language) and because our students are expected to be at least to some extent familiar with Java. For the academic system, we used the POSH reactive planner with a graphical editor. This is because POSH has been already demonstrated for controlling UT agents [13] and because POSH has previously been investigated by our postgraduates and integrated into Pogamut.

For both the tasks and in both programming environments, the students' task was to organize low-level action and sensory primitives to produce complex behavior, but not to program the primitives as such. The drag-and-drop graphical editor we developed for POSH disguised its Lisp-like underlying plan syntax students might have struggled with. The study was only possible because the Pogamut platform provided the same development environment for both tasks and allowed us to predesign the same sets of behavior primitives, isolating the features of the language as the subject of the study.

We collected various quantitative and qualitative usability data in four questionnaires. Our main hypothesis was that subjects' attitude towards POSH would be at least as high as towards Java. As this is a pilot study, we kept the research question as simple as possible. Of course, for practical, commercial application of POSH, it would be an advantage to specifically identify its benefits compared to Java (and other systems), but this was not our aim for this study and is left for future work.

The rest of the paper proceeds as follows. We introduce POSH in Section 2 and detail the methods of our study in Section 3. The results are presented in Section 4 and discussed in Section 5, and Section 6 concludes.

2   POSH

POSH action selection was originally developed in the late 1990s in response to criticism of what was at the time an extremely popular agent design approach (at least in academic discussion): the Subsumption Architecture (SA) [27]. SA was used to produce considerable advances in real-time intelligent agents, particularly robotics. It consists primarily of two components: a highly modular architecture where every action is coded with the perception it needs to operate; and a complex, highly distributed form of action selection to arbitrate between the actions that would be produced by the various modules. Although extremely well-known and heavily cited, the SA was seldom really used outside of its developers. Bryson hypothesized that the emphasis on modular intelligence was actually the core contribution of SA, but that the complexity of action selection, while successfully enforcing a reactive approach, confused most programmers who were not used to thinking about concurrent systems.

POSH was developed then to simplify the construction of action selection for modular AI. Briefly, a programmer used to thinking about conventional sequential programs is asked to first consider a worst-case scenario for their agent, then to break each step of the plan to resolve that scenario into a part of a reactive plan. Succeeding at a goal is the agent's highest priority, so should be the thing the agent does if it can. The programmer then describes for the agent how to perceive that its goal has been met. Then for each step leading up to the goal the same process is followed: a perceptual condition is defined allowing the agent to recognize if it can take the action leading most directly to its goal [12, 18]. The actions are each small chunks of code that control the agent, so-called behavior primitives (see Tab. S2 – all supplementary figures and tables can be found in the appendix), and the perceptions are sensory primitives (Tab. S4).

After a period of experimenting with the system, Bryson embedded POSH in a more formal development methodology called Behavior Oriented Design (BOD). BOD emphasizes the above development process, and also the use of behavior modules written in ordinary object-oriented languages to encode the majority of the agent's intelligence, and to provide the behaviour and sensory primitives. BOD includes a set of heuristics for recognizing when intelligence should be refactored either from a plan towards a behavior module or from a module into a plan. BOD and POSH have now been adopted or recommended by a number of leading thinkers and toolkits in AI, including Pogamut [21], RePast [28] and AIGameDev [6].

Recently, a graphical editor for POSH plans has been developed as part of the Pogamut effort. Its new version is used in the present study (Fig. S1).

3   Method

3.1   Experimental Design

As explained earlier, the study compares the usability of an academic reactive planner, POSH, and an unenhanced classical programming language, Java. Low-level behavior primitives were prepared for both groups in advance by the authors of the study. The set of primitives were fully sufficient for solving the presented tasks.

The study was set in an AI course for computer science students in Charles University in Prague. The syllabus of course is described in [20, 22]. Subjects were given a pretest (3 hours) after the course to ensure that they have acquired elementary skills for solving sub-problems from the final exam. Only subjects that have passed the pretest were admitted to the final exam.

The final exam was structured to obtain comparative data on Java and POSH usability. In the final exam, each subject had to solve two tasks, the Hunter Task (3 hours) and the Guide Task (3 hours), see Sec. 3.3. Subjects were split into two groups, Group A and Group B. Group A was instructed to solve Hunter Task in POSH first and Guide Task in Java second while Group B was instructed to solve Hunter Task in Java first and Guide Task in POSH second. For both tasks, syntax highlighting was available for Java and a graphical editor for POSH plans (Fig. S1).

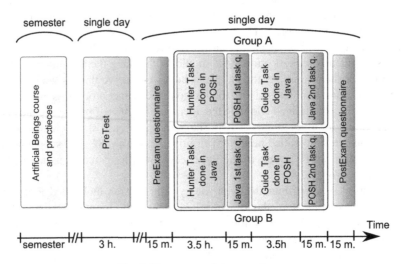

Fig. 1. The course of the experiment

Subjects were given 4 questionnaires in total during the exam (15 minutes each). There was a 30 minutes long break for a light lunch between the tasks. The course of the experiment is summarized in Fig. 1. Subjects were informed that the study will take about 8 hours in total in advance, but the structure and the exact content were revealed only during the study. The assignments were administered immediately prior to each task and the subjects given 30 minutes to read them.

3.2   Participants

We recruited 30 students for the study out of 52 attendants of the AI course. The study was the course's final exam and if students succeeded in its both parts, they were given a final grade based on their agent's performance. Students had the option of withdrawing from the study if they preferred a different kind of final exam.

We excluded 3 students from the analysis due to data incompleteness. In total, we analyzed data from 27 students of which 2 were female. Students were sampled into two groups. Due to the low number of subjects, the groups were not assigned to conditions entirely at random. Rather the students were ranked by their ability as determined by their pretest performance, and then the two groups were matched with as close to equal sums of rank status as possible. The number of students according to their years of study and assigned groups is presented in Tab. S1.

3.3   Materials

The Course. The students attended an introductory course on the control of virtual characters. The course is intended for students without previous AI or 3D graphics knowledge but with previous programming experience. Only students from the second or a higher year of study can attend. The course comprises of 12 theoretical lectures (90 minutes each) and 6 practical lessons at computers (90 minutes each). The theoretical classes are detailed in [20, 22]. During practical lessons, the students are taught how to work with Pogamut 3 platform library (2 lessons) and develop behavior of virtual agents using both Java (2 lessons) and POSH (2 lessons) [23].

The Pretest. The general aim of the Pretest was to rule out subjects that were not sufficiently prepared for the final exam. Unprepared subjects would bias the data as they would likely fail during the final exam which would influence their answers in questionnaires.

The Pretest task was to create an agent capable of exploring the environment of UT2004 game and collect items of a specific type only. The agent had no adversaries in this task. Subjects were not given behavior primitives in advance; they had to create them in Java for themselves. Regarding programming of a high-level behavior, subjects had the opportunity of choosing between Java and POSH. This approach was chosen to test the level of subjects' comprehension of the Pogamut library so that they would be able understand behavior primitives provided to them during the final exam.

Three programmers skilled in VR technology solved the pretest task in advance to calibrate the difficulty of the test. The time allotment (3 hours) was at least three times longer than average time needed by these programmers to finish the task. Subjects had 3 attempts to pass the Pretest. Most passed on their first attempt.

Task Hunter. The Hunter Task was designed as a game-like scenario. Subjects were to create an agent (called Hunter) that explores the environment collecting blood samples of another computer-driven agent called Alien either by finding them around in the environment or by shooting Alien. Alien was an adversary agent that was capable of killing Hunter when nearby. If Hunter or Alien got killed, they were restarted in the environment far from each other. In addition, Hunter started with no weapons. Thus, the AI behavior must correctly prioritize the following intentions: 1) finding a weapon, 2) collecting blood samples, 3) responding to Alien. For instance, the Hunter agent should stop pursuing a blood sample item and responded to Alien if Alien has approached, otherwise Hunter could be killed resulting in the loss of weapons and blood samples collected so far.

In contrast to the Pretest, subjects were given a full set of behavior primitives (canSeeEnemy, runToItem, shootEnemy etc., see list in Tab. S2) that were sufficient to solve the task. All behavior primitives were carefully commented inside the code to make their usage clear. Action primitives did not contain any decision making logic, e.g., shootEnemy action did not contain any checks whether the agent has a loaded weapon to shoot from or whether the enemy is close enough for the weapon to be effective. Such logic was to be created by each subject using proper sensors, e.g., hasWeapon and getEnemyDistance (example can be seen in the Fig. S1). The task was again solved by two skilled programmers in advance using these primitives and their feedback was used to adjust them.

After filling in a pre-exam questionnaire, each subject was given the assignment written on the paper and was provided a sufficient time (30 minutes) to read it and ask questions to clarify any ambiguities. Group A was then instructed to solve the task in Java while Group B in POSH. Time allotment was 3 hours, which is roughly three times more than was required by the skilled programmers. Both groups had the same set of primitives. The POSH version of the primitives differed only in implementation details so that they could be easily used inside POSH reactive plans.

Group A and Group B were working in parallel in two different rooms. Subjects were not allowed to cooperate on the solution but they were allowed to utilize any documentation about the Pogamut library available on the Internet [24].

Task Guide. The Guide Task was designed to be more cognitive than the Hunter Task. Subjects were to create an agent called Guide that can find a Civilian agent inside the environment and guide it back to its home. The Civilian agent was created to wander aimlessly around the environment far from its home unless the Guide agent instructed it otherwise. The Guide agent must communicate with the Civilian agent if it wants the Civilian agent to follow its lead. The communication has a fixed and rather simplistic protocol described in the assignment (see Tab. S3).

Communication was reliable and the two agents could hear each other up to a specific distance. Apart from finding Civilian, there were three obstacles that Guide had to overcome in order to successfully lead Civilian home. First, Civilian was willing to start to follow Guide only if it can see it. Second, if Civilian lost Guide from view, it stopped following. Third, Civilian was created to be absent-minded and ceased to follow the Guide agent from time to time for no reason. Thus, the challenge was not only to find Civilian and persuade it to follow the Guide agent to its home, but also to constantly observe whether Civilian is doing so.

As in the previous task, subjects were given a full set of behavior primitives (Tab. S4) and the task was tested by two skilled programmers both in Java and POSH. The only exception was the handling of the communication was always in Java, but it was sufficient to write three lines of Java code to solve the task in the POSH variant.

Group A was instructed to solve the task in POSH while Group B in Java. Everything else (the assignment description, the space for questions, the prohibition of cooperation, the allowance of Internet usage, slight differences in the POSH primitives) remained the same as in the previous task.

3.4   Questionnaires

Every subject was given four questionnaires in total. The timing of administration of each questionnaire is pictured in Fig. 1. Questionnaires were:

1) PreExam questionnaire,
2) Hunter Task questionnaire (in Java and POSH variants),
3) Guide Task questionnaire (in Java and POSH variants),
4) PostExam questionnaire.

The PreExam questionnaire contained questions about the subject's biographical background and their AI/Agent/Programming literacy. Only relevant results are presented in this paper. The main questions for the present interest are: "How many person-months of programming/AI/Java experiences do you have?" and "How many hours have you spent experimenting with Pogamut at home?"

The two task questionnaires were designed to elicit data about comprehensibility of sensory and behavior primitives and subjects' preferences for the programming formalism used in the task. The main questions for present interest are:

"Did you find POSH/Java sensor/action primitives comprehensible?"
Answers (Likert item with 5-point Likert scale):

1) I had a lot of troubles understanding them.
2) I did not understand a few primitives.
3) I had no troubles at all, everything was perfectly clear.

"Did you find the number of POSH/Java sensor/action primitives sufficient?"
Answers (Likert item with 5-point Likert scale):

1) Totally insufficient.
2) I had to create a few for myself.
3) Totally sufficient.

"Which formalism do you prefer, Java or POSH?"
Answers (Likert item with 5-point Likert scale):

1) Strong Java preference.
2) Weak Java preference.
3) Cannot tell which is better.
4) Weak POSH preference.
5) Strong POSH preference.

The PostExam questionnaire contained many questions about the comfort of the Pogamut library API, Java, POSH GUI and other features of the Pogamut platform. It also contained the final question about the overall preference between POSH and Java:

"Which formalism do you generally prefer for high-level behavior specification, POSH or Java?"

Answers (Likert item with 5-point Likert scale):

1) Strong POSH preference.
2) Weak POSH preference.
3) Can't tell which is better.
4) Weak Java preference.
5) Strong Java preference.

Subjects were also given a space for a free-text explanation of their answer.

The POSH/Java preference question was given three times in total and they have appeared in both (POSH/Java) variants of task's questionnaires. Our aim was to observe subject preferences with regard to the different tasks (Hunter Task vs. Guide Task) they had to solve as well as their overall. The questionnaires were not anonymous so we were able to pair them with concrete agents later on (see 4.2).

3.5   Data Analysis

Answers of subjects from questionnaires of both groups were analyzed. We used χ^2-tests of independence to test whether both groups had same or different language preferences. As the number of subjects in each group is rather small, we have grouped subjects with Java/POSH preferences into 3 classes (instead of 5) for the purpose of the χ^2-tests. Answer 1-2 is considered as *Java preference*, answer 4-5 as *POSH preference* and answer 3 as indifference.

Additionally, all agents were tested for quality. We executed a corresponding task scenario for every agent 15 times and checked whether the agent fulfilled the task's objective within the time frame of 10 minutes. We marked every run with either 0 (agent failure) or 1 (agent success). Average number of successes was counted as the *agent success rate (ASR)*. Even though every run was identical (the same environment setup was used, the same starting positions of bots were used, the same random seeds, etc.), we had to perform multiple runs due to small non-determinism caused by UT2004 and by asynchronous execution of agents' behaviors which resulted in different outcomes from the behavior deliberations.

ASR was taken as the degree of agent quality. An ASR of 1 indicates the agent always succeeded, while an ASR of 0 indicates the agent always failed – real values could fall between these. Logistic regression was used to identify relationships between the agent quality and the chosen technique, subject experiences and their understanding of the provided primitives. The regression was made for every task/group combination (4 regression models) as well as for all agent runs for Task 1 and for Task 2 (combining data from Group 1 and Group 2, model is including the group parameter) and is presented in 4.2.

There were 4 questions testing subject understanding of the behavior primitives. For the subsequent analysis, we averaged responses of these questions and used this average as the *Primitives apprehension* variable.

4   Results

4.1   Comparison of the Two Groups with Regards to Subjective Java/POSH Preference

The attitude of the students towards the languages in the two tasks is shown in Tab. 1, 3, S2-S7 together with their means and standard deviations.

Regarding the first task, Group A exhibits a strong preference to POSH (Hunter in POSH) while Group B (Hunter in Java) was more indifferent. The contingency table of Java/POSH preference after the first task is shown in Tab. 2. The preferences in Group A and B are not significantly different (p-value = 0.12).

Table 1. Left: Group A, Hunter Task (in POSH), Java/POSH preference. Right: Group B, Hunter Task (in Java), Java/POSH preference.

Ans.	#	%	Ans.	#	%
1	0	0	1	0	0
2	2	15.4	2	5	35.7
3	1	7.6	3	4	28.6
4	3	23.1	4	1	7.1
5	7	53.9	5	4	28.6
Mean	4.15±1.14		Mean	3.29±1.27	

Table 2. Contingency table of the Java/POSH preferences after the first task

	Java pref. (1-2)	Can't decide (3)	POSH pref. (4-5)	Total
Group A	2	1	10	13
Group B	5	4	5	14
Total	7	5	15	27

Concerning the second task, Group A (using Java) was indifferent and Group B (using POSH) exhibited preference to Java (Tab. 4). The preferences in Group A and B are not significantly different (p-value = 0.36). In general, the students shifted their preference to Java after the second task, which is summarized by Tab. S5.

General preference between Java and POSH, as assessed by PostExam questionnaires, is not a clear one. The preferences in Group A and B were significantly different with Group A preferring POSH while Group B preferring Java (p-value = 0.01) (summarized in the Tab. 5).

Table 3. From left to right: i) Group A, Guide Task (in Java), Java/POSH preference, ii) Group B, Guide Task (in POSH), Java/POSH preference, iii) Group A, PostExam, Java/POSH preference, iv) Group B, PostExam, Java/POSH preference

Ans.	#	%	Ans.	#	%	Ans.	#	%	Ans.	#	%
1	2	15.4	1	3	21.5	1	0	0	1	3	21.5
2	4	30.8	2	7	50.0	2	3	23.1	2	6	42.8
3	1	7.6	3	2	14.3	3	2	15.4	3	4	28.6
4	4	30.8	4	1	7.1	4	3	23.1	4	1	7.1
5	2	15.4	5	1	7.1	5	5	38.4	5	0	0
Mean	3.00±1.41		Mean	2.29±1.14		Mean	3.77±1.19		Mean	2.21±0.86	

Table 4. Contingency table of the Java/POSH preferences after the second task

	Java pref. (1-2)	Can't decide (3)	POSH pref. (4-5)	Total
Group 1	6	1	6	13
Group 2	10	2	2	14
Total	16	3	8	27

Table 5. Contingency table of the general Java/POSH preferences as answered in the PostExam questionnaire

	Java pref. (1-2)	Can't decide (3)	POSH pref. (4-5)	Total
Group A	3	2	8	13
Group B	9	4	1	14
Total	12	6	9	27

4.2   Comparison of the Two Groups with Regards to Objective Task Solution Quality

Logistic regression was used to identify relationships between an agent's quality (dependent variable) and chosen technique (Java or POSH), subject experiences and apprehensions of provided primitives. The parameter for the group was not statistically significant and was left out from the model for the sake of simplicity. We have created 3 models (using data from both Group A and B, from Group A only and from Group B only) for both tasks (6 models in total).

Models Description. The models' parameters are summarized in Tab. 6. Some dependencies between model variables and agent's quality are presented in Figs. S8 – S10. Every figure contains graphs for Task 1 (left) and Task 2 (right) models separately. Models using data from both groups contain the additional discrete variable *Technique* (Java / POSH), therefore they are visualized with two graphs separately in each picture (for the Java and POSH cases separately). As all models amount to a function from the n-dimensional space (yielded from the Cartesian product of model variables' ranges) into <0;1> (agent success rate, model dependent variable), every presented graph can be seen as a planar cut through chosen variable of the whole model's n+1-dimensional graph where all other variables are fixed at data's means.

Tasks Comparison. Task 1 was solved considerably better by subjects from higher years of study (Fig. S8, left). The data for Task 1 also suggests that subjects' comprehension of provided primitives affects the quality of their agents (Fig. S9, left); this is more pronounced in Group A's subjects. Additionally, solutions from Group B (implementing the Hunter agent in Java) indicate correlation with previous Java experiences (Fig. S10, left). The chosen technique (Java or POSH) did not influence the agents' success (see first row *POSH-influence* column in Tab. 6) in Task 1.

The interpretation of results of Task 2 is not as clear. Task 2 was also sensitive to Java experience as well as primitive comprehension (Fig. S10, S9, right), but results were more widely distributed this time. Also, agents of Group B driven by POSH did considerably worse than agents of Group A that were controlled by Java (see the fourth row *POSH influence* column in Tab. 6).

Table 6. Logistic models of agent success with respect to programming technique, subject's year of study, his/her experiences and primitives comprehension. Every row contains the parameters of one model. Column *POSH-influence* (discrete variable) explains how the probability of an agent's success changes when the agent was programmed using POSH (present only when data from both groups are used). All other columns (continuous variables) show how respective variables contribute to ASR. *Odds ratio* describes how the variable influences the probability of an agent's success. Values greater than one indicate that the probability grows proportionally with the variable and vice versa. Values in bold are discussed in Section 5.

Data used	Model fit comp. against empty model	POSH influence		Year of study		Java experience		Pogamut used at home		Primitives comprehension	
	P-Value	Odds ratio	Sig.	Odds ratio	Sig.	Odds ratio	Sig.	Odds ratio	Sig.	Odds ratio	Sig.
GA+B, T1	10^{-12}	**1.10**		**2.08**	***	1.08		0.96		**2.58**	***
GA, T1 (POSH)	10^{-10}	X		**2.10**	**	1.19		1.04		**1.24**	***
GB, T1 (Java)	10^{-6}	X		**1.81**	***	**1.30**	**	0.96		**0.74**	
GA+B, T2	10^{-5}	**0.44**	**	0.88		**1.11**	**	1.05	.	1.58	*
GA, T2 (Java)	0.057	X		0.99		**0.91**		0.91	*	2.37	**
GB, T2 (POSH)	10^{-7}	X		0.81		**1.09**		1.23	**	1.46	

Significance (P-Value): $0 < *** < 0.001 < ** < 0.01 < * 0.05 < . < 0.1$

5 Discussion

This pilot study compared the usability of an academic reactive planning system to the usability of a common programming language when applied to programming the behavior of virtual agents in 3D game-like tasks. The POSH reactive planner empowered by a graphical editor of plans was chosen for the former and the Java programming language for the latter. This quantitative experimental study is, to our knowledge, the first in the field of virtual agent programming techniques (but see also [29]). The purpose of the study was twofold. First, we aimed at investigating objectively the usability of the two techniques, making a small step towards the grand goal: isolating features that contribute to usability of different approaches to control virtual agents in 3D videogames and simulations. Secondly, we aimed at answering the question whether the chosen experimental method *per se* is promising for future studies. We now discuss these two points.

5.1 Results

Summary of the Data. The answer for the question of usability of Java and POSH has two sides which are intertwined. First, there is a subjective answer of comfort in using a chosen system as presented in Sec. 4.1. Second, there is an objective answer that comes of assessing the quality of agents as presented in Sec. 4.2.

Regarding the subjective answer, there are two main outcomes:

a) Subjects, in general, reported that they preferred POSH for the first task (Tab. 1, 2, S2, S3) while they preferred Java for the latter (see Tab. 3, 4, S4, S5);

b) group A subjects tend to prefer POSH while Group B subjects tend to prefer Java (Tab. 5).

The objective answer as showed by logistic regression indicates several outcomes:

c) Students in a higher year of study tend to perform better in the first task while there was no such influence in the second task (see Fig. S8);

d) previous Java experience was important in Task 1 in Group B (using Java in that task) but not in Task 2 in Group A (using Java in that task) (Fig. S10, left; Tab. 6);

e) comprehension of the provided primitives was high in general (Fig. S9 left; means in both tasks were higher than 4.1) and seems to influence ASR a bit (Fig. S9 left; Tab. 6);

f) the first task was done equally well in both POSH and Java (see *Odds ratio* of *POSH influence* in the first row of Tab. 6) while in the second task, subjects using POSH performed significantly worse (see *Odds ratio* of *POSH influence* in the third row of Tab. 6).

General Comments. Arguably, the main underlying theme is that the data indicates different outcomes for the two groups. Why? Let us start with comments on distribution of subjects into Group A and B with respect to major variables (Comment 1), proceed with comments on several uncontrolled variables that may have influenced the outcome (Comments 2, 3, 4), and finally return to the individual outcomes A-F above.

1. Is the average programming experience of the subjects the same for the two groups? Tab. S6 indicates that Group B may have consisted of slightly more Java experienced subjects, but the difference between the groups is rather small. Data for the total previous programming experience look similarly (note that mean is not a useful aggregative variable here since the learning curve is not linear). Students from Group B also have higher years of study on average (A: mean=3.3; SD=1. B: mean=4.4; SD=1.5). This is the outcome of the rank-based sampling procedure, which will be commented in Sec. 5.2. For present purpose, it is important that Group B may have comprised slightly more experienced programmers on average than Group A.

2. Subjects were undergoing a coding marathon as the final exam lasted 8 hours so the results from the second task could have been biased by subjects' tiredness. However, it seems reasonable to assume that both groups were equally tired.

3. It may be that the second task is harder in general, independently of the tiredness. We did not consider the complexity of tasks beforehand; therefore we have asked *post hoc* four independent VR experienced programmers to judge tasks' complexity out of the assignments (they did not perform them, we

have just presented them written assignments) and task suitability for the chosen technique. The second task was perceived as easier only by one of them; the others thought that the second task is harder. Their comments regarding the suitability of techniques diverged.

4. It also may be that POSH fits better for solving the first task while Java for the second. This idea is actually supported by free-report parts of questionnaires. Some subjects indicated that Java was more suitable for the second task while none the other way round. Some subject's comments to the 2nd task:

   "There were more if-then rules in the first task than here, therefore POSH would have suited the first task more, using it here was mere overkill."

   "Using POSH for this task would be a nuisance."

   "In contrast with the first task, this was too complex to niggle with POSH plan graphical editor. It was better to address it in Java."

Main Interpretation. In our opinion, the most plausible explanation of the results is that they are produced by combination of two effects: the fact that the second task can be more easily solved using Java (unlike the first task), and the fact that the graphical drag&drop editor and POSH (it is not clear which of these or whether both of them together) is more appealing to a less skilled audience and such an audience can use it more effectively than Java. This statement agrees with Results (A) and (B) and partly with (C), and is further supported by Comments 1 and 4. Of course, our data only indicates that this can be the case; a useful hypothesis for further testing rather than a conclusive result.

It is also possible that the essential difference was that Task 2 was best completed by altering or adding to the provided the primitives. Because of the way POSH was introduced with the emphasis on the graphical tool, most subjects appeared to feel obliged not to alter any Java code while they were in the POSH condition. One student did provide an exceptionally good agent in Task 2 by combining POSH and altered Java primitives. This strategy is more in keeping with the way POSH is presented in the academic literature as a part of a development methodology (Behaviour Oriented Design) rather than a stand-alone approach. However, only one exceptional programmer tried this strategy.

Another way of looking at the data is that POSH scored surprisingly well (Tab. 2, 4, 5) given many subject's initial Java experience but no initial POSH experience. Investigation of steepness of the learning curve might be fruitful in the future. Useful information could also come out of studies of programmers already skilled in using an agent-based technique. Sadly, finding such a subject pool is presently a difficult task.

It is not surprising that understanding the primitives (Result (E)) has a positive effect on ASR. In fact, the influence is rather small, which is most likely caused by a ceiling effect: the average understanding of primitives was high in general, suggesting that our primitives were well chosen, prepared and documented.

Several questions remain open. We do not know why there was no influence of the students' years of study on the agents' performance in the 2nd task (Result (C), 2nd part); perhaps the assignment was not sensitive enough, or perhaps the difference on the 1st task indicated more advanced students become more adept at a new problem more quickly, whether through learning more quickly or due to being less stressed by exam conditions.

Concerning Result (D), it is not surprising that previous Java experience was important in Task 1 in Group B but not A, because the former group used Java. We do not know why previous Java experience had no influence on Group A in Task 2; again perhaps the 2nd assignment was not sufficiently sensitive to this variable. Also the sensitivity to previous Java experience in Task 1 suggests that classical programming languages are not as suitable for less-experienced programmers such as game designers as higher-level graphical tools and planning languages are.

Generalization. The results of this study indicate that academic techniques may in certain cases provide advantages over classical programming languages, but it is too soon to generalize based on the results of one study performed on two particular approaches and tasks. More studies are needed to obtain more conclusive data for further supporting or refuting such a claim. Nevertheless, it is a good sign for developers of various agent-based languages such as Jason [26] or GOAL [11]. Closer examination is needed to identify different complexities underlying virtual agents' development. Such examination may help recognize possibilities and limits of various techniques and uncover their strong and weak points. For instance, it may be that when augmented by drag&drop graphical editors (as POSH was in our study), some of these languages may be better suited than scripting languages for people with mediocre programming skills, such as some game designers. We believe that without such analysis the gaming industry would unlikely embrace academic techniques for virtual agent's development.

5.2   Lessons Learned

As the comparative study of different techniques usable for virtual behavior development is new, we report lessons learned and suggest improvements for future studies. The main lessons are:

1. Performing the study in two consecutive parts promotes biased data on the second part due to subjects' tiredness. This can be addressed by altering the experiment design either by a) dividing subjects into 4 groups giving every group only *one* combination from the task-technique pairs, which would however require at least twice as many subjects, or b) by dividing each group into two subgroups, which would solve both tasks each but in the reverse order; that would allow the statistical computation of the effect of tiredness, or c) to perform the second task in another day.

2. It would be beneficial to administer one more questionnaire during the pretest to obtain the initial preferences of subjects regarding the techniques compared in the study. In general, several other variables could be controlled better, e.g. the task difficulty (see also Comments 2, 3, 4 in Sec. 6.1).

3. The analysis should be complemented with qualitative studies to gain more insight. This may have several forms. a) Interesting data can be obtained by analyzing the agent code as has been previously done by Hindriks and

colleagues [19]. We may still do this with the code from the present study. b) Focus groups or structured interviews can be conducted after the main study to obtain more precise explanations for subjects' preferences and their solutions' quality. c) Questionnaires should encourage subjects to describe reasons for their preference (the importance of this has been highlighted in Comment 4 in Sec. 5.1).

4. Attention should be paid to the evaluation's tasks. Each task should be judged not only for its general difficulty by programmers skilled with VR technologies, but also for its difficulty regarding the technique being tested. In general it is presumably a good thing to make assigned tasks varied so that an over-general conclusion is not reached without adequate justification. After the evaluation, subjects should be asked for their own assessment of the tasks to check if it correlates with the experts'. Note that both subject and expert assessment should be checked against actual quantifiable results.

5. The sampling procedure should be carefully considered. Evidently, even a rank-based sampling may produce unequal groups (with respect to some variables). When there are a lot of variables and a relatively small sample size, such an outcome may be inevitable. The sampling procedure will also be different for different questions asked, e.g., if one would like to assess group of experienced Java programmers against inexperienced ones, the criterion for sampling would be previous Java experience.

6. Pretests are important in order to ensure that students have certain minimal skills for the main study, e.g. from the present study the ability to understand behavior primitives. Pretests are also important for obtaining data for the sampling procedure.

5.3   Future Work

Our results clearly indicate a need to continue with comparative studies and to begin to identify the different aspects of the complex task of virtual behavior development. We are considering performing another study this year, taking into account the lessons learnt, possibly utilizing GOAL [10] as an academic reactive planning technique that is based on the BDI paradigm. We may also run the same test again but with POSH clearly set forward not as an alternative to Java but rather as a way to supplement it. AI action selection systems are intended to simplify the development of agent intelligence, not to replace it.

6   Conclusions

This pilot study compared an academic reactive planning technique (namely POSH) against a common programming language (namely Java) with respect to their usability for programming behaviors of virtual agents in 3D game-like tasks. The study has investigated the performance of subjects' agents with respect to the technique used as well as subjects' preferences towards the techniques.

The conclusion, stated with caution, is threefold. First, from a general perspective, POSH scored comparable to Java. Second, in a more fine-grained manner, usability of Java and POSH seem to be task-sensitive and subjectively perceived usability of the techniques as well as objective quality of the subjects' agents with respect to the techniques may change with subjects' programming experience. Third, the experimental method is useful, but should be complemented by other approaches.

Taken together, these are promising news for agent-based control mechanism developers. Future studies are needed and they should focus on isolating mechanisms' features that contribute most to the mechanisms' usability for different target groups of users, e.g., game designers vs. programmers.

Acknowledgement. Students' assignments were developed at Charles University in Prague as part of subproject Emohawk developed under the project CZ.2.17/3.1.00/31162 that is financed by the European Social Fund and the Budget of the Municipality of Prague. The subsequent research was partially supported by grant P103/10/1287 (GA ČR) (C.B., J.G., J.B.), SVV project number 263 314 (J.G., M.B.), research project MSM0021620838 (MŠMT ČR) (C.B.) and by students grant GA UK No. 0449/2010/A-INF/MFF (M.B.). We thank our students. The questionnaires were designed by J.G. and C.B. Human data were collected respecting APA ethical guidelines.

References

1. Fu, D., Houlette, R.: The Ultimate Guide to FSMs in Games. In: AI Game Programming Wisdom II, pp. 283–302. Charles River Media (2004)
2. Champandard, A.J.: Behavior Trees for Next-Gen Game AI. Internet presentation (January 18, 2011), http://aigamedev.com/insider/presentations/behavior-trees
3. Schuytema, P.: Game Development with Lua. Charles River Media (2005)
4. UnrealScript programming language (January 18, 2011),
   http://unreal.epicgames.com/UnrealScript.htm
5. Schwab, B.: AI Game Engine Programming, 2nd edn. Charles River Media (2008)
6. AiGameDev community (January 18, 2011), http://aigamedev.com/
7. Rabin S.: AI Game Programming Wisdom series (January 18, 2011),
   http://www.aiwisdom.com/
8. Gamasutra webpage (January 18, 2011), http://www.gamasutra.com/
9. Magerko, B., Laird, J.E., Assanie, M., Kerfoot, A., Stokes, D.: AI Characters and Directors for Interactive Computer Games. In: Proceedings of the 2004 Innovative Applications of Artificial Intelligence Conference, San Jose, CA. AAAI Press (July 2004)
10. Best, B.J., Lebiere, C.: Cognitive agents interacting in real and virtual worlds. In: Sun, R. (ed.) Cognition and Multi-Agent Interaction: From Cognitive Modeling to Social Simulation. Cambridge University Press, NY, NY (2006)
11. Hindriks, K.V., van Riemsdijk, B., Behrens, T., Korstanje, R., Kraayenbrink, N., Pasman, W., de Rijk, L.: UNREAL GOAL Bots: Conceptual Design of a Reusable Interface. In: Dignum, F. (ed.) Agents for Games and Simulations II. LNCS (LNAI), vol. 6525, pp. 1–18. Springer, Heidelberg (2011)

12. Bryson, J.J.: Inteligence by design: Principles of Modularity and Coordination for Engineering Complex Adaptive Agent. PhD Thesis, MIT, Department of EECS, Cambridge, MA (2001)
13. Partington, S.J., Bryson, J.J.: The Behavior Oriented Design of an Unreal Tournament Character. In: Panayiotopoulos, T., Gratch, J., Aylett, R.S., Ballin, D., Olivier, P., Rist, T. (eds.) IVA 2005. LNCS (LNAI), vol. 3661, pp. 466–477. Springer, Heidelberg (2005)
14. Köster, M., Novák, P., Mainzer, D., Fuhrmann, B.: Two Case Studies for Jazzyk BSM. In: Dignum, F., Bradshaw, J., Silverman, B., van Doesburg, W. (eds.) Agents for Games and Simulations. LNCS (LNAI), vol. 5920, pp. 33–47. Springer, Heidelberg (2009)
15. Dignum, F., Bradshaw, J., Silverman, B., van Doesburg, W. (eds.): Agents for Games and Simulations. LNCS, vol. 5920. Springer, Heidelberg (2009)
16. Tyrrell, T.: Computational Mechanisms for Action Selection. Ph.D. Dissertation. Centre for Cognitive Science, University of Edinburgh (1993)
17. Bryson, J.J.: Hierarchy and Sequence vs. Full Parallelism in Action Selection. In: Simulation of Adaptive Behavior 6, Paris, pp. 147–156 (2000)
18. Bryson, J.J.: Action Selection and Individuation in Agent Based Modelling. In: Proceedings of Agent 2003: Challenges of Social Simulation, Argonne National Laboratory, pp. 317–330 (2003)
19. Hindriks, K.V., van Riemsdijk, M.B., Jonker, C.M.: An Empirical Study of Patterns in Agent Programs. In: Desai, N., Liu, A., Winikoff, M. (eds.) PRIMA 2010. LNCS, vol. 7057, pp. 196–211. Springer, Heidelberg (2012)
20. Brom, C.: Curricula of the course on modelling behaviour of human and animal-like agents. In: Proceedings of the Frontiers in Science Education Research Conference, Famagusta, North, Cyprus (2009)
21. Gemrot, J., Brom, C., Kadlec, R., Bída, M., Burkert, O., Zemčák, M., Píbil, R., Plch, T.: Pogamut 3 – Virtual Humans Made Simple. In: Gray, J. (ed.) Advances in Cognitive Science, pp. 211–243. The Institution Of Engineering And Technology (2010)
22. Brom, C., Gemrot, J., Burkert, O., Kadlec, R., Bída, M.: 3D Immersion in Virtual Agents Education. In: Spierling, U., Szilas, N. (eds.) ICIDS 2008. LNCS, vol. 5334, pp. 59–70. Springer, Heidelberg (2008)
23. Artifical beings course, practical lessons slides (January 18, 2011),
    http://diana.ms.mff.cuni.cz/pogamut-devel/doku.php?id=lectures
24. Pogamut 3 platform documentation (January 25, 2011),
    http://diana.ms.mff.cuni.cz/
    main/tiki-index.php?page=Documentation
25. Artificial beings course, final exam package (January 18, 2011),
    http://diana.ms.mff.cuni.cz/pogamut-devel/doku.php?id=
    human-like_artifical_agents_2009-10_summer_semester_exam_info
26. Bordini, R.H., Hübner, J.F., Wooldridge, M.: Programming Multi-Agent Systems in AgentSpeak Using Jason. John Wiley & Sons, Ltd. (2007)
27. Brooks, R.A.: Intelligence Without Representation. Artificial Intelligence 47(1-3), 139–159 (1991)
28. Bozada, T.A., Perkins, T.K., North, M.J., Kathy, K.L., Simunich, L., Tatara, E.: An Applied Approach to Representing Human Behavior in Military Logistics Operations. In: Fall Simulation Interoperability Workshop, Simulation Standards Interoperability Organization, Orlando, FL USA (September 2006)
29. Desai, N.: Using Describers To Simplify ScriptEase. Master Thesis. Department of Computing Science, University of Alberta, Edmonton, Alberta, Canada (2009)

Appendix

This section contains additional tables, figures and some additional text concerning presented study.

Reusable Package. The package containing the assignment texts, Pogamut 3 platform, template agent projects and the scenario map can be downloaded from [25].

Table S1. Number of students in groups according to their types of study and years of study. Master students have number of years spent for their bachelor studies included into their years of study. Note that bachelor studies last 3-4 years typically and master studies takes usually extra 2-3 years.

Group A

Study / Year of study	2nd	3rd	4th	5th	Total
Bachelor	4	2	0	0	6
Masters	0	0	6	1	7
Total	4	2	6	1	13

Group B

Study / Year of study	2nd	3rd	4th	5th	6th	8th	Total
Bachelor	2	1	3	0	0	0	6
Masters	0	0	3	2	2	1	7
Total	2	1	6	2	2	1	14

Table S2. List of all behavior primitives that were provided in the Task 1

Sensors		
class of primitives	*X parameter*	*Y parameter*
canSee X	AlienBlood, Ammo, Enemy, Weapon, WeaponOrAmmo	
get/know X	NavPointToExplore	
know X Y	SpawningPoint	AlienBlood, Ammo, Weapon, WeaponOrAmmo
	Spawned	AlienBlood, Ammo, Weapon, WeaponOrAmmo
get X Y	Random	NavPoint
	Nearest	NavPoint
	NearestVisible	AlienBlood, Ammo, AmmoOrWeapon, Enemy, NavPoint, Weapon
	NearestSpawned	AlienBlood Ammo Weapon WeaponOrAmmo
	AlienBlood, Ammo, Item, Weapon, DistanceToTarget	
has X	Ammo, Weapon	
is X	Moving, Shooting, RunningToItem, RunningToPlayer, RunningToNavPoint	
wantToSwitchToItem		

Actions		
run X	ToItem ToNavPoint ToPlayer	
shootEnemy		
stop X	Movement, Shooting	

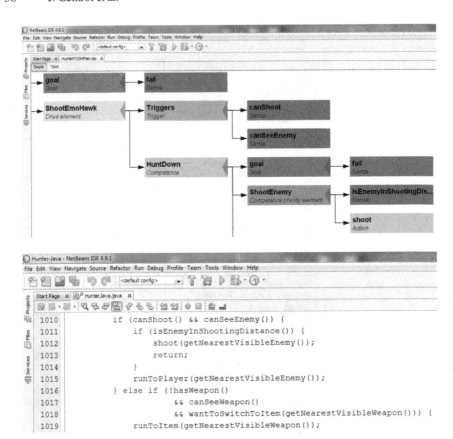

Fig. S1. Example of the code that the subjects were creating. Top: part of a POSH plan of the Hunter task as visualized by the graphical editor. Below: Hunter code in Java. The code and the plan were taken from an exemplary solution created by one of VR experienced programmers.

Table S3. List of possible commands that can be issued by the Guide and corresponding possible answers

Guide commands	Possible Civilian answers
commandCivilianCanSee	answerAngry
	answerDontUnderstand
	answerCanSee
	answerCantSee
commandCivilianFollowMe	answerAngry
	answerDontUnderstand
	answerCantFollowingCantsee
	answerFollowingOk
commandCivilianStop	answerAngry
	answerDontUnderstand
	answerStopped
commandCivilianTurn	answerAngry
	answerDontUnderstand
	answerTurning

Table S4. List of all behavior primitives that were provided in the Task 2

	Sensors	
class of primitives	*X parameter*	*Y parameter*
can X Y	See	Civilian, Player
	FollowCivilian	
get/know X	NavPointToExplore	
get X Y	NearestVisible	NavPoint, Player
	DistanceTo	Civilian, NearestPlayer, Target
is X	CivilianFollowing, CivilianMoving, CivilianNear PlayerInTalkingDistance, Moving, RunningToPlayer,	

	Actions	
command X Y	Civilian	CanSee, FollowMe, Turn, Stop
faceCivilian		
followCivilian		
run X	ToNavPoint, ToPlayer	
set X	CivilianSpeed, GuideSpeed	
stopMovement		

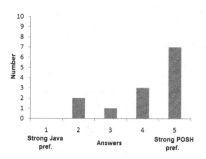

Ans.	#	%
1	0	0
2	2	15.4
3	1	7.6
4	3	23.1
5	7	53.9
Mean	4.15±1.14	

Fig. S2. Group A, Hunter Task (in POSH), Java/POSH preference

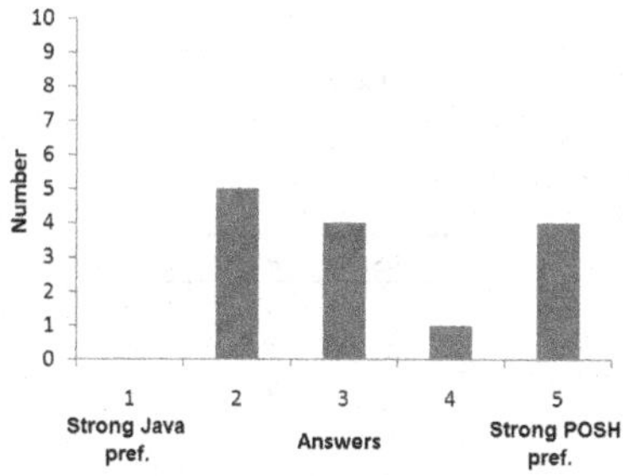

Ans.	#	%
1	0	0
2	5	35.7
3	4	28.6
4	1	7.1
5	4	28.6
Mean	3.29±1.27	

Fig. S3. Group B, Hunter Task (in Java), Java/POSH preference

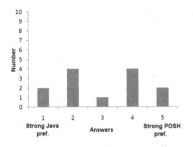

Ans.	#	%
1	2	15.4
2	4	30.8
3	1	7.6
4	4	30.8
5	2	15.4
Mean		3.00±1.41

Fig. S4. Group A, Guide Task (in Java), Java/POSH preference

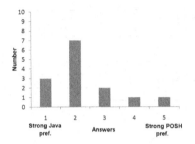

Ans.	#	%
1	3	21.5
2	7	50.0
3	2	14.3
4	1	7.1
5	1	7.1
Mean		2.29±1.14

Fig. S5. Group B, Guide Task (in POSH), Java/POSH preference

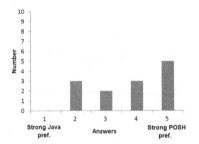

Ans.	#	%
1	0	0
2	3	23.1
3	2	15.4
4	3	23.1
5	5	38.4
Mean		3.77±1.19

Fig. S6. Group A, PostExam, Java/POSH preference

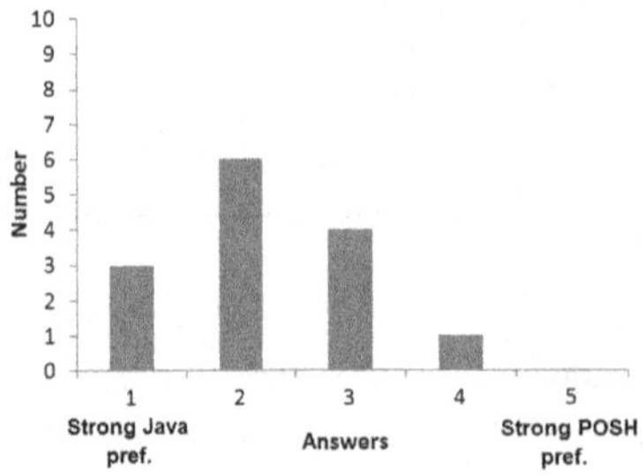

Ans.	#	%
1	3	21.5
2	6	42.8
3	4	28.6
4	1	7.1
5	0	0
Mean		2.21±0.86

Fig. S7. Group B, PostExam, Java/POSH preference

Table S5. Contingency table of the Java/POSH preferences shift

Change in preferences of Group A

	T2 - Java	T2 - Can't decide	T2 - POSH	Total (Task 1)
T1 - Java	2	0	0	2
T1 - Can't decide	1	0	0	1
T1 - POSH	3	1	6	10
Total (Task 2)	6	1	6	13

Change in preferences of Group B

	T2 - Java	T2 - Can't decide	T2 - POSH	Total (Task 1)
T1 - Java	5	0	0	5
T1 - Can't decide	3	1	0	4
T1 - POSH	2	1	2	5
Total (Task 2)	10	2	2	14

Table S6. Table summarizing previous Java experiences in both groups (in man-months)

	0-1 months	2-5 months	6-9 months	> 9 months	Total
Group A	9	2	0	2	13
Group B	6	4	1	3	14
Total	15	6	1	5	27

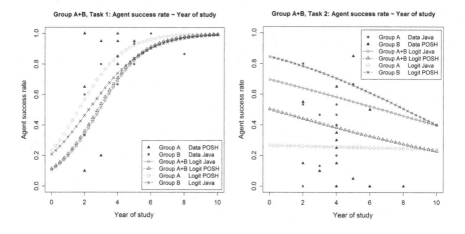

Fig. S8. Dependency of ASR on subject's year of study (Left – Task 1; Right – Task 2)

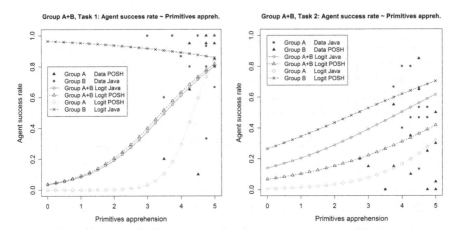

Fig. S9. Dependency of ASR on primitives' comprehension (Left – Task 1; Right – Task 2)

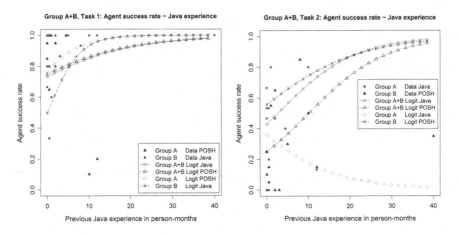

Fig. S10. Dependency of ASR on previous Java experience (Left – Task 1; Right – Task 2)

Dialog Designs in Virtual Drama: Balancing Agency and Scripted Dialogs

Edward Chao-Chun Kao and Von-Wun Soo

Institute of Information Systems and Applications, National Tsing Hua University
101, Section 2, Kuang-Fu Road, Hsinchu City, Taiwan 30013, R.O.C.
{edkao,soo}@cs.nthu.edu.tw

Abstract. Scripts are automatically generated by a story generator and subsequently played by virtual agents. The scripts for actors consist of two parts: movements and dialogs, however, the dialogs are insufficiently addressed in current research of story generation, thereby limiting the generated stories. Therefore, our initial goal was to enable story generators to generate dialogs as sets of character-based actions that are integrated with original story plots. This paper presents a speech-act-based dialog generation framework to define the relationship between dialogs and story plots. In addition, we introduce the manner in which agents may improvise scripted dialogs by selecting various courses of actions. Lastly, a sample scenario was generated according to this framework and demonstrated by virtual agents with the Unreal Development Kit. Our initial results indicated that this framework maintains a balance between agency and scripted dialogs, and that improvised dialogs of virtual agents do not affect the consistency of stories.

Keywords: speech act theory, dialog generation, virtual drama.

1 Introduction

The rise of intelligent virtual agents has formed a new interdisciplinary research community comprising artificial intelligence, computer graphics, cognitive science, natural language processing, and narrative theories.

Although the future direction of virtual agents may vary according to the major domain of researchers, a significant domain is virtual drama because it occurs in existing applications, such as computer games, emotion counseling, and simulation-based training. We identified virtual drama as a play with the following characteristics:

1. Virtual environments: rendering computer graphics with either realistic or cartoon-style pictures as the scenes in the play. The virtual environments often serve as the engine that integrates other components, such as camera controllers and physics.
2. Virtual actors: virtual agents may be implemented by various methods in virtual environments and intended to act as characters in the play. They are equipped with the abilities to display believable gestures and facial expressions, and to synthesize voices and other interactions.

M. Beer et al. (Eds.): AEGS 2011, LNAI 7471, pp. 63–78, 2012.

3. Play scripts: the actions of virtual actors and virtual environments are described in the play scripts, which are either manually written or automatically generated. Although they differ from movie scripts, which are intended for human actors and directors, play scripts in virtual drama are often defined with formalisms and/or markup languages, for example, PDDL [14] in the planning domain and BML [29] to describe the action timing of virtual actors.

Although the virtual environments and virtual actors are important research topics in virtual agents, we focused on the generation of the third part, which is identified as story generation or narrative generation in academic terms.

The need for automated story generation is because audiences consume stories markedly faster that human authors write stories. The scripts are automatically generated with the use of a story generator and are subsequently played out by virtual actors who are situated in virtual environments. Therefore, we argue that story generation is the starting point for virtual drama to become completely automated and to provide on-demand digital content.

However, although recent research in story generation applies various types of planning [8][25] and theories in narrative analysis to generate plots, these plots contain only high level actions that consist of physical actions only , and the dialogs between characters are often ignored or are hand-crafted, resulting in speechless or domain-specific scenarios. The high level actions require human authors to fill in the dialogs; however, the dialogs of the characters are limited to current storylines, and are difficult to apply to other generated stories.

To address this problem, the main aim of our research was to model a generative framework of dialogs to generate dialogs for various stories and actors without losing its generality. Because the entire domain of natural language generation is beyond our research problem, our framework is based on a simplified yet well-structured form of language that is known as speech acts, which are treated as ordinary actions in the planning domain, therefore, the state-of-the-art techniques of story planning may use them during the planning process without several modifications.

In particular, this novel dialog framework is flexible to both virtual actors and story plots. It allows virtual agents to choose more detailed dialogs based on internal character profiles and the play scripts, and also allows human authors to specify constraints at the level of story discourse.

The remainder of this paper is described as follows: section 2 presents reviews of related literatures in the domains of agent communication and story generation, which focuses our work and identifies its scope; section 3 provides a description of our desiderata and an explanation for the selection of hierarchical speech acts as the foundation of our framework; section 4 provides a formal representation of virtual drama and our dialog framework in Z notation; section 5 presents the application of this framework to an abstract scenario to evaluate the use of our model to generate balanced dialogs between characters and plots;

and a sample scenario is illustrated in section 6 to demonstrate the whole frame-work. Lastly, section 7 offers conclusions by summarizing our main findings and future work.

2   Related Work

2.1   Narrative Generation

In general, research of narrative generation is based in literary structuralism. Based on their work, a narrative world is described by a series of events, which are known as fabula. The pieces of fabula that are chosen by storytellers to be retold to the audience are identified as sujet. Because story discourse (the sequence of sujet) may differ from fabula in temporal order and appearance (for example, not every piece of fabula will appear in sujet), various stories may be generated, including those based on the same fabula.

Fabula and sujet, when formulated as actions, may be generated with POP-based planning. Although structuralists [7][24] analyzed stories as a set of specific patterns of sujet, the goal of narrative generation is to generate stories according to these patterns. The further decompositions of these overall story patterns lead to the formulation of causal constraints in planning. By contrast, the continuity of character intention that is expressed in sujet is also a crucial factor to stories and is identified as intentional constraints by Riedl et al. and was utilized by their story planner IPOCL [25].

The POP-based narrative planning yields optimal stories, which may be fur-ther processed into various styles of sujet, such as suspense. Riedl extended his method by incorporating vignettes [27], which are considered good scenarios and used as existing plan fragments during the planning process, enabling the story to be reused. However, the actions used by planners are defined as major events at the level of overall fabula rather than at the level of sujet, which consists of lines of dialogs between characters.

2.2   Interactive Narratives

A parallel trend of research in narrative intelligence is interactive narratives, which focuses on interactions between human users and virtual actors. In the I-Storytelling system [4], each virtual actor interacts with users and other virtual actors based on a pre-scripted HTN plan, allowing others to change its behavior based on the actual interactions on-stage. The sujet emerges from real-time interactions without definite fabula, and therefore, this method is also identified as emergent narratives. The method of emergent narratives leads to multiple possible fabula, as it may generate inconsistent stories with the same set of HTN plans.

The formulation of interactive narratives may be more suitable in describing dialogs because dialogs are a type of interaction. As the number of pre-scripted interactions increase, users may experience varied dialogs. In most applications, the definition of story directions at various levels is still preferred to avoid virtual actors from becoming random chat bots and thereby losing the focus of the intended stories. Therefore, a drama manager is required to determine appropriate interactions according to the current development of stories. With fine-grained interaction segments, such systems can yield highly interactive stories of excellent quality, as exemplified by Faade [19]. However, in contrast to those actions which are general events in POP-based story planning, all the dialogs and other interactions in interactive narratives are domain (story) specific. Consequently, recent development about dialog generation in interactive narratives demonstrates the differences among characters regarding various forms of expressions [5], character archetypes [28], personality [18], culture [11], and multi-modal dialogs [22]. These dialogs require time to build and refine, however, they are difficult to reuse in new stories due to the lack of explicit notations related to high level plots because they intertwine with implicit and possibly multiple fabula.

2.3   Simulation-Based Training

By contrast, negotiation formalisms from agent communication languages were introduced into applications of simulation-based training [30]. The virtual actors must interact with users through protocols of normal coordination and communication because their goal is to train human users with virtual agents in virtual environments. Although the actual lines of dialogs are pre-recorded, the virtual actors reason about their communication with users and evaluate it as various, based on explicit task models of standard operation procedures. A set of negotiation-related speech acts were used to allow users to negotiate with virtual actors, , and either the actors or the users interacted with each other through speech acts and related parameters that were defined in the task models, and the speech acts of the user were identified automatically with voice recognition and further natural language processing. If negotiated properly, the virtual actors take various courses of actions and hence change the following story.

This method is applied in several related training projects [10][31]. From our point of view, the task models and speech acts are defined explicitly within interactions, and the gestures, facial expressions, and other movements of virtual actors are configured independently in the visualization process, making this dialog model modularized and plausible to stories. Based on this research, our study introduces a speech act classification system to serve as the foundation of the dialog framework that is revealed in the next section, and to integrate it with the narrative generation process.

3   Dialog Framework

In this section, we clarify the purpose and the definition of dialogs with formalisms.

Dialogs, which are either a monologue or a conversation involving multiple participants, are conducted in any part of the narratives and describe a part of the story from the point of view of particular characters. The presented story may change, depending on the points of view of various characters [23]. However, Austin indicated that the purpose of statements is not only to describe, but also to do things with words [1], and that the purpose of dialogs in narratives is not just to describe the story, but also to represent the actions of characters toward the narrative world. To model these actions, we used the theory of speech acts and viewed dialogs as sequences of various speech acts.

Although the model of domain knowledge in dialog contents were conducted in recent research [17], the speech acts in interactive narratives are usually customized according to the tasks in stories [6][19][30] in an ad-hoc manner without a determined hierarchy or relations among the various speech acts, therefore, speech acts are difficult to use by either story planners or virtual actors that intend to emerge narratives. Considering these findings, we progressively introduce what we assume to be the essential classification of speech acts, and the manner in which it is applied to build a consistent schema that captures the dialogs in narratives.

Although we intended to only allow virtual actors to adopt and mimic the structures of human dialogs to generate similar sentences, we first categorized and identified the relations among numerous speech acts that are used by humans. Our approach was based on Ballmer and Brennenstuhls speech act classification [2] because it provided explicit relationships among various groups of speech acts. Their classification identified four main groups of speech activities as hierarchical linguistic functions. The functional effect of each category of speech acts does not overlap although a semantic verb may appear in various categories. Consequently, we believe it is possible for story generators to select corresponding categories based on the effects of speech acts. We explain groups of speech acts in the context of narratives, as follows:

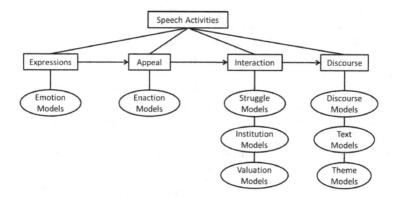

Fig. 1. Speech Act Classification from [2]

- Level1-Expression: including all emotional reactions. Expression contains the most primitive and direct speech acts that present the profiles of characters, such as angry, afraid, and grateful.
- Level2-Appeal: Appeal represents speech acts in a focused sense, where the speaker attempts to influence and control the listener (for example, order, threaten, encourage).
- Level3-Interaction: similar to Appeal, however, the listener can influence the speaker, whereas the speaker may try to avoid the influence, which forms a series of Appeals in various directions.
- Level4-Discourse: appropriately conducted and more rigidly organized Interaction(s), which implies that Interactions occur in a particular order and appearance according to the definition of this Discourse.

Although we only used a subset of speech acts in our system, we argue that it is the relationship among these levels that link character dialogs (low levels) to narrative discourses (high levels). As indicated in the classification definition, there is a vital property that allows us to utilize this speech act model in narratives.

Property 1. (Speech Act Hierarchy): Being the higher linguistic functions imply being the lower ones.

That is, if a Discourse is described between two actors, it should contain one or more interactions, all of which lead to several Appeals in both directions. These Appeals occur with various (emotional) Expressions.

With this property, the plot symbols in narrative structures are expanded into one or more speech acts (which are later realized as dialogs) in addition to ordinary actions. For example, when two persons A and B argue about something in a play script (its the performance of which is sujet), if we describe this speech act as primitive actions in the domain theory of planning, this speech act can be illustrated as:

$$argue(A, B, sth) \qquad (1)$$

During the process of argue, a number of forms of protocols must exist in the knowledge of both participants, such as rebut, undercut, and negotiate. These protocols contain a series of speech acts that designate verbal attacks and defenses toward each other, which may be chosen by both parties during the run time. When A and B execute these speech acts, they may also express their current emotions.

In the previous example, argue belongs to the Discourse (level-4); and rebut, undercut, and negotiate are its associated Interactions (level-3). Those attacks, defenses, and evasions that follow the Interaction protocols are Appeal (level-2), and their emotional behaviors are considered Expression (level-1).

Based on this property, we defined a *dialog frame* based on *speech acts* within narratives.

Definition 1. *(Speech Act): four major groups of speech acts occur, which are Expression, Appeal, Interaction, and Discourse, from low to high levels.*

A high level speech act may include speech acts from the lower levels.

Definition 2. *(Dialog Frame): a dialog frame must contain more than one speech act.*

Although these definitions do not provide precise information as to what type of speech acts are included in each model, we indicate the rules among each group. Although our focus was not to re-examine whether speech acts in each model are appropriate in human language, we provide several examples to demonstrate the manner in which these models are used as parameters for virtual drama, and explain the pros and cons with various approaches. The users are responsible for customizing their own sets of speech acts in each level, and the associated relations among these groups. Interested readers may refer to speech act classification for further details.

4 Virtual Drama

As stated in section 1, an automated virtual drama system must contain a minimum of 3 components, as follows: story generators to generate play scripts, virtual actors to play according to the scripts, and a virtual environment that integrates these components. Although the mechanism of story generation is outside the scope of this paper, we assume that the scripts are already generated as a sequence of high level actions such as those in [13][25]. Under this assumption, we specify the manner in which dialog frames are elaborated in virtual drama as these high level actions, and how virtual actors may improvise during the play of dialog frames.

4.1 Virtual Actors

To specify without losing generality, we define the schema of each component based on environment and autonomous agents of the SMART Agent Framework [9] in Z notation.

Virtual Enviromnent. The main difference between virtual drama systems and general agent systems is the existence of play scripts. These play scripts should be perceived by virtual actors to indicate the play, therefore, they must be defined in the virtual environment, above the original environment schema Env.

Definition 3. *(Virtual Environment)*

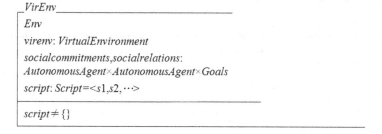

In Definition 3, the virtual environment includes not only play scripts, but also the social commitments and social relations among virtual actors. All of these attributes may affect the play of virtual actors. As Karunatillake et al. indicated, *since most (social) relationships involve the related parties carrying out certain actions for each other, we can view a relationship as an encapsulation of social commitments between the associated roles.*[16] We omitted the notion of social roles in favor of this notion, and only used them as parameters during the play, especially the play of dialog frames.

Character Profiles. In addition to social relations, the virtual actors should have particular internal parameters to maintain consistency between various states during the play to not interrupt the character believability, as proposed by Riedl and Young [26]. In addition to the intention of characters, we argue that the continuity of affective states also plays a vital role in maintaining character believability because if a character suddenly laughs whereas it cried a few minutes ago, this will cause unpredictable expressions to the audience. During a scene of dialogs, a virtual actor must be able to interact in various manners based on its affective states and the changes of affective states.

We defined the affective states as *character profiles*, following the ALMA affective model [12]. The reason that we used ALMA is due its elegant notation, which integrates emotions, mood, and personality in a single three-dimension space where the axes are pleasure, arousal, and dominance, rather than defining each of them in a different model [3][20][21].

Definition 4. *(Character Profile)*

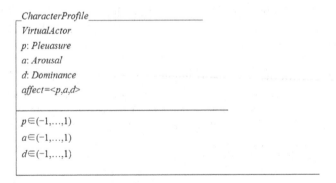

The difference between virtual actors and autonomous agents is its definition of motivation, which is based on script and character profiles.

Virtual Actors. Scripts and character profiles are independent of each other, although their combination determines the motivation of virtual actors. As we defined motivation in terms of scripts and character profiles, the definitions of agent perceptions and actions may not require further modification from those in autonomous agents because they percept and act upon virtual environments instead of environments. The action and perception schema of virtual actors was omitted to maintain the clarity of this paper.

Based on the previous definition, we may define the virtual actor state as follows:

Definition 5. *(Virtual Actor State)*

$$
\begin{array}{|l}
\_VirtualActorState_____ \\
AutonomousAgentState \\
VirtualActorPerception \\
VirtualActorAction \\
\hline
willact{=}actoractions\ motivation \\
\ goals\ actualpercepts\ virenv \\
\end{array}
$$

Three possible effects occur on the virtual environments and virtual actors during the play, as follows:

1. Change of character profiles, which change the motivation of virtual actors and leads to various choices of Interaction in the case of dialogs.
2. Change of social commitments, which lead to the change of available options in Interaction because social commitments serve as preconditions of Interaction.
3. Changes of scripts: because scripts are also a part of the virtual environment, the result of speech acts may also change the scripts and cause re-planning of scripts. Although we acknowledge its importance and effects, the topic of story re-planning is outside the scope of this paper.

Dialog Frame. The usage of dialog frames is summarized in this paragraph. First, because dialog frames are considered high level actions in a play script, the mapping of speech act models should also be specified in the script to provide virtual actors with available courses of actions during the play. Second, the character profiles of each virtual actor determine its goal selection on the courses of actions. Conversely, the effects of dialogs not only change character profiles, but also change social commitments, which alter the available options of speech acts within the script. Lastly, speech acts may also change scripts in the Discourse level, which leads to the re-planning of scripts.

4.2 Improvisation of Dialog Frames

Although dialog frames provide virtual actors with various options to select from during the play, these options are occasionally insufficient to reflect the character profiles of virtual actors because a script is a linear sequence of action events. Although each event may be divided into various sub events (speech acts in lower levels), these sub events are limited to the script, and defining specialized mapping among speech act models for individual virtual actors is ad-hoc and inflexible. Based on Gebhards justification to the ALMA model [12], we propose an improvisation mechanism to achieve a higher degree of believability. This improvisation allows virtual actors to use particular speech acts in the Appeal and Expression levels to reflect extreme cases of character profile values and changes.

The add-on of improvisation mechanisms satisfies the previous specification of virtual actors. Because character profiles are one of the determinants of motivation, improvisation is defined in terms of affecting the thresholds and changes of $< p, a, d >$ vectors in virtual actors instead of virtual environments.

Furthermore, improvisation is triggered despite the current script, therefore, other virtual actors must be able to cope with improvisation at the time that improvisation occurs; otherwise, the behaviors that follow will contrast audience prediction and sabotage character believability. These coping behaviors are limited to insert right after improvisation occurs, and thus, the entire play script will not require re-planning. By defining the coping behaviors in secondary scripts parallel to play scripts, the virtual actors may conduct improvisation and coping speech acts by selecting various scripts to play, without re-planning the primary play scripts. The coping behaviors between improvised speech acts and coping speech acts are defined as follows:

Definition 6. *(Script of Coping Behaviors)*

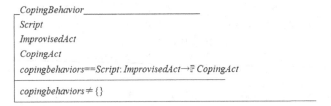

The overview of dialog frames is illustrated in Fig. 2 with an intuitive script of a detective story, which is illustrated in section 6.

5   System Implementation

To demonstrate this dialog framework, we used a first-stage implementation of a virtual drama system according to the specifications. The system overview is illustrated in Fig 3.

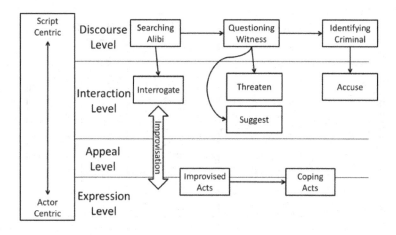

Fig. 2. Dialog Frames in Detective Scenario

The system was divided into two main parts, as follows:

1. Virtual Drama Server: The server was implemented with a JACK [15] agent platform because it supports the capacity, plan, and communication of autonomous agents. The Virtual Environment was also implemented in JACK as the data set. Consequently, the server may generate various sujet of play scripts in a plain-text format.
2. Visualization Frontend: The frontend is responsible for providing visual and audio experience for the audience of virtual drama. We chose the UDK3 (Unreal Development Kit 3) [32] as our frontend platform because it comprises a built-in full functional GUI editor and APIs that were written in Unreal Scripts that allowed us to write drama manager within it. Once the server passed sujet of a play script, the drama manager allocated the corresponding virtual actor, customized the SoundNodeWave library corresponding to speech acts with a built-in text-to-speech function, and gestures, all of which were regarded as parameters of matinee in cinematic mode.

At this stage of the implementation, the purpose of the virtual drama system was to achieve full automation of sujet performance; therefore, user interaction was not implemented to simplify the process.

6   Sample Scenarios

In this section, we provide a sample scenario to demonstrate the effect of dialog frames in our implemented system, which is illustrated in Fig. 3.

This sample scenario is a typical detective story, as the play script only contains three high level speech actions in Discourse, as follows: search for alibi, question the witness, and identify the criminal. Assuming that this play script is

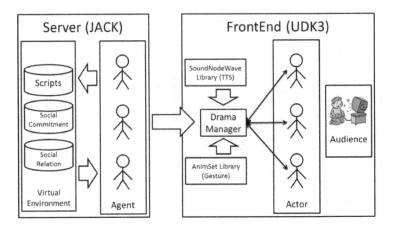

Fig. 3. System Implementation Overview

sufficiently simple to be generated by state-of-the-art story planners; our system was demonstrated the following functionalities:

1. Our dialog framework simplified each speech act into the Interaction level, which corresponds to various interaction protocols.
2. When these protocols were provided as dialog options, each virtual actor chose protocols in which the preconditions matched its character profiles while playing that part of the script.
3. Improvised dialogs may occur during the play, because each move in the Interaction protocol affects the character profiles of the opponent, which triggers improvisation in the stipulated thresholds. After improvisation, the virtual actors return to the former part of the script and continue the main storyline.

7   Conclusion and Future Work

The development of story planning led to the possibility of an automated drama system, in which play scripts are generated by story generators and subsequently played by virtual actors in a virtual environment with the ability of visual and audio expression. Although few studies attempted to generate dialogs based on the provided fabula, we used speech act classification that was derived from empirical studies of speech act designating verbs to generate dialog in a virtual drama. This study offers three contributions, as follows:

1. We propose a dialog framework with the ability to promote flexible dialog selection and to improvise character-based dialogs from existing play scripts.
2. The core specifications of virtual actors and virtual environment are specified in Z notation to elaborate the desiderata of virtual drama components without losing generality.

3. A first-stage virtual drama system was implemented to demonstrate the selection of dialogs during a sample scenario.

Although the initial results were satisfactory, several components must be addressed in future studies to achieve a fully automated virtual drama system, as follows:

1. Generating natural dialogs from speech acts to advance the automation of dialogs.
2. Treating Discourse-level speech acts as vignettes [27] in story planning may lead to improvements in script generation. Because Discourse-level speech acts are combinations of Interaction-level protocols, they may represent a source of vignettes.
3. The domain knowledge of speech acts and their parameters may be further elaborated as more structured data, therefore, virtual actors may reason with the play script rather than profile-based selection in the available options.

Acknowledgement. This research is supported by National Science Council of ROC under grant number NSC 99-2221-E-007-090-MY3.

References

[1] Austin, J.L.: How to Do Things with Words. Oxford University Press, London (1962)
[2] Ballmer, T., Brennenstuhl, W.: Speech Act Classification: a Study of the Lexical Analysis of English Speech Activity Verbs. Springer, Berlin (1981)
[3] Campos, A.M., Santos, E.B., Canuto, A.M., Soares, R.G., Alchieri, J.C.: Flexible Framework for Representing Personality in Agents. In: 5th International Joint Conference on Autonomous Agents and Multiagent Systems, pp. 97–104. ACM, New York (2006)
[4] Cavazza, M., Charles, F., Mead, S.J.: Interacting with Virtual Characters in Interactive Storytelling. In: 1st International Joint Conference on Autonomous Agents and Multiagent Systems, pp. 318–325. ACM, New York (2002)
[5] Cavazza, M., Charles, F.: Dialogue Generation in Character-based Interactive Storytelling. In: AAAI First Annual Artificial Intelligence and Interactive Digital Entertainment Conference, Marina del Rey, California, USA (2005)
[6] Cavazza, M., Pizzi, D., Charles, F., Vogt, T., Andr, E.: Emotional Input for Character-based Interactive Storytelling. In: 8th International Conference on Autonomous Agents and Multiagent Systems, pp. 313–320. ACM, New York (2009)
[7] Cavazza, M., Pizzi, D.: Narratology for Interactive Storytelling: a Critical Introduction. In: Göbel, S., Malkewitz, R., Iurgel, I. (eds.) TIDSE 2006. LNCS, vol. 4326, pp. 72–83. Springer, Heidelberg (2006)
[8] Charles, F., Lozano, M., Mead, S.J., Bisquerra, A.F., Cavazza, M.: Planning Formalisms and Authoring in Interactive Storytelling. In: Gobel, S., et al. (eds.) 1st International Conference on Technologies for Interactive Digital Storytelling and Entertainment. Fraunhofer IRB Verlag, Darmstadt (2003)

[9] D'Inverno, M., Luck, M.: Understanding Agent Systems. Springer, New York (2004)

[10] Endrass, B., Andr, E., Huang, L., Gratch, J.: A Data-driven Approach to Model Culture-specific Communication Management Styles for Virtual Agents. In: 9th International Conference on Autonomous Agents and Multiagent Systems, pp. 99–108. ACM, New York (2010)

[11] Endrass, B., Rehm, M., Andr, E.: Planning Small Talk Behavior with Cultural Influences for Multiagent Systems. Comput. Speech Lang. 25, 158–174 (2011)

[12] Gebhard, P.: ALMA: A Layered Model of Affect. In: 4th International Joint Conference on Autonomous Agents and Multiagent Systems, pp. 29–36. ACM, New York (2005)

[13] Gervs, P., Daz-Agudo, B., Peinado, F., Hervs, R.: Story Plot Generation Based on CBR. Know.-Based Syst. 18(4-5), 235–242 (2005)

[14] Helmert, M.: Concise Finite-domain Representations for PDDL Planning Tasks. Artif. Intell. 173(5-6), 503–535 (2009)

[15] JACK (Java Agent Compiler and Kernel), http://aosgrp.com/index.html

[16] Karunatillake, N.C., Jennings, N.R., Rahwan, I., McBurney, P.: Dialogue Games that Agents Play Within a Society. Artif. Intell. 173(9-10), 935–981 (2009)

[17] Larsson, S., Traum, D.R.: Information State and Dialogue Management in the TRINDI Dialogue Move Engine Toolkit. Nat. Lang. Eng. 6(3-4), 323–340 (2000)

[18] Mairesse, F., Walker, M.: PERSONAGE: Personality Generation for Dialogue. In: 45th Annual Meeting of the Association of Computational Linguistics, pp. 496–503. ACL, Stroudsburg (2007)

[19] Mateas, M., Stern, A.: Structuring Content in the Faade Interactive Drama Architecture. In: First Artificial Intelligence and Interactive Digital Entertainment Conference, pp. 93–98. AAAI, Palo Alto (2005)

[20] Mehrabian, A.: Pleasure-arousal-dominance: A General Framework for Describing and Measuring Individual Differences in Temperament. Curr. Psychol. 14(4), 261–292 (1996)

[21] Ortony, A., Clore, G.L., Collins, A.: The Cognitive Structure of Emotions. Cambridge University Press, Cambridge (1988)

[22] Piwek, P., Hernault, H., Prendinger, H., Ishizuka, M.: T2D: Generating Dialogues between Virtual Agents Automatically from Text. In: Pelachaud, C., Martin, J.-C., André, E., Chollet, G., Karpouzis, K., Pelé, D. (eds.) IVA 2007. LNCS (LNAI), vol. 4722, pp. 161–174. Springer, Heidelberg (2007)

[23] Porteous, J., Cavazza, M., Charles, F.: Narrative Generation through Characters' Point of View. In: 9th International Conference on Autonomous Agents and Multiagent Systems, pp. 1297–1304. ACM, New York (2010)

[24] Propp, V.: Morphology of the Folktale. University of Texas Press (1968)

[25] Riedl, M.O., Young, R.M.: An Intent-Driven Planner for Multi-Agent Story Generation. In: 3rd International Joint Conference on Autonomous Agents and Multiagent Systems, pp. 186–193. ACM, New York (2004)

[26] Riedl, M.O., Young, R.M.: Narrative Planning: Balancing Plot and Character. J. Artif. Intell. Res. 39, 217–268 (2010)

[27] Riedl, M.O., Sugandh, N.: Story Planning with Vignettes: Toward Overcoming the Content Production Bottleneck. In: Spierling, U., Szilas, N. (eds.) ICIDS 2008. LNCS, vol. 5334, pp. 168–179. Springer, Heidelberg (2008)

[28] Rowe, J.P., Ha, E.Y., Lester, J.C.: Archetype-Driven Character Dialogue Generation for Interactive Narrative. In: Prendinger, H., Lester, J., Ishizuka, M. (eds.) IVA 2008. LNCS (LNAI), vol. 5208, pp. 45–58. Springer, Heidelberg (2008)

[29] Thiebaux, M., Marsella, S., Marshall, A.N., Kallmann, M.: SmartBody: Behavior Realization for Embodied Conversational Agents. In: 7th International Joint Conference on Autonomous Agents and Multiagent Systems, pp. 151–158. ACM, New York (2008)

[30] Traum, D., Rickel, J., Gratch, J., Marsella, S.: Negotiation over Tasks in Hybrid Human-agent Teams for Simulation-based Training. In: 2nd International Joint Conference on Autonomous Agents and Multiagent Systems, pp. 441–448. ACM, New York (2003)

[31] Traum, D., Swartout, W., Marsella, S., Gratch, J.: Virtual Humans for Non-team Interaction Training. In: AAMAS Workshop on Creating Bonds with Embodied Conversational Agents (2005)

[32] Unreal Development Kit 3, http://www.udk.com/

Appendix

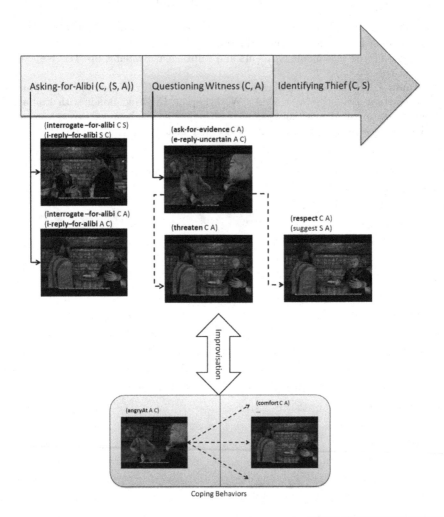

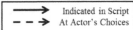

Learning by Playing in Agent-Oriented Virtual Learning Environment

Yundong Cai[1] and Zhiqi Shen[2]

[1] School of Computer Engineering
[2] School of Electrical and Electronic Engineering,
Nanyang Technological University, Singapore
{ydcai,zqshen}@ntu.edu.sg

Abstract. Virtual environments have gained tremendous popularity among young generation in recent years. Learning in the virtual environment becomes a new learning perspective that helps to promote the learning interests of students. However, there is a lack of methodology to develop and deploy a personalized and engaging virtual learning environment to various learning subjects. In our paper, we propose an *Agent-oriented VIrtual Learning Environment (AVILE)* as a new "learning by playing" paradigm, in which each learning object is built up as a goal of a *Goal-Oriented Learning Agent (GOLA)*. In AVILE, students conduct the personalized virtual experiments through the simulations and engaging role-playing games for knowledge acquisition by interacting with the intelligent *GOLAs*. Each *GOLA* provides most appropriate instructions by analyzing the students' learning process, and stimulates the students to make deeper learning within the exploration and knowledge transfer on real problems in the virtual learning environment. We adopted this methodology to teach plant transportation for secondary school students and received very positive results.

Keywords: Virtual learning environment, agent, virtual experiment, personalization.

1 Introduction

Virtual environments have gained tremendous popularity among young users in recent years for its openness, convenience, and mobility, e.g. World of Warcraft, Second life. People are able to communicate with each other in the virtual community and share information easily and efficiently in 3D virtual presentation, which is rather limited in the real world. Learning in the virtual environment becomes a new learning perspective that helps to promote the learning interests of students in the new era. The potential for innovative and ground breaking research in virtual learning environments has been recognized by leading education research scientists [1] [7]. Preliminary studies on using virtual worlds as learning environments to promote highly immersive experiential learning have achieved encouraging results [6]. However, it is still a big challenge to make a personalized

M. Beer et al. (Eds.): AEGS 2011, LNAI 7471, pp. 79–93, 2012.
© Springer-Verlag Berlin Heidelberg 2012

virtual learning environment for designers (e.g. teachers), based on the students' preferences and real-time interactions, due to a lack of systematic methodologies. Agent-based learning environment has been studied by researchers as a research tool for investigating teaching and learning [2], which presents a new perspective to the future learning method in virtual environment with intelligent virtual entities.

In this paper, we propose an Agent-oriented Virtual Learning Environment (*AVILE*) as a "teaching by learning" paradigm targeting to the raised challenges. In our system, each learning object is modeled as the goal of a goal-oriented learning agent (*GOLA*). *AVILE* is constructed as a multi-agent system of *GOLAs*, which construct the virtual laboratory that students perform the virtual simulations, and a virtual world environment that students can engage and interact with. *GOLAs* are created to perceive the students' actions and simulate customized laboratory and playing experience in the virtual environment, in the form of non-player characters (NPCs) or invisible observers (or instructors). In order to model different related learning objects in consequences, Fuzzy Cognitive Goal Net (FCGN) is used to model the hierarchical goals with alternatives, through which *GOLA* selects the goals and actions by reasoning the real-time interactions and context variables. Evolutionary Fuzzy Cognitive Maps (E-FCMs) is used as the reasoning model about the dynamic causal relationships among the user interactions, contexts and agent goals, thus to present a personalized learning object.

The rest of the paper is organized as below. Section 2 will illustrate our agent oriented virtual learning environment system and the involved agents. Section 3 will focus on Fuzzy Cognitive Goal Net which models leaning objects as the goals and cognition model to provide personalized playing and learning. We will show a case study of using the paradigm to teach secondary school students plant transportation system in Section 4. Lastly we will draw the conclusions and future plan.

2   Agent-Oriented Virtual Learning Environment (*AVILE*)

Agent-oriented virtual learning environment (*AVILE*) provides a new approach for students to learn by playing in the virtual environment, which might not be easy to achieve in the conventional classroom learning (CL) or the real-life experiments, due to the communication constraint, physical limitation, and building cost etc. Each student is unique, in terms of the learning curve of new knowledge and learning habit, while a generic virtual learning environment or virtual laboratory might not suit the needs of all the students easily. Therefore, there is a need to customize the virtual learning experience with many alternatives to serve different learners.

In current agent-based virtual learning environment, learning contents are mainly delivered through the non-player characters [5, 8, 9, 11] with limitations of delivering knowledge. In our approach, agents are not only used to model non-player characters, but also to model any learning object which can be either visible or invisible.

2.1   Learning Structure

Personalization is a key to promote the learning experience of the student at knowledge acquisition. Agent-oriented virtual learning environment (*AVILE*) augments the virtual learning environment with a number of intelligent goal-oriented learning agents (*GOLAs*), which enable personalized virtual learning to students by reasoning the students' preferences and real-time interactions with the students.

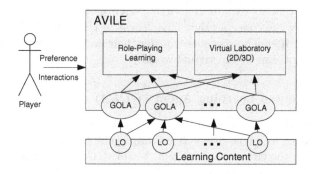

Fig. 1. Learning structure in the Agent-oriented Virtual Learning Environment

Figure 1 shows the learning structure of agent based virtual learning environment. Learning content is decomposed to a series of learning objects (LO), e.g. "diffusion" and "osmosis" are two learning objects in plant transportation chapter. Each LO is assigned to one or more *GOLAs* as their goals. For example, water molecules and plat root are two *GOLAs* to show the "diffusion" concept. The *GOLAs* are created in the role-playing learning virtual environment and virtual laboratory that the students can learn from the interactions.

In order to provide a fast-responsive and personalized learning experience, the user preferences are firstly gathered off-line for each student, e.g. age, gender, interests and prior knowledge. After that, the students play and learn in the agent mediated virtual learning environment by two methods: virtual laboratory and role-playing learning. In the virtual laboratory, the students are able to conduct 2D or 3D simulations of learning objects, by acting as a "God". Moreover, the students are able to immerse through a role-playing learning by acting as a "Player", to verify the concepts they have learnt in the virtual laboratory. Stories are created to motivate the students in the role-playing learning by linking the learning objects together seamlessly. Agents perceive the real-time interactions of a student, reason about them and act back to the student, i.e. to provide a unique learning experience eventually.

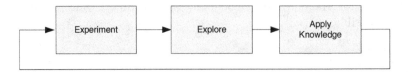

Fig. 2. Learning model in *AVILE*

There are three learning phases in *AVILE* as shown in Figure 2, which are carried out iteratively:

Experiment: The students conduct the virtual simulation in the virtual laboratory to study the basic concepts of learning objects.

Explore: The students explore the virtual environment and interact with *GOLAs* to verify the concepts they have learnt in the virtual laboratory.

Apply Knowledge: The students transfer their knowledge they have learnt to solve real problems in the virtual world.

2.2 Goal Oriented Learning Agent (*GOLA*)

Different from other agent-based virtual environment, each learning object in *AVILE* is modeled as a goal-oriented learning agent (*GOLA*), which can be visible or invisible in the virtual environment. Visible *GOLAs* include the non-player characters (e.g. humans, animals, and context objects) that deliver the knowledge to students directly through interactions; while invisible *GOLAs* include the contexts (e.g. temperature, weather, time and instructions) that deliver the knowledge indirectly.

A capable agent is able to perceive, reason and act in the virtual environment by defining its goals and cognitive variables initially. Fuzzy Cognitive Goal Net is used as the goal model for *GOLAs* to act in the agent-oriented virtual learning environment, which is explained in details in next section.

In the *AVILE*, the following agents interact with students to help them and to analyze the learning process in real-time:

- **Instructor Agent** Each instructor agent is responsible to provide meaningful instructions to the students. By monitoring the learning process of the students (e.g. difficulty, speed), the agent is able to tune the instructions in terms of difficulty, speed and detail.
- **Assessment Agent** An assessment agent evaluates the learning progress of the students, in order to master the learning efficiency of the students. Then it will send feedbacks to the instructor agent.
- **Inhabitant Agent** Inhabitant agents are the believable non-player characters to deliver the learning contents in the virtual learning environments, which could be a human or a tree, etc.

In order to provide an engaging learning experience, each *GOLA* presents the following properties:

Interactive: The agents are able to interact with the students in real-time. Protocols of interactions are defined, e.g. dialog or interaction mechanisms.

Intelligent: The agents are able to "perceive, reason and act" in real-time in order to create intelligent interactions.

Adaptive: The agents are able to learn from the students' behaviors and context changes, in order to provide "believable" interactions to the students.

Emotional: The agents are emotional as a feedback to user interactions.

As a result, the students are able to immerse into the virtual learning environment.

2.3   Virtual Laboratory

3D virtual laboratory is a good place that allows students to do experiments intuitively. In our *AVILE*, both 2D and 3D virtual experiments are designed as simulations in the virtual laboratory.

Table 1. Comparison of 2D and 3D Simulations

	2D Experiment	3D Experiment
Implementation	Easy	Hard
Immersion	Low	High
Role	"God"	"Player"
Collaboration	No	Yes
Suitable Contents	Intuitive	Explorative

2D or 3D virtual simulations have their own strengths and limitations. Table 1 shows a brief comparison between the two kinds of simulations. 3D simulation provides a better immersive experience to the students, and allows the interactions and collaborations of students at the learning. It is more suitable for students to explore and induct new knowledge in the science learning. However, the implementation of 3D simulation is more expensive at the implementation. On the other hand, 2D simulation is more suitable to present the intuitive concepts, e.g. specific science terms. In our real implementation, we use a hybrid of 2D and 3D simulations as a balance of production cost and user experience.

Virtual laboratory provides a basis of concepts for the students to learn through the simulation. Thus, the students are able to recall the simulation when they explore the virtual learning environment and explain the concepts in the real activities.

2.4   Role-Playing Learning

In *AVILE*, role-playing learning is a main concept that the student can immerse into the virtual environment to learn. Inhabitant agents are distributed in the virtual environments to deliver the related learning objects. Thus, the students need to compare, evaluate and induct the knowledge gathered at different places, which would help them to achieve the deeper learning. Moreover, students are encouraged to apply the knowledge they have learnt in the virtual experiments or exploration to solve real problems in the virtual learning environment. Stories are incorporated in the virtual learning environment to motivate the students to acquire new knowledge step by step.

3   Fuzzy Cognitive Goal Net

How to model numerous earning objects in an organized way is a big challenge. Fuzzy Cognitive Goal Net is a computational model to simulate the goals that *GOLA* pursuits in the virtual environment. As shown in Figure 3, *goals*, denoted as circles, are used to represent the goals that an agent pursues. *Transitions*, represented by arcs and vertical bars, connecting from the input goal to the output goal, specify the relationship between the two goals. Each transition is associated with a task list which defines the possible tasks that an agent needs to perform in order to transit from the input goal to the output goal. Here, each learning object is modeled as a goal of *GOLA*. A simple learning object (e.g. "diffusion") is modeled as an atomic goal; while a complex learning object (e.g. "molecule movement" is modeled as a composite goal, which can be further divided to "diffusion" goal and other goals.

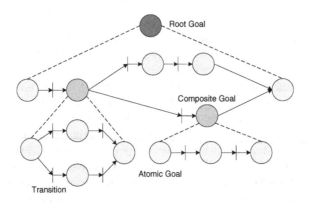

Fig. 3. A sample Fuzzy Cognitive Goal Net which is composed of goals and transitions

As an extension to generic Goal Net model [10], Fuzzy Cognitive Goal Net perceives and reasons the goal-related variables/events to choose the suitable goals in real-time [3]. With the "choice" transition, different goals can be achieved based on fuzzy context, user preferences or real-time interactions. For example, the agent can present different learning objects to different learners based on the learners' levels, past activities etc.

The pseudo code of running fuzzy cognitive goal net is shown here to select learning objects in real-time. By modeling the learning objects as goal net in

---

Algorithm 1. $Running of Fuzzy Cognitive Goal Net to Select Learning Object$

Require: Root Goal G
 1: Push G into Goal Queue Q
 2: **while** Q is not empty **do**
 3:   Pop goal g from Q
 4:   Perceive Environment e
 5:   **if** g requires e **then**
 6:     **if** g is Atomic **then**
 7:       Get action A from g
 8:       Execute action A
 9:     **else**
10:       Get Sub-goals $g_1, g_2, ..., g_n$
11:       Push Sub-goals $g_1, g_2, ..., g_n$ into Goal Queue Q
12:     **end if**
13:   **end if**
14: **end while**

---

a hierarchical way, the students are able to take a smooth learning curve systematically, from the easy learning object to difficult learning object, and from atomic learning object piece to complex learning object cluster.

In the "learning by playing" paradigm, a personalized learning is achieved by the goal selection mechanism of *GOLAs*. Each *GOLA* can use different goal selection mechanisms to choose an appropriate goal to handle user interactions correctly at playing. Evolutionary Fuzzy Cognition Map is a soft computing model to simulate the dynamic context variables and to conduct real-time reasoning [4]. It is adopted as the reasoning and simulation tool in the Fuzzy Cognitive Goal Net for goal selection. It models two main components: *concepts* S_i and *causal relationships* R_i. *Concept* can be input (context variables, user interaction variables), intermediate (i.e. variables that connect input and output), or output (agent goals, states etc). *Causal relationship* represents the interconnection from one concept to another. In the virtual learning, the concepts includes students' preference (i.e. gender, age, interests), students' activities in the learning environment and learning objects. By studying the causal relationships among the students and the learning objects, *GOLA* is capable to select a most appropriate learning curve to each student in real-time. The details of the model and its inference process can be found in [4].

4   Case Study: Plant Transportation in Banana Tree

4.1   Learning Content

The agent-oriented virtual learning environment is used for secondary level science learning about plant transportation in Catholic High Secondary School, Singapore in year 2011. The learning content of the virtual learning environment is plant transportation system. The related learning concepts (LO) include:

Xylem and Phloem of Root, Stem and Leaf: the cross section and functionalities of xylem and phloem inside the plant.

Osmosis and Diffusion: different movement methodologies of the water and mineral molecules.

Photosynthesis: chemical reaction of how the energy and oxygen are generated inside the leaf with water, light and carbon-dioxide.

4.2   Implementation

In order to motivate the students to learn the concepts in the plant transportation, we generate a story scenario, namely "saving the dying banana tree".

> "The banana trees in Singapura town are quite sick. The farmer *Uncle Ben* asks the investigators to explore the whole plant transportation system of the tree, in order to find how to save them."

We have implemented our agent-oriented virtual learning environment with Torque 3D Game Engine.

4.3   Sample *GOLAs*

There are a set of agents involved in the virtual learning environment to facilitate the students at the learning of plant transportation system as investigators. Three main *GOLAs* that provide the personalized learning are illustrated here.

Lab Supervisor. Lab supervisor "Miss Lee" is a tutor in the virtual laboratory, who determines the learning objects of the student based on the student's current level and preferences.

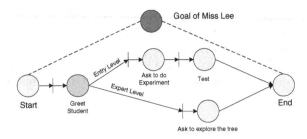

Fig. 4. Fuzzy Cognitive Goal Net of lab supervisor agent to choose the learning object

The goal net used by the supervisor agent is shown as Figure 4. If the student is at the entry level, she will lead the student to do the virtual experiment, e.g. diffusion or osmosis; otherwise, she will recommend the student to enter into the banana tree to watch the diffusion or osmosis process of water molecules at the

Fig. 5. Lab supervisor "Miss Lee" greets students with an introduction ('greet student' goal in Figure 4)

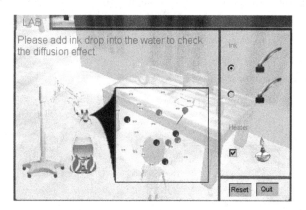

Fig. 6. Diffusion experiment with 2D simulation: add ink drops to observe the movements of molecules of diffusion ('experiment' goal in Figure 4)

root. Figure 5 shows a snapshot that the lab supervisor "Miss Lee" greets the student with some introductions by pursuing "greet student" goal (Figure 4). Figure 6 illustrates a 2D diffusion simulation that the student can play. Through this observation, the students are able to learn the diffusion concept by checking how the ink molecules move in the water and the variables that might affect the diffusion process.

Director Agent. Besides the simulations in the virtual laboratory, the students can watch the diffusion or osmosis at plant root immersively, which is impossible in the real world experiments. The invisible director agent directs the whole role-playing learning. It provides hints and analyzes the students' behaviors at the students' playing.

The goal net used by the director agent is shown as Figure 7. It can schedule the students to talk to different non-player characters to find the sick banana tree to start the plant transportation journey. The "visit plant transportation" is a composite goal. When the director agent pursues this goal, it will load the sub-goals of it, which is shown as Figure 8. Figure 9–11 are some screenshots of the students at the playing when the goals of the director agent are executed. In Figure 9, the student is exploring the stem xylem through flying upward. Through this, the students are able to observe the inner structure of the stem xylem and the molecules that flow in it. Figure 10 shows the cross section of the leaf (i.e. xylem is on top of the phloem), which is different from the cross section at the root or at the stem. Figure 11 shows that the student pushes the water molecule to carbon-dioxide molecule to generate food and oxygen in the leaf. Through this process, the students are able to learn the photosynthesis intuitively.

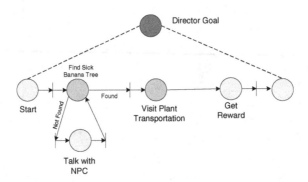

Fig. 7. Fuzzy Cognitive Goal Net of director agent to control the role-playing of students

Water Molecule. Water molecule is an inhabitant *GOLA* in the learning adventure, who asks for help from the student to take them into the leaf where the photosynthesis is carried out. The goal net used by the water molecule agent is

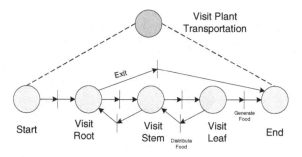

Fig. 8. Sub-goal of director agent to visit plant transportation

Fig. 9. Student meets panic water molecules at the root ('visit root' goal in Figure 8)

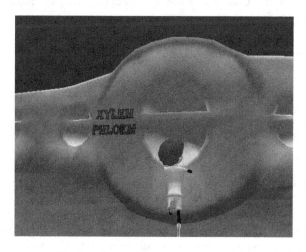

Fig. 10. Cross section of leaf: xylem on top and phloem at bottom ('visit leaf' goal in Figure 8)

Fig. 11. The student pushes the water molecule to carbon-dioxide molecule to generate food ('generate food' transition in Figure 8)

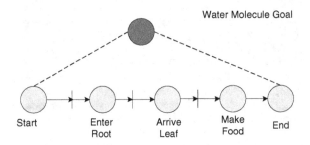

Fig. 12. Fuzzy Cognitive Goal Net of water molecule agent to go through root, stem, leaf and generate the food

shown as Figure 12. Depending on the learning scenario, the water molecule's goal is composed of a series of goals linearly.

4.4   Assessments

We conducted a comparative study in the Catholic High School to evaluate the students' performance in the agent oriented virtual learning environment. One group of 36 students (Group 1) used the agent-mediated virtual learning environment to learn and another group of 34 students (Group 2) used the formal classroom learning as a comparison. Group 1 used a same learning time as group 2 which is around 2 hours. After the learning, both groups were given a MCQ test about plant transportation. The group using *AVILE* has a mean score of 13.55 and the group using CL has a mean score of 14.05. As shown in Figure 13, *AVILE* group's learning result is quite close to that of CL. Considering that the students need to use around 1 hour to be familiar with the virtual learning

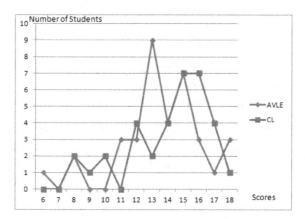

Fig. 13. Distribution of scores in agent-oriented virtual learning environment group (*AVILE*) and classroom learning (CL) group

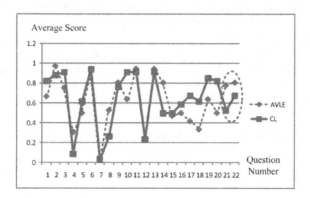

Fig. 14. Average of each question in agent-oriented virtual learning environment (*AVILE*) and classroom learning CL

environment, *AVILE* students still learn quite well. Moreover, more students got highest score (18 scores) in *AVILE* than those in CL. Because MCQ questions include some open questions that require the reasoning of concepts, the students perform well in *AVILE* which stimulates the exploration and thinking at the learning process, rather than just memorizing the knowledge. Figure 14 shows the average score of each question in both *AVILE* group and CL group. It is found that, students of the two groups perform well in different questions.

Some questions require the students to make the reasoning based on what they know, e.g. question 21.

> Suppose you killed the plant cell in the Figure of question 14A with poison (that does not destroy the cell membrane) and immediately placed the dead cell in a 25% saltwater solution.
> 1. Osmosis and diffusion would not occur.
> 2. Osmosis and diffusion would continue.
> 3. Only diffusion would continue.
> 4. Only osmosis would continue.

In this case, students in *AVILE* perform better. On the other hand, students in CL perform slightly better in the questions about concepts memorizing. The students in *AVILE* might focus on the exploration process with less concept memorization, as agents help them at all the memorizing.

4.5 Discussions

Through the test results, we found that agent-oriented virtual learning environment helps the students at deep learning by encouraging them gain knowledge through thinking and reasoning. The students can also transfer their knowledge easily, e.g. they apply the "osmosis" knowledge learnt in the virtual laboratory to help molecules enter into the root.

According to our observation and interview, the students are very engaged and motivated in the learning in the virtual environment. With the similar computer game experience, they adapt to the virtual learning environment very fast. The students are excited to experience in the virtual world differently with their classmates, and assisted well by the learning agents. However, the test results are not as good as expected, which might be due to the following reasons:

1. The students have little training time to be familiar with the virtual learning environment. They need more time to be comfortable with the learning method.
2. AVILE is a good compensation but not a replacement to the classroom learning. Especially when we conduct the virtual learning with the teachers supervised, the students are easy to be panic.
3. We choose the students who have very good academic performance as the test groups, which might not be very sensitive of the different learning methods.

In the future, it will be used an informal learning method as a testbed to prove the concepts which are learnt in the classroom, rather than replacing the whole classroom teaching.

5 Conclusion

In the paper, we have proposed an agent oriented virtual learning environment (*AVILE*) with a mixture of 3D virtual laboratory and role-playing learning. The learning objects are modeled as goals of goal-oriented learning agents (*GOLAs*), which provide personalized learning experiences through real-time goal selection. The results prove the learning efficiency and students' interests boost over that of the classical classroom learning.

Currently, mouse and keyboard are the main interaction methods for students to conduct the virtual experiments. In the future, we expect to have a more intuitive user-computer interfaces to enhance the engaging experience. Moreover, we will continue to improve the learning ability of the agent to study the students' behaviors in real-time in order to provide a better personalization of learning contents.

Acknowledgment. The authors would like to acknowledge the grant support of NRF/MOE, Singapore.

References

1. Bainbridge, W.S.: The scientific research potential of virtual worlds. Science 317(5837), 472–476 (2007)
2. Baylor, A.L.: Agent-based learning environments as a research tool for investigating teaching and learning. Journal of Education Computing Research 26(3), 227–248 (2002)
3. Cai, Y., Miao, C., Tan, A.-H., Shen, Z.: Modeling believable virtual characters with evolutionary fuzzy cognitive maps in interactive storytelling. In: AAAI Spring Symposium on Intelligent Narrative Technologies II. AAAI Press (November 2009)
4. Cai, Y., Miao, C., Tan, A.-H., Shen, Z., Li, B.: Creating an immersive game world with evolutionary fuzzy cognitive maps. IEEE Computer Graphics and Applications 30(2), 58–70 (2008)
5. Cavazza, M., Charles, F., Mead, S.J.: Interacting with virtual characters in interactive storytelling. In: Proceedings of the First International Joint Conference on Autonomous Agents and Multiagent Systems, Bologna, Italy, pp. 318–325 (2002)
6. Dede, C.: Immersive interfaces for engagement and learning. Science 323(5910), 66–69 (2009)
7. Dillenbourg, P., Schneider, D.K., Synteta, P.: Virtual learning environments. In: Proceedings of the Third Hellenic Conference Information & Communication Technologies in Education, pp. 3–18 (2002)
8. Figa, E., Tarau, P.: The vista architecture: experiencing stories through virtual storytelling agents. ACM SIGGROUP Bulletin 23(2), 27–28 (2002)
9. Gratch, J., Marsella, S.: Tears and fears: modeling emotions and emotional behaviors in synthetic agents. In: Proceedings of the Fifth International Conference on Autonomous Agents, pp. 278–285. ACM, New York (2001)
10. Shen, Z., Miao, C., Miao, Y., Tao, X., Gay, R.: A goal-oriented approach to goal selection and action selection. In: Proceedings of IEEE International Conference on Fuzzy Systems, pp. 114–121. American Association of Artificial Intelligence (2006)
11. Theune, M., Faas, S., Heylen, D.K.J., Nijholt, A.: The virtual storyteller: Story creation by intelligent agents. In: Göbel, S., Braun, N., Spierling, U., Dechau, J., Diener, H. (eds.) Technologies for Interactive Digital Storytelling and Entertainment, pp. 204–215. Fraunhofer IRB Verlag, Darmstadt (2003)

Collection and Analysis of Multimodal Interaction in Direction-Giving Dialogues: Towards an Automatic Gesture Selection Mechanism for Metaverse Avatars

Takeo Tsukamoto[1], Yumi Muroya[2], Masashi Okamoto[2], and Yukiko Nakano[2]

[1] Seikei University, Graduate School of Science and Technology, Tokyo, Japan
[2] Seikei University, Faculty of Science and Technology, Tokyo, Japan
{dm106216,us072149}@cc.seikei.ac.jp,
explicature@gmail.com, y.nakano@st.seikei.ac.jp

Abstract. With the aim of building a spatial gesture generation mechanism in Metaverse avatars, we report on an empirical study for multimodal direction-giving dialogues and propose a prototype system for gesture generation. First, we conducted an experiment in which a direction receiver asked for directions to some place on a university campus, and the direction giver gave directions. Then, using a machine learning technique, we annotated the direction giver's right-hand gestures automatically and analyzed the distribution of the direction of the gestures. As a result, we proposed four types of proxemics and found that the distribution of gesture directions differs with the type of proxemics between the conversational participants. Finally, we implement a gesture generation mechanism into a Metaverse application and demonstrate an example.

Keywords: Gesture, Direction giving, Proxemics, Empirical study, Metaverse.

1 Introduction

Online three-dimensional virtual worlds based on Metaverse applications as typified by Second Life have been growing steadily in popularity. Communication in such a virtual world is mainly through online chat using an avatar, which is a user's representation of himself/herself. However, the current avatar's chat has a limitation in its expressiveness in that it largely depends on speech balloons except in some extended systems that allow avatars to communicate based on speech and gesture.

Moreover, many communication studies suggest that a large part of human face-to-face communication depends on nonverbal behavior, which can compensate for verbal information [1,4,5]. In particular, many spatial gestures are used in direction-giving dialogues to illustrate directions and physical relationships of

M. Beer et al. (Eds.): AEGS 2011, LNAI 7471, pp. 94–105, 2012.

buildings and landmarks. Therefore, a spatial gesture generation mechanism in multimodal direction-giving dialogues between two avatars in a virtual world is expected to facilitate their users' communication.

We thus report on an empirical study for multimodal direction-giving dialogues with the goal of building a spatial gesture generation mechanism in Metaverse avatars. First, we collected multimodal interaction data by conducting an experiment in which a direction receiver asked for directions to some place on a university campus, and the direction giver gave him/her directions. Then, using a machine learning technique, we annotated the direction giver's right-hand gestures automatically and analyzed the distribution of the direction of the gestures. As a result, we illustrated that the distribution of gesture directions differs with the proxemics of the conversational participants.

2   Related Work

Gestures frequently accompany speech, emphasizing its important points or coordinating its rhythm. McNeill [6] classifies speech-accompanying gestures, in view of function, into iconic gestures, metaphoric gestures, beats, and so on. Based on this classification, several automatic gesture generation systems have been developed. Nakano et al. [7] implemented an embodied conversational agent system, which selects appropriate gestures and facial expressions based on linguistic information and calculates a time schedule for the set of agent actions. Breitfuss et al. [3] built a system that automatically adds different types of gestural behavior and eye gaze to a given dialogue script between two virtual embodied agents. Their gestures, generated based on the analysis of linguistic and contextual information of the input text, are generally limited to "beat" gestures represented by the repetitive up-and-down motion of hands or arms.

However, these studies have not fully dealt with iconic or metaphoric gestures, the shape and motion of which should be decided according to their meaning. The difficulty in implementing these types of gestures lies in their differences among individuals, thus preventing their coherent subclassification. It is nevertheless indispensable to precisely determine the shape and motion of a gesture as well as its functional type to be able to achieve genuine automatic gesture generation.

To tackle this problem, Tepper et al. [8] focused on direction-giving dialogues and proposed a new method for the generation of novel iconic gestures. They used spatial information about the locations and shapes of landmarks to represent the concept of words with multidimensional properties. Novel iconic gestures can be generated from a set of parameters without relying on a lexicon of gesture shapes. Moreover, Bergmann & Kopp [2] represented the individual variation of gesture shape using the Bayesian network. Based on the transcription of spoken words and the segmentation and coding of coverbal gestures, they built an extensive corpus of multimodal behaviors in the direction-giving and landmark description task, from which both general and personalized networks were built. As a result, they could simulate a variety of gestures of different speakers for the same referent in the same situation.

Fig. 1. Snapshot of experiment

We thus focus on the direction-giving situation, aiming at establishing an automatic gesture selection system. Though the previous methods described above were largely dependent on the form of landmarks, we pay more attention to the relationship between the proxemics and the gesture distribution.

3   Experiment

To determine appropriate gesture shapes for direction-giving utterances in Metaverse avatars, we conducted an experiment to collect direction-giving conversations and analyzed human gestures used in the conversations.

3.1   Experimental Procedure

A Seikei University student, who acted as a direction giver (DG), stood in front of a big screen on which a snapshot of a virtual university campus was displayed (Fig. 1). DGs were students of that university, and they knew the directions to any place on campus. Another student, who acted as a direction receiver (DR), approached the DG and asked for directions to a specific building. Then, the DG explained how to get to the building.

Instructions: The DR was instructed to completely understand the direction to the target destination through a conversation with the DG. Moreover, the DG was instructed to ensure that the DR understood the direction correctly. To confirm the DR's understanding, the DG asked the DR to repeat the direction after the DG finished explaining. If the explanation by the DR was not correct, the DG explained the direction again. In each session, the DG was requested to remember two landmarks to which the DG must refer during the conversation.

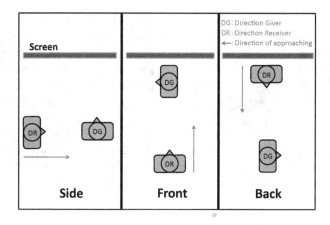

Fig. 2. Three experimental conditions

Experimental Materials: As the experimental materials, six pictures were created by screen capture. Target destinations, which were not visible in the picture, were assigned to each picture.

Experimental Conditions: The following three types of initial positions of the DG were used as experimental conditions (Fig. 2).

(a) **Side:** The screen was on the left-hand side of the DR. The DG was facing the screen.
(b) **Front:** The screen was in front of the DR and was on the right-hand side of the DG.
(c) **Back:** The screen was at the back of the DR and was on the left-hand side of the DG.

Note that a 50cm square sheet was used to mark the position of the DG, and the DG was instructed to remain one leg on the sheet. In this way, the movement of the DG was restricted. Since we plan to implement a proxemics coordination system by guiding (or automatically moving) the DR avatar, we needed to collect human interaction data in a similar situation.

Under all the conditions, the DR approached the DG from her/his side and initiated the conversation by asking for a direction. Six scene pictures were randomly assigned to three conditions. Therefore, two conversations were recorded for each condition.

Equipment: Subjects used a wireless (Bluetooth) headset microphone to record their voice, and each wore a cardigan on which motion-capture markers were mounted. An OptiTrack motion-capture system with 10 cameras was used to capture the subject's upper body motions. The subject's interactions were video-recorded from their side and above. Fig. 3-(a) (side) and Fig. 3-(b) (overhead) show pictures for the "Back" experimental condition.

(a) Side camera

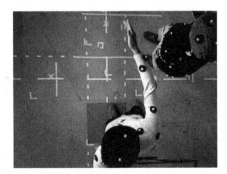
(b) Overhead camera

Fig. 3. Videos in "Back" condition

Subjects: Fourteen university students (7 male and 7 female) joined as DRs, and fourteen male students of Seikei University joined as DGs. Thus, we had 14 pairs of subjects in this experiment.

3.2   Collected Data

We collected video data from two directions, speech audio of each subject, transcription of utterances, and motion-capture data tracking each subject's upper body motions. Each subject's motion was tracked for her/his head, shoulder, back, right arm, and left arm at 100 fps.

We had 14 pairs of subjects, and each pair had 6 sessions. Therefore, we collected 84 direction-giving dialogues in all. The average length of conversation was 68.6 s.

4   Analysis

By analyzing the collected data, we investigated how a DG's gesture directions for indicating the spatial information differ with the proxemics between the DR and the DG. We analyzed 30 dialogues collected from 10 pairs for further analysis.

4.1   Automatic Gesture Annotation

Since it is very time consuming to manually annotate nonverbal behaviors, we automatically annotated the gesture occurrence (start and end time of a gesture).

Since more than 77% of the gestures observed in this study were right-hand gestures, we built a decision tree that judges the occurrence of right-hand gestures using Weka J48. From the motion-capture data of the DG's right arm and the right shoulder, 10 features were extracted: position (x, y, z), rotation (x, y, z), movement of the z position, relative position of the right arm to the right

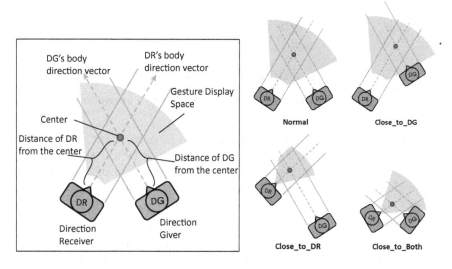

Fig. 4. Definition of proxemics

shoulder (x, y, z), and distance between the centroid of the right arm and that of the right shoulder. We annotated right-hand gestures for two subjects for six sessions to create training data.

As the result of 10-fold cross validation, the accuracy of binary judge (gesturing or not gesturing) was 97.5%, which is accurate enough for automatic annotation. Thus, we applied the decision tree to the rest of the data and automatically annotated right-hand gestures. Through this process, we obtained 161 right-hand gestures for further analysis.

4.2 Proxemics between the Direction Giver and the Direction Receiver

To characterize the proxemics between DG and DR, we defined a gesture display space. As illustrated in Fig. 4, the gesture display space is specified as the overlap between the DG's front area and the DR's front field of vision towards the screen. The width of the DG's front area is determined by the distance between the left shoulder and the right shoulder. Then, the center of the display space is calculated as follows. First, a shoulder vector is defined by connecting the left shoulder position and the right shoulder position. Then, another vector, which is orthogonal to the shoulder vector, is defined as a body direction vector. The intersection between the DG's body direction vector and the DR's body direction vector is defined as the center of the gesture display space.

Then, we categorized the pair's proxemics based on the distance from the center of the gesture display space. We assumed that if the gesture display space is far from the DG, the gesturer needs to stretch her/his arm to show her/his gestures to the DR. In contrast, if the gesture display space is very close to

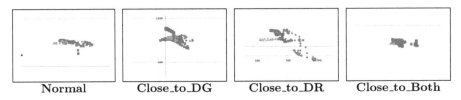

| Normal | Close_to_DG | Close_to_DR | Close_to_Both |

Fig. 5. Distribution of gestures with respect to proxemics

both participants, the DG does not need to use large motions; small gestures are enough to communicate. Since human arm length is 60 to 80 cm, by adding a 15-cm margin we defined 450 to 950 mm as the standard distance from the center of the gesture display space. Based on this, we defined the following five categories of proxemics.

(i) **Normal:** Both participants are standing within the standard distance (450 to 950 mm) from the center of the gesture display space.
(ii) **Close_to_DG:** The DG is standing close (less than 450 mm from the center) to the gesture display space, and the DR is maintaining the standard distance.
(iii) **Close_to_DR:** The DR is standing close to the gesture display space, and the DG is maintaining the standard distance.
(iv) **Close_to_Both:** Both participants are standing close to the gesture display space.
(v) **Far_from_Both:** Either of the participants is standing far (more than 950 mm from the center) from the gesture display space.

As a result of analyzing the motion data for 30 sessions, 11 were categorized as Normal, 4 as Close_to_DG, 9 as Close_to_DR, 2 as Close_to_Both, and 4 as Far_from_Both. Far_from_Both is a very inconvenient proxemics because it is almost impossible for the DR to see the DG's gesture. For example, both participants were facing the screen, or the DG was standing behind the DR. Thus, for gesture analysis in the next section, we will exclude the data classified as belonging to this category. Table 1 lists the average distances from the center of the gesture display space for each category.

4.3   Relationship between Proxemics and Gesture Distribution

To investigate the relationship between the proxemics and the DG's right-hand gestures, we analyzed the distribution of gestures by plotting the DG's right arm position, which was the centroid of the right forearm calculated from four data points: one on the right elbow and three on the right wrist. Fig. 5 shows some examples. As shown in the plots, Normal and Close_to_DG are similar in gesture distribution range. In Close_to_Both, the range of gesture distribution is much smaller. This suggests that the DG uses smaller gestures because both participants were close to each other and the gesture display space was smaller than that in other proxemics. In contrast, in Close_to_DR, the range of gesture distribution was much wider, specifically in the z position. This suggests that the DG was slightly far from the display space and tried to show her/his gestures by stretching her/his arm to the front.

To confirm this observation, we measured the area of the gesture distribution. Table 1 shows the average width, length, and the square measure for four types of proxemics.

Table 1. Gesture distribution area

	Normal	Close_to_DG	Close_to_DR	Close_to_Both
Distance to DG (mm)	665.9	395.0	596.4	392.0
Distance to DR (mm)	706.5	638.7	281.9	359.0
Width (mm)	197.2	214.0	237.6	189.5
Length (mm)	246.2	188.0	368.9	119.5
Area (mm^2)	48557.1	46388.0	91257.8	23218.0

The data support our discussion above. The gesture distribution range (Area) is similar in Normal and Close_to_DG because, in both categories, the gesture display space is not far from the DG and the DG can choose the directions of gestures in a wide space. In Close_to_DR, the distribution range is much larger, specifically in length (z position), because the gesture display space is slightly far from the DG and the DG needs to stretch her/his arm to make the gestures reach the gesture display space. In Close_to_Both, the gesture space is not very wide, because the participants are too close to each other and there is insufficient space for gesturing.

5   Gesture Generation Mechanism for a Metaverse Avatar

In this section, we propose a gesture generation mechanism for a direction-giving Metaverse avatar.

5.1   System Architecture

The system consists of four modules: (1) Second Life Manipulator (SLM), (2) Direction Coordinator, (3) Gesture Decision and Speech Production Module (GDM), and (4) Action-Voice Controller (AVC). We use OpenSim as an open source platform for Second Life. Fig. 6 shows the system architecture of our gesture generation mechanism.

(1) Second Life Manipulator (SLM). In Second Life, avatars can be controlled via an object called a prim. A prim contains a script described in Linden Scripting Language (LSL), which is the scripting language for Second Life, and the prim is attached to the avatar. The SLM used this feature to control the avatar, to get chat text, or to obtain location information.

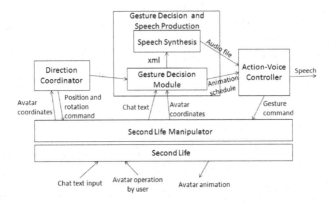

Fig. 6. System architecture for a direction-giving Metaverse avatar

(2) Direction Coordinator. The Direction Coordinator determines the appropriate position of the Direction Receiver Avatar (DR avatar) if it is too far from the Direction Giver Avatar (DG avatar), and it moves the DR avatar if it is necessary. It also coordinates the direction of both avatars to make them redirect towards the destination.

(3) Gesture Decision and Speech Production Module. Gesture timing is determined by CAST [7], which receives text as input and makes a Japanese morphological analysis using JUMAN and a dependency analysis by KNP to determine where in the sentence gestures are assigned. The GDM also determines the viseme animations for lip synchronization.

Then, the GDM determines proxemics types based on the DR and DG avatars' coordinates and the body orientation obtained from Second Life. The intersection of the DR avatar's orientation vector and that for the DG avatar is the center of the gesture display space. The distances from the center to the position of the DG avatar and to the position of the DR avatar are calculated. Then, according to the distances, the proxemics type is determined by referring to Table 1.[1].

Hand shape and trajectory are determined by our shape-selection rules, which were manually formulated by analyzing the video data in Section 3 [9]. In addition, the arm direction and stretch are determined based on the proxemics. These parameters are applied to the shape-selection rules and a gesture animation ID is determined. The gesture animation ID is added to the input text in XML format, and the text is sent to TTS (Text-To-Speech) to generate synthesized speech and save it as an audio file. Then, the animation time schedule is determined using the phoneme timing obtained from the TTS.

---

[1] Since the scale in the Second Life is different from the real world. We used normalized distance values.

7-1   7-2   7-3

Fig. 7. Snapshots of the direction-giving system

(4) Action-Voice Controller (AVC). In addition to playing the audio file, the AVC sends animation commands to the SLM according to the animation schedule. Then, the SLM applies the animation to the DG avatar to execute the gesture.

The mechanism described above allows the users to create DG avatars that express gestures synchronized with synthesized speech by only typing Japanese text in the Second Life chat window.

5.2   Example

This section presents an example of gesture generation. First, when a user for a DR avatar clicks on the DG avatar, a menu opens on the right corner (Fig. 7-1). If the user of the DR avatar chooses "Building 7" from the menu as her/his destination, the SLM obtains the coordinates <101.8, 104.2> and the orientation <107> of the DG avatar as well as the coordinates <102.2, 103.2> and the orientation <76> of the DR avatar, and finally the coordinates of the destination, <74.6, 15.5>. The SLM sends these data to the Direction Coordinator, which computes the rotation angle to redirect the DG and DR avatars towards the destination and sends the angle data back to the SLM. The rotation command is executed on OpenSim through the SLM. As a result, the coordinates are changed as follows: The coordinates of the DR avatar are <101.8, 104.2>, its orientation is <172> , the coordinates of the DG avatar are <102.2, 103.2>, and its orientation is <167> (Fig. 7-2). The coordinate information is sent to the GDM. Then, the user of the DG avatar inputs a direction-giving statement in the chat window (e.g., "When you turn left, there is a connecting corridor"). The SLM obtains the input text and sends it to the GDM.

The GDM performs a morphological and dependency analysis, as well as a search for synonyms for the input text, and selects words and phrases to which avatar gestures should be assigned. In this example, the system decides to assign gestures to "turn left" and "a connecting corridor." Then, the GDM calculates the center of the gesture display space based on the coordinates received from the SLM and determines the proxemics type. In this example, the proxemics type is "Normal." Next, the gesture animation ID is determined based on the proxemics type and the information for hand shape and trajectory determined by our shape-selection rules. The gesture animation ID "A-Left-M" is assigned to "turn left," and "LaR" is assigned to "a connecting corridor."

Then, synthesized speech is generated for the sentence and an animation time schedule is computed based on the phoneme information. Once the AVC receives the time schedule, it executes "A-Left-M" and "LaR" animations at the right timing on the DG avatar (Fig. 7-3).

6   Conclusion and Future Work

With the goal of automatic generation of direction-giving gestures in Metaverse avatars, we conducted an empirical study to collect human gestures in direction-giving dialogues. Then, we investigated the relationship between the proxemics and the gesture distribution, and we proposed four types of proxemics characterized by the distance from the gesture display space. Finally, we proposed a mechanism that determines the timing and the form of avatar gestures using proxemics information and the language information obtained from the chat text. We also showed an example of how the proposed mechanism can generate animation and speech on a Metaverse avatar in Second Life.

In future work, we need to investigate other factors that may influence the gesture shape. One important aspect is the relationship between the experimental conditions and the gesture distributions. We intend to analyze whether the preferable proxemics differs with the direction from which the direction receiver is approaching. Another important future objective is to evaluate the effectiveness of the gesture generation mechanism by testing whether the users perceive the avatar's gestures as being appropriate and informative.

Acknowledgment. This work was partially funded by JSPS under a Grant-in-Aid for Scientific Research (S) (19100001) and by MEXT Grant-in-Aid for Building Strategic Research Infrastructures.

References

1. Argyle, M.: Non-verbal communication in human social interaction. In: Hinde, R.A. (ed.) Non-verbal Communication. Cambridge University Press, Cambridge (1972)
2. Bergmann, K., Kopp, S.: GNetIc – Using Bayesian Decision Networks for Iconic Gesture Generation. In: Ruttkay, Z., Kipp, M., Nijholt, A., Vilhjálmsson, H.H. (eds.) IVA 2009. LNCS, vol. 5773, pp. 76–89. Springer, Heidelberg (2009)
3. Breitfuss, W., Predinger, H., Ishizuka, M.: Automatic generation of gaze and gestures for dialogues between embodied conversational agents. Int'l Journal of Semantic Computing 2(1), 71–90 (2008)
4. Bull, P.E.: Posture and Gesture. Pergamon Press, Elmsford (1987)
5. Kendon, A.: Some functions of gaze-direction in social interaction. Acta Psycholigica 26, 22–63 (1967)
6. McNeill, D.: Hand and Mind: What Gestures Reveal about Thought. University of Chicago Press, Chicago (1992)

7. Nakano, Y.I., Okamoto, M., Kawahara, D., Li, Q., Nishida, T.: Converting Text into Agent Animations: Assigning Gestures to Text. In: Human Language Technology Conference of the North American Chapter of the Association for Computational Linguistics (HLT-NAACL 2004), Companion Volume, Boston (2004)
8. Tepper, P., Kopp, S., Cassell, J.: Content in Context: Generating Language and Iconic Gesture without a Gestionary. In: Proc. of the Workshop on Balanced Perception and Action in ECAs at AAMAS 2004 (2004)
9. Tsukamoto, T., Nakano, Y.: Gesture Generation for Metaverse Avatars using Linguistic and Spatial Information. In: Proc. of the 74th National Convention of IPSJ (in Japanese) (to appear)

Organizing Scalable Adaptation in Serious Games[*]

Joost Westra[1], Frank Dignum[1], and Virginia Dignum[2]

[1] Universiteit Utrecht
[2] Delft University of Technology

Abstract. Serious games and other training applications have the requirement that they should be suitable for trainees with different skill levels. Current approaches either use human experts or a completely centralized approach for this adaptation. These centralized approaches become very impractical and will not scale if the complexity of the game increases. Agents can be used in serious game implementations as a means to reduce complexity and increase believability but without some centralized coordination it becomes practically impossible to follow the intended storyline of the game and select suitable difficulties for the trainee. In this paper we show that using agent organizations to coordinate the agents is scalable and allows adaptation in very complex scenarios while making sure the storyline is preserved the right difficulty level for the trainee is preserved.

1 Introduction

In serious games, quality is measured in terms of how well the components in the game are composed, how they encourage the player (or trainee) to take certain actions, the extent to which they motivate the player, i.e. the level of immersiveness the game provides, and how well the gaming experience contributes to the learning goals of the trainee [3]. Thus believability is a main driver of game development. The search for enhanced believability has increasingly led game developers to exploit agent technology in games [11] in order to preserve believable storylines.

Dynamic difficulty adjustment is an important aspect in training applications that need to be suitable for a large variety of users with different skill levels. Having the correct difficulty level ensures that the game will contribute to the learning goals of the trainee. Current approaches of dynamic difficulty adjustment in games use a purely centralized approach for this adaptation [21,9]. This becomes impractical if the complexity increases and especially if past actions of the non player characters (NPC's) need to be taken into account while trying to adapt to the skill level of the trainee (as is needed for serious games [18,20]). The

[*] This research has been supported by the GATE project, funded by the Netherlands Organization for Scientific Research (NWO) and the Netherlands ICT Research and Innovation Authority (ICT Regie).

M. Beer et al. (Eds.): AEGS 2011, LNAI 7471, pp. 106–122, 2012.

use of software agents has also been advocated as a means to deal with the complexity of serious games [11]. Distributing the responsibility of staying believable and adjusting to game progress, over the different non player characters creates a much more manageable situation, but this might lead to unwanted situations if their adaptation is not well coordinated.

Current agent approaches have no coordination over the adaptation at all. We argue that a system without any coordination will not result in good adaptation if the complexity of the game and the number of different adaptable elements increases. Multiple elements could adapt in the same direction and will overshoot the desired target difficulty for the trainee. Or the agents all adapt in a very similar way, resulting in state where the NPC's are not performing all the tasks required by the scenario. We will also show in this paper that a nave centralized approach will become too slow if the numbers of tasks that NPC's can perform becomes too big. While this might not be problematic with the current entertainment games yet where adaptation to the user is very limited, it will be a problem with more complex serious games. In this paper we propose to use agent organizations plus a related adaptation engine to manage the control of the coordination and adaptation of the agents, while leaving them enough autonomy to determine their next actions. We will show that this gives the right balance between distributing decision making (leading to scalability) and keeping the game believable and immersive.

The paper is organized as follows. In the next section we will look at the requirements for the adaptive serious games we are investigating. In section 3 we will look at the current approaches that are used in games. In section 4 we further explain the agent organization based framework we are using. We show how this framework can be used to create scalable serious in section 5. In section 6 we will show the order of magnitude of a resulting design compared to a nave centralized approach. Conclusions are discussed in the last section.

2   Adaptation

The type of adaptive serious games we are investigating have certain requirements and properties that are usually not found in current entertainment games. The biggest difference is that the NPC's in these games can perform a lot of different types of actions. In most commercial games that do adapt to the user, the NPC's can only perform a very limited number of different tasks and the adaptation isn't done on the task type level but only by adjusting certain simple parameters within the same task definition. In most serious games we want to expose the trainee to a much larger variety of different tasks. This is partly caused by the fact that the trainee needs to learn separate skills and different combinations of these skills. For example, the trainee needs to learn to extinguish fire while making sure the victims are safely extracted from the building. For each skill we also want to expose the trainee to a larger variety of challenges that do not only differ in simply tunable parameters but require a substantially different response from the trainee. For example the trainee should learn to extinguish basic home fires but also chemical fires at a chemical plant. Even within the basic home fire category we want the trainee to be able to cope with fire that started on the ground floor and fires that started on the higher floors.

Also if current games progress each character type will keep performing very similar throughout the game. In serious games we want the NPC to exhibit different behaviors throughout the game. This is required because we want to expose the trainee to significantly different scenarios with different skill combinations to allow the trainee to learn to handle a larger variation of different situations. The behavior of the NPC's also has very big influence on the difficulty level for the trainee. Because we want these serious games to be suitable for a large variation of trainees with different skill levels and different learning rates we want the game to continuously adapt. This also requires a much larger number of plans that can be performed by the agent (while keeping an overall goal) because they do not only need to operate in varying scenarios but also to operate in these scenarios with different difficulty levels.

Without a clear organization structure, adaptation can quickly lead to a disturbed storyline and the believability of the game will be diminished and will lead to an explosion of possible combinations. Furthermore, characters in serious games are usually active for relatively long periods. This poses an extra burden on the believability of the game, namely coherence of long-term behavior [13]. When there are multiple NPC's that all have their own preferences and can all adapt to the trainee independently, it becomes almost impossible to create a coherent game that has a natural progression of the game and is the right difficulty for the user. The game progression is much more controllable if there is a monitoring system in the application where the desired progression (could have different paths) is specified. We propose a system where we do not only have a monitoring system that specifies the desired storyline but that also tracks the current progression within the storyline. The NPC's are still programmed with their own preferences but they receive updates of the game progression. The agents can then easily be programmed to perform different plans, not only dependent on their own beliefs but also dependent on the game progression.

Coordination of agent actions (that are still autonomous most of the time) also becomes a lot more manageable if there is a central control system that allows the designer to put restrictions on the possible plans performed by the agents. A very simple example is that the designer can specify that at a certain point in the game, one of the NPC's should always check the left hallway. A possibility would be that all the agents are programmed with this restriction in mind and that they communicate directly with each other to make sure that one goes left. We propose an efficient coordination system where all the agents propose multiple actions with preference weights corresponding to each of these proposals. From these proposals the adaptation engine will select the optimal solution that also keeps the restrictions of the designer and the preferences of the agents in mind. In this example, this means that at least one agent prefers to check the left hallway but it puts a lot less burden on the designer to allow autonomy within the agents while making sure that certain critical criteria are always met.

An added challenge for user adaptation in games is that it can only be done while the user is playing the game [2,5]. Online adaptation requires that the algorithm adapts quicker with a lot less episodes and learning data. Because the game is adapting while the user is participating in the game, it is also important that no unwanted and unpredictable situations are introduced by the adaptation. This means that the adaptation should only try promising and believable solutions while exploring different options.

Another important aspect of adaptation in (serious) games is the distinction between direct and indirect adaptation. Direct adaptation occurs when the designer specifies possible behavior of the agents in advance and specifies how and when to change this behavior. The designer also specifies what input information should be used. Direct adaptation only allows adaptation to aspects that the designer has foreseen. No unexpected behavior can emerge when using direct adaptation. On the other hand, in indirect adaptation performance is optimized by an algorithm that uses feedback from the game world. This requires a fitness function and usually takes many trials to optimize. If indirect optimization is used the algorithm also needs to be able to cope with the inherent randomness of most computer games.

In previous work [23,22] we proposed the use of multi-agent organizations to define a storyline (defining coordination restrictions on the agents) in such a way that there is room for adaptation while making sure that believability of the game is preserved. This approach has the benefits of direct adaptation without the need for the designer to directly specify how the adaptation should be done. The designer is able to specify certain conditions on the adaptation to guarantee the game flow but does not have to specify which implementations are chosen after each state. In this paper we show how the agents are implemented and show the coordination of tasks and proof that it is scalable enough and works in practice

3   Current Approaches

Even though many commercial games do not use any dynamic difficulty adaptation [15], already some research has been done on difficulty adaptation in games. Most of this research focuses on adaptation of certain simple quantitative elements in the game that do not influence the storyline of the game. For example better aiming by opponents or adding more or a stronger type of opponents.

Current research on online adaptation in games is mostly based on a centralized approach [21,10]. Centralized approaches define the difficulty of all the subtasks from the top down. This is only feasible if the number of adaptable elements is small enough and if the separate adaptable elements have no separate time lines that need to be taken into account. In shooting games, for example, these requirements are not problematic. The games only adapt to the shooting skill of the trainee and most characters only exist for a very limited amount of time. In the type of adaptable serious games we are researching, completely centralized approaches will not be scalable enough.

Research has been done on using reinforcement learning in combination with adaptation to the user [21,1]. Most of these algorithms rely on learning relatively simple subtasks. Moreover, the aim of these adaptation approaches is learning the optimal policy (i.e. making it as difficult as possible for the user). In order to avoid that the game becomes too difficult for the user, some approaches filter out the best actions to adjust the level of difficulty to the user. This results in unrealistic behavior where characters that are too successful suddenly start behaving worse again.

Little attention is paid to preserving the storyline in present online adaptation mechanisms, because they only adjust simple subtasks that do not influence the storyline of the game. Typical adjustments are, for example, changing the aiming accuracy of the opponents or adding more enemies.

Some work has been done on preserving the storyline with adapting agents [12,4] but they focus on preserving the plot, not on adapting to the trainee. Other work [16] has also been done on interaction between the agents and the storyline while adjusting to the trainee. This framework adjusts to the trainee to preserve and repair the plot of the game, this is very different from adapting the difficulty level for the trainee. Some work has been done [19] on adjusting the goals of the agents to facilitate learning of the trainee, but they also do not take skill levels of the trainee into account.

4   Framework

To get a better understanding of the different elements of the whole framework we first briefly describe the different elements and the information that is passed between them. Figure 1 shows a schematic overview of all the different elements of the framework. We are currently using a custom Java environment as our *game world*, but our approach is also applicable to other games. The *NPC's* and

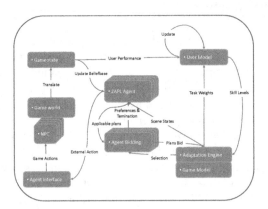

Fig. 1. Framework overview

other dynamic game elements in the game are controlled by *2APL agents*. The agents in the game have the capability to perform basic actions, like walking to a certain location or opening a door. The higher level behaviors are specified in the *2APL agents* which sent the basic *external actions* to the *agent interface* which translates these commands to basic game actions.

The *game state* is used to update the beliefs of the agents, update the progression of the game and pass the performance of the trainee to the user model. The *user model* uses this information and the *task weights* from the adaptation engine to update the estimated skill level for each state. These updated *skill levels* can then be used again to find better matching agent behaviors.

The 2APL agents can perform different actions depending on their beliefs and dependent on the scene states. The *game model* contains information about the desired storyline of the game and keeps track of how far the game has progressed in the storyline. This information is passed to the *2APL agents* to influence the possible actions they can perform. The *agent bidding* module specifies the agent preferences for all the *applicable plans*. The *adaptation engine* uses this information and the information from the *user model* to find the plan assignment for the agents that best serves the situation for the trainee. The bidding module of the agent uses this information to control the plans that are selected by the agents.

4.1 Agent Organizations

Adapting the game to the trainee for complex learning applications requires both learning capabilities and decentralized control. However, in order to guarantee successful flow of the game and the fulfillment of the learning objectives, the system needs to be able to describe global objectives and rules. Although many applications with learning agents exist, multi-agent systems with learning agents are usually very unpredictable [14]. In order to limit unpredictability in MAS, organization-oriented approaches have been advocated such as OperA [7] and MOISE+ [8]. In this framework it is possible to define conditions when certain plans are allowed or not. The ordering of the different possible plans can also be defined in this framework. This allows the designer to make sure that the users are not exposed to tasks that are not suitable yet or would ruin the storyline. In previous work we have shown how to use agent organizations to specify the boundaries of the game [22,23].

The OperA model for agent organizations enables the specification of organizational requirements and objectives, and at the same time allows participants to have the freedom to act according to their own capabilities and demands. In OperA, the designer is able to specify the flow of the game by using landmarks. The different sub-storyline definitions of the game are represented by scenes which are partially ordered without the need to explicitly fix the duration and real time ordering of all activities. That is, OperA enables different scenes of the game to progress in parallel. In the scenes, the results of the interaction are specified and how and in what order the different agents should interact.

4.2   Adaptation Engine

The adaptation engine consists of two different parts. One part selects the best combination of plans for all the different agents. The other part keeps track of the game progress and is responsible for checking if the combinations of plans are currently valid depending on the state of the game. The adaptation engine has to optimize on two possibly conflicting objectives. On the one hand we want to optimize on the preferences of the agents while on the other hand we want to select the combination which is the optimal difficulty for the user. Because we focus on adapting to the trainee, we give the highest priority to finding the best match for the trainee. Remember that we optimize on different skills of the trainee. Slight variations in difficulty level are not problematic but we do want to prevent large deviations from the desired skill levels for each separate skill. This means that we rather have deviations that are a bit larger for each skill than have multiple skill levels that are perfectly chosen but a large deviation in one remaining skill.

While optimizing on the skills of the trainee we also want to optimize on the preferences of the agents to keep their preferences into account to keep the game as believable as possible. This process uses a form of a combinatorial auction [17]. This needs to be a combinatorial auction because the agents can give a higher score for performing a certain action depending on which plans the other agents will perform. This preference dependence is only used for tasks that require coordination between the agents. For example, it is more believable for a fireman to lift a heavy object if another agent helps him. We try to limit the amount of preference dependencies because it is much more labor intensive for the game designer to specify the preferences of the agents and it is also more computationally expensive to find the best solution. Similar to finding the best match for the skill level we also want to avoid large deviations from the preferences. This means that we do not optimize on the highest combination of preferences from the agents but on the smallest squared deviations from the preferred proposal. The deviation in the skill levels are combined with the deviation of the agent preferences, giving more influence to the skill deviation.

In the game model we do not only allow the designer to specify the progress of the game but we also allow the designer to specify different difficulties corresponding to certain phases in the storyline. We also allow the designer to specify an absolute difficulty level, which can be a desired option especially for serious games because one would like to be able to know that if the trainee finishes the training that the skill level of the trainee is high enough. Updating the user model can be done in different ways. Our proposed user model update function is beyond the scope of this paper but is described in [22].

Selecting the best combination of plans from the different agents is easiest if they all terminate at the same moment. If all plans are terminated and started at the same time the optimal combination for the trainee can be selected. However, the time to execute the different plans by the agents is not always the same, and to keep the storyline flowing, it is not always a possibility to terminate plans of all the agents when a few agents have completed their task. In our framework we specify different subtasks of the game application by using scenes. The scenes usually begin when certain agents start interacting and end when that group of agents end their interaction or an organizational objective has been reached. The end of a scene usually is a natural time for all the participating agents to terminate or change their behavior. This gives enough control to make the necessary changes both for the gameflow and to optimize learning for the user.

Because multiple scenes can be active at the same time, it also does not mean that if a scene is finished all agents have terminated their plans. The goal is to have the most suitable task combination for the trainee during the whole game. Our solution is to assume that all plans that have not terminated are fixed and that newly created plan combinations keep these active plans into account. This results in a good combination for the trainee when the new plans are started. If plans are terminated the difficulty of the task changes again (becomes easier most of the time), but this can usually be compensated very quickly with new plans from the same agents (instant correction) or new plans from other agents. This results in a system that adapts quickly while keeping the behavior of the agents realistic.

4.3 Agent Implementation

The high level actions of the NPC's are implemented using the 2APL [6] language. This allows modeling of the NPC's using the BDI architecture. Using BDI agents is a suitable implementation because it allows us to create intelligent characters that are goal directed and able to deliberate on their actions. 2APL is an effective integration of programming constructs that support the implementation of declarative concepts such as belief and goals with imperative style programming such as events and plans. Like most BDI-based programming languages, different types of actions such as belief and goal update actions, test actions, external actions, and communication actions are distinguished. These actions are composed by conditional choice operator, iteration operator, and sequence operator. The composed actions constitute the plans of the agents. The agents are created with the game model structure in mind. This is done in such a way that the applicable plans are not only dependent on the game state and the internal state of the agent but also on the scenes that are currently active. This process makes it a lot easier for the developer to ensure the certain behaviors are only performed at the right moment in the game progress. The 2APL agents are created in such a way that multiple plans are applicable at the same time. These applicable plans can vary in difficulty for the trainee but they can also have the NPC perform substantially different tasks in the game.

When the agents receive a request to perform a new behavior they reply with a number of different applicable plans according to the game state, the active scenes and the internal state of the agent. This bidding process is not part of the normal 2APL deliberation cycle but is a separate part of the agent. We separated these tasks because it would be very inefficient and unnecessarily complex if the agents use the BDI reasoning process to decide why they want to perform a certain plan. This separate bidding part of the agent is also responsible for estimating the believability of each action. One important factor in estimating the believability of a new plan is dependent on the difference compared to the previous plan.

5   Designing Scalable AI

In this section we will show how our design approach can be used and why it gives a natural and effective implementation. One simple example is used throughout this section to show how the different aspects of the framework function. Figure 2 shows part of an interaction structure of a possible game. In the same figure we also display the partial ordering of the *Evacuate Victims* scene. On the interaction structure level we only define the ordering of the scenes and when it is allowed to transition to the next scene. The scenes are defined by scene scripts that specify which roles participate and how they interact with each other. The definition of the organization can be so strict that it almost completely defines the strategy. But it is also possible to specify the organization in such a way that all the agents in the game work towards achieving the goals of the game but are still able to do this using different strategies. In these scenes the results of the entire scene is specified and how and in what order the different agents should interact. It is also possible to defines norms in the scene description. This makes it possible to put extra restriction on the behavior of the agents. The agents can be programmed to break the norms. Agents that do not follow norms can be an essential part of the training. In a scene script is also possible to define certain time constraints to make sure that the game progresses fast enough.

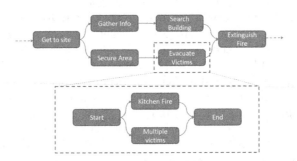

Fig. 2. Interaction structure

When scripting languages or hard coding of NPC behavior is used, it will become very difficult to read and understand the intended behavior if the project becomes more complex. In our approach we use NPC's that are based on BDI agents. This means that agent behavior is specified using high level goals and act according to their internal believes. This makes it much easier to identify why a NPC why an agent performs a certain plan. We specially use the term "high level" goals because some of the lower level behaviors can better by specified by other approaches then BDI. For example path planning can much better be handled by an A* algorithm then to incorporate this into the BDI part of the NPC. The BDI part still selects where to go but the lower level behavior handles exactly how this is done. This also results in a nice and modular approach. Using a combination of BDI agents with an agent organization architecture, results in very natural agent objectives. The whole storyline of the game is build from a collection of partially ordered different scenes. In each scene we specify the scene objective and the roles that are being played in this scene. Each participating agent plays one of these roles and therefore helps to complete the scene objective. This results in agents goals and plans that are very natural and relevant to the scene and therefore relevant to the storyline.

An obvious danger of coordinating actions between agents is that, if all possibilities are always sent to a central point which finds the best the combination, we can run into scaling problems and you might as well use completely central control instead of an agent based approach. One of the differences between a completely centralized approach and our approach is that the agents make a pre-selection of the plans that are applicable in regards to their internal state and the current game state.

5.1   Scenes

As discussed earlier the rough outline of the game is specified in the interaction structure. This interaction structure is build up from the scenes where the action required behavior of the participating agents is outlined. Only a limited number of scenes can be active at the same time. Each arrow in the interaction structure defines a scene transition with its corresponding transitions requirement. A transition always means that the old scene is no longer active (a scene transition could spawn multiple new scenes). From Figure 2, where we show a small part of an interaction structure, it can be seen that in this specific case only one or two scenes can be active at the same time. The scene *get to site* has two outgoing arrows, this type of arrow is used for situations where both transition are valid at the same time. In our framework the agents are always informed which scenes are currently active. The agents are designed in such a way that they know which plans are applicable in which scene. This allows the agents to make a very fast selection on all the plans. They do not have to check the applicability of these plans according to their believes. Because the kind of serious games we investigate have a lot of specialized plans for each scene this filtering has a very big influence on the performance of the whole system. Every scene is also build of a partial ordered collection of sub-scenes. This allows the agents to make an even more fine grained pre-selection.

Technically it functions as follows. As can be seen in Figure 1 the *adaptation engine* updates every 2APL agent with the most current *scene states*. Each 2APL agent extends a basic *GameCharacter* agent. From this definition every agent will inherit the standard ability to update its believes according to the *scene states update*. This specific 2APL plan adds the current active sub-scene to the beliefbase of the agent.

Example 1

```
Include: GameCharacter.2apl
//handles scene transition messages
//and characters movement

BeliefUpdates:
[...]

Beliefs:
 SubScene(MultipleVictims)
 Subscene(KitchenFire)

Goals:
    ExtractVictims(disasterArea)
    StoveOff(disasterArae)

Plans:
  @disasterArea( enter( 8, 8, red ), _ )

PG-rules:
true<-SubScene(MultipleVictims)//init sub-scene
 |{[...]}

true<-Scene(KitchenFire)//init sub-scene
 |{[...]}

ExtractVictims(disasterArea)<-SubScene(MultipleVictims)
//easy
 |{[...]}

ExtractVictims(disasterArea)<-SubScene(MultipleVictims
)//hard
 |{[...]}

StoveOff(disasterArae)<-Scene(KitchenFire)//easy
 |{[...]}

StoveOff(disasterArae)<-Scene(KitchenFire)//hard
 |{[...]}

PC-rules:
[...]
```

Example 1 shows a simplified version of the code of a fireman agent. In this example only the *Evacuate victims* scene is active. As can be seen the agent has the current active sub-scene available as beliefs. These beliefs are used as conditions for the PG-rules of the agents. A planning goal rule (PG-rule) specifies that an agent should generate a plan if it has certain goals and beliefs. This means that these plans are only generated if the sub-scene conditions is true. Some generic plans can be used in multiple scenes. This can easily be achieved because the conditions check is a belief query that can also include the logical OR.

For every sub-scene we use a special rule that will be applicable when the corresponding belief is added to the belief base. These specific rules will be applicable independent of the agents current goals (it could have no goal at all). In this plan we specify which goals should be added to the added goals base (and which should be removed). These goals that are added to goal base match the goals that should be fulfilled in the scene. For example in the *evacuate victims* scene each victim agent will have the goal to play a victim in that specific scenario while a fireman agent could have a goal to locate the victims and a goal protect them from harm. In Example 1 it can be seen that the scenes are already initialized because the corresponding goals are already active.

Most of the time when a sub-scene is finished the participating agents are finished with their sub-scene specific goals and plans. However this is not always true. In some cases a different agent satisfies the requirements to move to the next sub-goal while a different agent is in the middle of a task. The agent will now have more applicable plans then just the new plans corresponding to the new sub-scene. In other systems it would be very difficult to manage these kinds of situations. In our system the agent would just propose the applicable from the old task and from the new sub-scene. The agent can also give a much higher believability rating to the old plan if terminating the plan would disrupt the flow of the game.

An important thing to note is that the scenes start and end in natural situations in the games, it is not just split up into arbitrary pieces. Scenes correspond to natural occurring phases in the training game. The scene *Get to site* in Figure 2 for example is clearly a separate and phase in the progress of the game. The goals of the agents that are active during this scene will correspond to the goal of the scene and will usually be fulfilled when the termination criteria of the scene are reached. This also makes the transition between scenes a very natural moment to adapt to the trainee and to coordinate this adaptation with the participating agents.

5.2   Believability

Besides the pre-selection on the scene level we also prune the number of suggested plans that the agent can suggest by using their believability preferences. This means that the agents will estimate the believability for all the remaining and exclude the plans that have a believability below the set threshold. In quite a number of cases there will be plans that have a believability that is very low or even zero. This is mainly caused by past events that are already observed by the trainee. It could happen for example, that the agent is currently playing a victim with a broken leg because that was the best fit with the current skill levels of the trainee. It would then be completely unbelievable if the agent suddenly switches to a plan where he runs away.

The believability filtering will have a larger influence if the characters are interacting for a larger part of the game. The trainee will have more knowledge about the NPC and the numbers of believable actions will be more limited. A factor that is frequently limited because of this is the intelligence or autonomy of the NPC. It is possible for an NPC to perform a task a bit more intelligent (as if the NPC would have learned) but it would be very strange if the NPC suddenly becomes much more intelligent or very stupid.

On the implementations level it works as follows. 2APL builds a list of all the applicable plans exactly in the same way as the default 2APL implementation. This list is already quite limited because of the scene restrictions we discussed earlier. For all these we calculate the believability number. This is always between zero and one. The actual calculation of the believability is domain dependent. For example, a fire agent can only increase or decrease the fire expansion rate within certain limits. NPC's that simulate humans will have very different limitations in order to make sure the agent does not appear schizophrenic while adapting to the trainee.

The calculation of the believability is done in a separate module in our intended 2APL implementation. The believability is usually dependent on past actions and believes from the agent. The agents for example need to keep track of the level of intelligence of its past actions to make sure it will stay consistent from the perspective of the trainee. We also store this data in the belief base of the agent. This means that not only the extra believability module has access to this but that the reasoning part of the agent is also able to use this data. This means that the agent can reason that it cannot run away because it is aware that it has a broken leg. This allows the designer to implement these dependencies on the past more naturally. It also helps to make the framework to scale better because more plans are excluded in an earlier phase. The believability calculations are allowed to be a bit more computationally expensive then some of the calculations in the framework because they only have to be performed on a relatively small number of plans. A cutoff threshold is set and all the plans that fall below this level will be excluded from the agent proposal. The threshold level for a part defines the tradeoff between accurate adaptation and believability. Only filtering out plans with believability zero will already help a lot in solving the disruptive changes that can be observed in some more traditional adaptive games.

5.3 Combinations

After all the agents have finished selecting the possible plans that possible fit in the current situation they send this proposal to the adaptation which checks the tasks that are currently performed by agents and then checks all the new proposals from possibly different agents (remember that the agents can use the coordination asynchronously). The adaptation engine uses the specifications from the game model of the scenes that are currently active (for example only the *extract victims* scene could be active). This means that number of plan combinations is not only limited by the number of plans proposed by the agents but also by checking the validity of the combinations before they are evaluated on skill difficulties. In some cases this pruning can have a big influence. If we for example assume that the (sub)scene defines that at least fireman should explore the left corridor and that there is currently only one fireman active then we can very quickly throw away all the combinations that contain the fireman performing a different plan than exploring the left corridor. In most cases however this pruning is little less efficient because most requirements require to really check the plans of multiple agents. For example, if the (sub)scene specifies that a stretcher needs to be carried by at least two agents then we need to check each combination until from all the corresponding plans there are at least two agents that perform the carry stretcher plan.

The agents also do not use the adaptation engine for all their plan selections. If there is no need for adaptation, then the agents will keep running their normal 2APL program with the current preferences. The adaptation engine will request a new bidding round if the deviation from the intended difficulty becomes too large. The bidding process is also started at fixed points in the game scenario where it is logical for the agents to start performing different actions. Updated preferences also do not mean that the agents have to stop performing their current plan but the selection of the first new plan is influenced. A third way of managing the scaling problem is that multiple scenes can be active at the same time and not all agents are part every scene. This splits the optimization problem into smaller subtasks which makes it more efficient to optimize.

6   Scalability Analysis

In this section we will analyze the scaling difference between a naïve centralized approach and our coordinated distributed approach. Both approaches will have a very similar approach of combining the actions of the NPC's but the main difference will be in the remaining number of plans proposed by the agents. We aim to use reasonable assumptions that correspond to the type of serious games we have encountered during our research. The example in Figure2 shows a part an interaction structure of a game. This part of the interaction structure shows six scenes. A reasonable assumption is that a whole game can be split into 30 different scenes of which on average two scenes are active at the same time. Because the scenes are independent of each other, the total number of scenes hardly influences the execution time if our distributed approach is used. In Figure 2 only one or two scenes can be active at the same time. In practice most interaction structures are very similar and it hardly ever happens that more than two scenes can be active at the same time. Using an average of two scenes at the same time will therefore give a pessimistic estimation of the performance. The ability of the agents to filter the possible actions depending on the active scenes makes a huge difference in the number of possible actions that can be proposed by the agents. In this example the agent will filter out more than 93% $((30-2)/30)$ from its complete plan base. In the same figure we also see an example of scene with different sub-scenes. In this case there are only two sub-scenes but an average of four will give a more realistic estimation. We again pessimistically assume that on average two sub-scenes are active at the same time (per scene). We assume that every agent has 6 unique plans for each sub-scene. The ability to also select plans according to the sub-scenes will cut the remaining number of plan in half again (2 of 4 sub-scenes are active for each scene). As explained in section 5 the agents can also filter out some of the remaining plans by cutting out the plan that are not believable enough. In some cases this filtering percentage will be very low but in the kind of serious games where the NPC also cooperate with the trainee a reasonable assuming will be that 50% of the remaining plans are filtered out. We will leave out the optimization on the invalid combinations because it is very difficult to give accurate estimations for this and it will also make it more difficult to compare to the nave approach. This means that we will compare the number of combinations that can be made from the actions proposed by the agents. For each of these combinations the difficulties for the different skill levels needs to be calculated. Even though this calculation itself is not very time consuming the exponential nature of making these combinations will really become a factor in complex scenarios.

The purely nave approach will have 720 (30 scenes * 4 sub-scenes * 6 actions per sub-scene) different plans for each agent active at the same time. Our approach will have 12 (6 actions per sub-scene *2 sub-scenes active per scene * 2 active scenes /2 for believability filtering) In figure 3 we plotted the out the number of combinations for both approaches depending on the number of agents. As can be seen the number of combinations already add up very quickly with our distributed filtering but it is much more manageable then without the filtering. Even with four agents the filtered approach is already 12960000 times as slow. With more than four agents the nave approach becomes completely impractical.

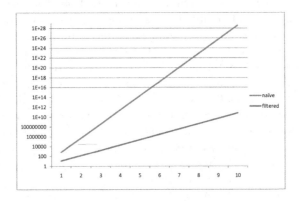

Fig. 3. Number of possible action combinations

Keep in mind that in practice our distributed approach will be much faster because we are also efficiently filtering out impossible combinations. This means that in practice the number of combinations that will be evaluated will be much lower than the estimations from our graph. We, however, also realize that the term scaling is relative. The coordination is fast enough by using our distributed approach for the type of games we are investigating and is much faster than the nave approach. But because of the exponential nature of the remaining coordination it will not scale to games with massive numbers of NPC's.

7   Conclusion

In this paper we discussed online adaptation in serious games. The adaptation is based on the use of learning agents. In order to coordinate the adaption of the agents we use an organizational framework that specifies the boundaries of the adaptation in each context. We argue that an agent based approach for adapting complex tasks is more practical than a centralized approach. It is much more natural when the different elements are implemented by separate software agents that are responsible for their own believability.

We mainly concentrated on the different phases of plan selection performed on the agent level. However, we also have shown that by using an agent organization framework we can segment the game in scenes in a natural way to describe which of the possible actions of the agents are relevant at the current moment. Every selection phases reduces the number of plans that need to be coordinated. This greatly reduces the scaling problems when coordination multiple agent with a large variety of possible actions.

The system is implemented using 2APL for the agents and tested with artificial trainees on the fire fighting example also used in this paper. The next step is to couple the system to a game engine and test it with real trainees.

References

1. Andrade, G., Ramalho, G., Santana, H., Corruble, V.: Extending Reinforcement Learning to Provide Dynamic Game Balancing. In: Reasoning, Representation, and Learning in Computer Games (2005)
2. Beal, C., Beck, J., Westbrook, D., Atkin, M., Cohen, P.: Intelligent modeling of the user in interactive entertainment. In: AAAI Spring Symposium on Artificial Intelligence and Interactive Entertainment, Stanford, CA (2002)
3. Brusk, J., Lager, T., Hjalmarsson, A., Wik, P.: Deal: dialogue management in scxml for believable game characters. In: Future Play 2007: Proceedings of the 2007 Conference on Future Play, pp. 137–144. ACM, New York (2007)
4. Cavazza, M., Charles, F., Mead, S.: Characters in search of an author: AI-based virtual storytelling. Virtual Storytelling Using Virtual Reality Technologies for Storytelling, 145–154
5. Chen, J.: Flow in games. Communications of the ACM 50(4), 31–34 (2007)
6. Dastani, M.: 2APL: A practical agent programming language. Autonomous Agents and Multi-Agent Systems 16, 214–248 (2008)
7. Dignum, V.: A Model for Organizational Interaction: based on Agents, founded in Logic. SIKS Dissertation, series (2004)
8. Hübner, J.F., Sichman, J.S., Boissier, O.: $S - Moise^+$: A Middleware for Developing Organised Multi-agent System. In: Boissier, O., Padget, J., Dignum, V., Lindemann, G., Matson, E., Ossowski, S., Sichman, J.S., Vázquez-Salceda, J. (eds.) ANIREM and OOOP 2005. LNCS (LNAI), vol. 3913, pp. 64–78. Springer, Heidelberg (2006)
9. Hunicke, R., Chapman, V.: AI for Dynamic Difficulty Adjustment in Games. In: Proceedings of the Challenges in Game AI Workshop, Nineteenth National Conference on Artificial Intelligence, AAAI 2004 (2004)
10. Hunicke, R., Chapman, V.: AI for dynamic difficulty adjustment in games. In: Challenges in Game Artificial Intelligence AAAI Workshop, pp. 91–96 (2004)
11. Lees, M., Logan, B., Theodoropoulos, G.: Agents, games and HLA. Simulation Modelling Practice and Theory 14(6), 752–767 (2006)
12. Magerko, B., Laird, J., Assanie, M., Kerfoot, A., Stokes, D.: AI characters and directors for interactive computer games. Ann Arbor 1001, 48109–2110

13. Moffat, D.: Personality Parameters and Programs. In: Petta, P., Trappl, R. (eds.) Creating Personalities for Synthetic Actors. LNCS, vol. 1195, pp. 120–165. Springer, Heidelberg (1997)
14. Panait, L., Luke, S.: Cooperative multi-agent learning: The state of the art. Autonomous Agents and Multi-Agent Systems 11(3), 387–434 (2005)
15. Rabin, S.: AI Game Programming Wisdom. Charles River Media (2002)
16. Riedl, M., Stern, A.: Failing believably: Toward drama management with autonomous actors in interactive narratives. Technologies for Interactive Digital Storytelling and Entertainment, 195–206
17. Sandholm, T.: Algorithm for optimal winner determination in combinatorial auctions. Artificial Intelligence 135(1-2), 1–54 (2002)
18. Schurr, N., Marecki, J., Lewis, J.P., Tambe, M., Scerri, P.: The DEFACTO system: Training tool for incident commanders. In: Veloso, M.M., Kambhampati, S. (eds.) AAAI, pp. 1555–1562. AAAI Press / The MIT Press (2005)
19. Si, M., Marsella, S., Pynadath, D.: Thespian: An architecture for interactive pedagogical drama. In: Proc. Of AIED, Citeseer (2005)
20. Silverman, B., Bharathy, G., O'Brien, K., Cornwell, J.: Human behavior models for agents in simulators and games: part II: gamebot engineering with PMFserv. Presence: Teleoperators and Virtual Environments 15(2), 163–185 (2006)
21. Spronck, P., Ponsen, M., Sprinkhuizen-Kuyper, I., Postma, E.: Adaptive game AI with dynamic scripting. Machine Learning 63(3), 217–248 (2006)
22. Westra, J., Dignum, F., Dignum, V.: Modeling agent adaptation in games. In: Proceedings of OAMAS 2008 (2008)
23. Westra, J., van Hasselt, H., Dignum, F., Dignum, V.: Adaptive Serious Games Using Agent Organizations. In: Dignum, F., Bradshaw, J., Silverman, B., van Doesburg, W. (eds.) Agents for Games and Simulations. LNCS, vol. 5920, pp. 206–220. Springer, Heidelberg (2009)

Inferring Pragmatics from Dialogue Contexts in Simulated Virtual Agent Games

Alex Yu-Hung Chien[1] and Von-Wun Soo[1,2]

[1] Department of Computer Science,
[2] Institute of Information Systems and Applications,
National Tsing Hua University,
30013 No. 101, Section 2, Kuang-Fu Road, Hsinchu, Taiwan, R.O.C.
knightsot@gmail.com, soo@cs.nthu.edu.tw

Abstract. Virtual agents in video games may conduct two types of interactions: physical and dialogical. While the former is recognized as gazes and gestures, which received significant attention, the latter is often simplified in simulated virtual agent games. However, dialogical interactions affect the mental states of individual agents, and the relations between them, therefore playing a more important role than physical interactions in games. An implemented dynamic Bayesian Network (DBN) based on speech acts is proposed to model the dialogical effects as dialogue contexts in different aspects, such as emotion states, social relations, and social roles. We adopt a scene in the famous movie Doubt that has 53 dialogue sentences as the test corpus and implement 21 types of speech acts in the experiments. The results indicate that, with our DBN model, agents have the ability of context awareness to infer indirect speech acts from given direct speech acts, and that this ability may assist agents to plan dialogues based on speech acts in future work.

Keywords: Speech act theory, Bayesian networks, Pragmatics, Context awareness, Agent dialogue, Virtual games.

1   Introduction

While computer entertainment and education games have evolved into a huge industry in recent years, they have brought us into a new era full of imagination and creativity. Computer games today could simulate virtual worlds more believably than before, and could immerse people with realistic presentations to their cognition. Various techniques including 3D graphics and sound effects have been implemented in the latest games to make them more vividly and lively in the virtual worlds, and we can act as a virtual character role and interact with non-player characters (NPCs) and the virtual environment in the virtual games for entertainment or education. Therefore, in virtual world, we need to enrich the NPCs ability in their reasoning, dialogues and context awareness, whereas NPCs are usually treated as a multi-agent system (MAS).

In MAS, either rational or non-rational agents rely on communication to solve problems, resolve conflicts, argue about disagreements, form teams for cooperation, come up with a joint plan, and conduct social activities. Different modes of communication for

M. Beer et al. (Eds.): AEGS 2011, LNAI 7471, pp. 123–138, 2012.
© Springer-Verlag Berlin Heidelberg 2012

agents have been developed for MAS. In 1993, DARPA KES defined a standard of agent communication language (ACL) called Knowledge Query Manipulation Language (KQML) that was based on the speech act theory for intelligent agents [7]. FIPA-ACL extended KQML and defined 22 performatives for agents to communicate. Both KQML and FIPA-ACL [8] basically pre-suppose that agent's dialogue pragmatics must to some extent follow Grice's maxims [10] in order to achieve effective communication and avoid ambiguity and misunderstanding. However, in computer games, the ability for NPCs to accurately interpret the semantics and pragmatics in a dialogue can be seriously restricted by the sanction of Grice's maxims, since indirect speech acts, which are appearing frequently in story dialogues such as metaphors, jokes, ironies, or even lies can easily violate the Grice's maxims. Therefore, if we insist agents to communicate strictly within Grice's maxims, it would be difficult for agents to infer different pragmatics from its semantics in the dialogue context.

Our research objective is to establish a dialogue context awareness model for virtual agents who play as NPCs in computer games so that they can "understand" the dialogue context to some extent and infer the true intentions of other agents in the dialogue from emergent narratives. From our point of view, a virtual agent who can conduct dialogue properly with other agents must have at least the following capabilities: 1. awareness of the situations in the dialogue including the observable environment and dialogue history; 2. ability to reason about other agent's mental states; 3. ability to predict possible consequence or other agent's possible reactions at current dialogue situations; 4. ability to explain what might have possibly happened based on current dialogue context situations. We consider these abilities all related to the dialogue context awareness, which is needed for a dialogue agent to be able to infer pragmatics from semantics of a dialogue under various dialogue contexts. On the other hand, for an agent to conduct dialogue properly, it implies the agent can select a proper speech act with respect to situated dialogue contexts. Therefore, agents must be able to model speech acts not only by considering its preconditions but also by projecting its post-conditions and effects in a dialogue, so they can select a speech act properly. However, unlike physical actions, speech acts normally involve contexts that are related to participants' mental states and social situations and are difficult to specify. The context models are needed to be clarified first before speech act models are defined. Besides, since mental states of agents and dialogue pragmatics are in general unobservable and uncertain, we need a probabilistic reasoning model to support the uncertain reasoning both forward and backward between the dialogue pragmatics and dialogue contexts. We adopt dynamic Bayesian networks [13] (DBN) as the framework to support the simulation of the context awareness reasoning based on a sequence of dialogue sentences in the dialogue.

This paper focuses on how to model the speech acts so that they can facilitate agents to be aware of dialogue contexts by mapping from the dialogue semantics to its pragmatics. In section 2, we survey related works. In section 3 we describe our method of modeling speech acts and various dialogue contexts, the computation models of DBN for context awareness. In section 4, we describe the simulation experiments against a test dialogue corpus from a movie script and we show our results and discuss their significance. We conclude in section 5.

2   Related Works

Traditionally, context-awareness refers to the extraction and purification of information with low-level signals from the real world. Dey and Abowd [6] defined the term "context" as "any information that can be used to characterize the situation of an entity". The closest related research to our work in context-aware applications is emotion detection from texts, speeches, or videos in human-machine interactions [11][12].

Stolcke et al. [18] used a hidden Markov model as a Bayesian network to determine the likelihood from speech signals to 42 dialogue acts based on 1,155 switchboard conversations with high accuracy. In contrast, our goal is to determine the likelihood from speech acts to contexts.

Galley et al. [9] applied a statistical approach for modeling agreements and disagreements in dialogues. They rank the maximum entropy, based on several observable features, to identify participants in conversation. In contrast, our approach uses a wider variety of unobservable dialogue contexts than it does agreements and disagreements.

In contrast to our statistical approach, Bentahar [3] designed the Commitment and Argument Network to enable agents to reason about communicative acts and conversation states with logical inference, as long as agents follow Grice's maxims (being honest and precise) [10]. In addition to difficulties in implementing Grice's maxims, it is advisable not to follow them in many dramatic scenes. Therefore, we aim to develop probability-based models to infer the mental states of each agent.

Conati [4] proposed a model based on a dynamic decision network to monitor the emotions of users in educational games by assessing the actions of users and agents as evidence of the causes and effects of users' emotional arousal. This model is closely related to our research. In addition to proposing theoretical models on evidences and hidden states at the same context level with a wider variety, we implement our models and conduct experiments to justify our assumptions.

3   Methods

In In speech act theory, all speech acts must accompany some context to be meaningful. For example, the speech act: *Order* must be used in the context that corresponds to a hierarchical relation, in which a person in a relatively higher position has the right to command, and people in a lower position have the obligation to obey this command. In other words, to define a speech act, it must be associated with relevant social situations and changes in mental states of both dialogue agents.

Figure 1 shows possible contexts involved in dialogue. Agents can obtain dialogue context information regarding their dialogue situations through the observation on the environment, such as the physical states of location, room arrangement, temperature, and brightness. In addition, agents can memorize all previous dialogues as contextual information. This type of contextual information can be obtained via agent sensors as evidence, and can become more reliable and refined as the sensor technologies available to the agents are improved and diversified.

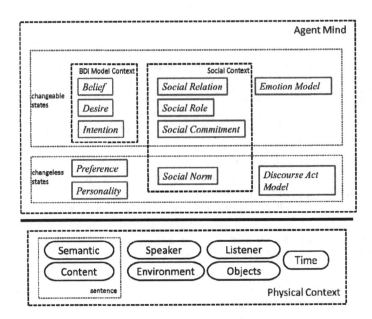

Fig. 1. Agent's mental states and physical context

Another type of contextual information is unobservable, and must be obtained by reasoning, based on prior knowledge and evidence gathered from the environment. The mental states of other agents, including their emotions, cognition of social relations, personalities, beliefs, goals, intentions, or even atmosphere of dialogue, are usually hidden and unobservable contextual information. Usually, agents cannot be 100 % certain that the contextual information inferred is correct, even by reasoning with sound logic. Since Grice's maxims cannot be assumed, agents cannot believe other agents. Agents must rely on unobservable contextual information to make decisions, even though there is uncertainty in such information. Therefore, unobservable contextual information is no less important than directly observable contextual information.

We refer to these two types of contextual information as the dialogue context of a speech act because they are useful in defining a speech act. This is described in Section 3.1. To design the reasoning of contextual information, based on the observable evidence and unobservable information, we adopt dynamic Bayesian networks, which are described in Section 4.

In a dialogue, agents can obtain contextual information directly from not only tones of speech and facial expressions of other agents, but also the content semantics in the dialogue sentences. The content semantics of a dialogue sentence could generally be obtained from complex natural language processing steps to simplify the discussions and focus on the theme of the paper. We assume that the content semantics of a dialogue have been extracted and processed separately.

3.1   Models of Speech Acts and Dialogue Context

Speech Acts
In traditional planning, each action must satisfy some physical states, referred to as preconditions, to be executed, after which it can cause a change to the world states as effects or post-conditions. These states are generally observable to ensure that the action is executed or successfully performed.

A speech act has similar properties, except that a speech act only changes the mental states of agents that cannot be verified via direct observation, without some mode of reasoning. Therefore, we must first define which dialogue contexts a particular speech act can affect, and the manner and degree to which it affects the dialogue context.

An action can only be applied when all preconditions are matched in the action model. However, the speech act model is less rigid than the action model. Although there are many related dialogue contexts that can trigger a speech act, we assume that a speech act can be triggered by a partial match with related dialogue contexts. For example, the emotion contexts "anger" and "reproach" are related to the speech act "blame." However, an angry agent might still blame someone even if they did not experience the reproach emotion. This is a major difference between the speech act model and the action model.

In our speech act model, a speech act affects not only the speaker's mind, but also the listener's mind. All mental contexts of the agents cannot be combined because the mental states of each agent are formulated by independent Dynamic Bayesian Network (DBN) models. This is explained further in Section 3.2.

In Figure 2, we show that a speech act is modeled by the changes in various contexts, which indicates that the mental states of an agent can affect the selection of a speech act, and that a speech act can affect the mental states of agents and others, based on the observation of current dialogue contexts.

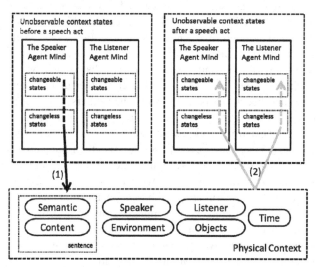

Fig. 2. A speech act affects both speaker's and audience's mental contexts. The effects to audience are hard to know until the agent conduct some speech acts in conversation.

As discussed above, if we assume that all agents conduct dialogues by obeying Grice's maxims, we could convert the dialogue content semantics directly into pragmatics (infer speech acts directly from their dialogue content semantics). However, in emergent narratives, we forego the assumption of Grice's maxims for agent communication, and therefore, could not directly obtain the pragmatics or speech acts from the dialogue content semantics. Since the agent mental states are essentially unobservable, we cannot confirm whether the pragmatics in a dialogue sequence of inferred speaker agents are indeed the true intentions (or speech acts) of the speakers. Therefore, we distinguish between two different dialogue sequences: (1) a coherent semantic sequence, in which all the dialogue semantics of speech acts in the dialogue sequence can be treated as pragmatics and no incompatible speech acts can be found in the sequence; and (2) an incoherent semantic sequence in which the dialogue semantics of speech acts are treated directly as pragmatics, and if so, the dialogue semantics of certain speech acts might be in conflict with their true pragmatics. Dialogues in the emergent narratives are generally incoherent semantic sequences, and therefore, we must find an explanation of the most likely pragmatic speech act sequence for a given dialogue sequence.

Dialogue Context. In the work of speech act classification [1], approximately 4,800 speech acts and 600 categories were divided into four major layers: expression, appeal, interaction, and discourse. Each speech act can be defined by the changing or triggering of specific contexts. It is impossible to list all applicable context conditions for a speech act since it falls into the frame problem, where all contingent conditions involved could not be specified. The ramification effects of a speech act on the mental states of other agents cannot be easily and clearly framed, due to the unobservable property of their mental states.

In designing the dialogue context model, we only considered the major conditions and effects that an independent speech act can achieve in a dialogue. Some principles and commonly encountered contexts, while considered arbitrary, can still be adopted in the dialogue context modeling to render the context awareness feasible.

We often encounter the matter of the degree of effect in describing the relationship between the dialogue context and a speech act; to distinguish whether an agent is more likely to choose a particular speech act over another under a certain context, or whether a particular speech act is more likely than others to affect a given context. Our solution is to divide the degree of effect into five levels. Each level maps a probability in the Bayesian network, as follows: Level 1: 15 %, Level 2: 35 %, Level 3: 50 %, Level 4: 65 %, and Level 5: 85 %. We then subjectively annotate the information into each speech act. Although the subjective annotation can cause inaccurate predictions in the beginning, we can later adjust the degree of effect dynamically at a separate learning stage based on the dialogue records, when the inaccurate predictions are found. For example, when we find that all agents tend to have low estimation toward the "angry" emotion, we could raise the levels of the effects of all speech acts that have affected the "angry" emotion.

To demonstrate our approach, we focus on three types of dialogue contexts: emotion context, social relations, and social roles.

Emotion Context. The OCC emotion model [2] proposed an emotion model for 22 types of emotions according to their triggering conditions in terms of an agent's appraisal on objects, agents and events with respect to his/her utility. Using OCC model to logically describe the emotion context for speech acts encounters not much difficulty. However, the strength of an emotion cannot have a common standard way to model. For example, if Peter *requests* Mary something, he will have emotions of *hope* if Mary accepts or have emotion of *fear* if Mary rejects. However, if there is no difference in the strength of emotions, it is hard to distinguish the emotional differences that could be brought from the use of three different speech acts: *request*, *beg*, and *order*. Intuitively speaking, speaker agents using *order* should have less *fear* and *hope* emotion than *beg* after using it. Table 1 shows an example of speech act models of *beg* and *order* respectively in their post-conditions to distinguish such a difference.

Table 1. The effects on speaker's emotion of speech acts of *order* and *beg*

.   A *order* B⬚ (effects on the speaker A only)
P(A_emotion_hope | order) = 0.15 P(A_emotion_fear | order) = 0.15
.   A *beg* B⬚ (effects on the speaker A only)
P(A_emotion_hope | beg) = 0.65 P(A_emotion_fear | beg) = 0.65

As discussed above, not only can a speech act affect an emotion at a different degree to an agent, but the strength of an emotion can also affect the selection of a speech act for an agent. In Ballmer's speech act classification, 155 speech acts have been identified under Expression Layer that are used to express agent's self-emotion. In other words, in dialogue context, expressing self-emotion can play a very important role in agent communication that can help an agent to make other agents understand his reactions to previous conversation or release his emotional pressure.

In Table 2, we show an example of model emotion expression speech act *blow-up* that is adopted by a speaker whose angry emotion has reached a higher degree than a specified threshold (according to his personality) in the precondition and that might also affect its listener's emotion toward negative in the post-condition. The figures in the parentheses indicate the tendency of increase or decrease emotion toward a positive or negative condition.

Table 2. The emotion context of speech act blow up

.   A *blow_up* B.
P(blow_up | A_emotion_anger) = 0.85   ⊐— trigger P(B_emotion_NEGATIVE | blow_up) = 0.5   ⊐— effect

On the other hand, in accompany with different emotions, the speech act adopted by an agent for a dialogue can be different even it has nothing to do with emotion expression. For example, if a boss has a very positive emotion toward his/her subordinate then he might use the speech act of *request* rather than *order*. We classify 22 emotions into categories of positive and negative as shown in Table 3. Then we could model speech acts in terms of positive and negative emotions.

Table 3. Classification of 22 OCC emotions into positive and negative emotion types

Positive Emotion	Love, Pride, Admiration, Happy-for, Gloating, Satisfaction, Relief, Hope, Joy, Gratification, Gratitude
Negative Emotion	Hate, Shame, Reproach, Resentment, Pity, Disappointment, Fear-confirmed, Fear, Distress, Remorse, Anger

Social Context. Besides emotion, a dialogue can be directed to different styles and directions according to different social relations among speakers and the listeners. After all, a dialogue can be conducted with more than one agent. To maintain a normal dialogue, agents will more or less respond with a proper speech act that follows some conventions or protocols. Random selection of speech acts among dialogue agents cannot possibly make the dialogue be pursued smoothly. Therefore under most situations, agents would choose certain speech acts according to the social context in the dialogue. For example, a subordinate rarely *yells* to his/her boss under a normal social context, while we would more than often see a warm greeting among friends. We therefore include social norms, agent social roles and social relations in the social context modeling for a speech act.

Social Relation. Social relations refer to organizational relations, friendship/enemy relations, or family relations. We focus on those relations in terms of two aspects that must be specified in the speech act: the relations that can be suggested or implied when a given speech act is adopted, and the relations that can be affected by the speech act. The social relations can affect the speech act at different degrees of influence toward the emotions of the listener agent. In table 4, we show an example of speech act order that has preconditions related to social relations. The positive and negative signs represent either a must or a must- not condition.

Table 4. The part of social role context in speech act *order*

.   A *order* B (partial trigger conditions only)
P(blow_up I A_social_relation_be_authority) = 0.85
P(blow_up I B_social_relation_be_subordinate) = 0.85

Social Role. Some speech acts can only be used by the agents having certain social roles. The speech acts "*Sentence* (in court)" or "*Diagnose* (a disease)" must be adopted by a judge or a medical doctor respectively to be considered as the proper utilization of a speech act. On the other hand, when a speech act is adopted by an agent, it might be naturally to make other agents believe that the speaker agent actually plays the social role that is implied in the speech act.

Social Norm. The social norm refers to the rules or conventions that are usually the common knowledge for all agents and that in a dialogue context can usually specify whether a given speech act should be used under certain social contexts. However, social norms can also be violated. For example, take *greeting* as an example, someone can ignore the step of *greeting* and directly cut in the main topics of the dialogue. To deal with this, we would maintain a personality context of an agent and record the frequency of violation of norms in the speech act behaviors of the agent so that it could predict more accurately the pragmatics and dialogue context of the agent in the future dialogue.

Personality Context. Personality context specifies the tendencies of the reactions of an agent toward certain emotions and social norms. At the current stage, we assume personality cannot be altered by speech acts, and thereby remain static during dialogue to simplify the evaluation of other contexts.

Preference Context. In the preference context, we record the frequencies of speech acts used by a particular agent toward other agents under certain dialogue situations so that the tendency of choosing a particular speech act for the agent can be analyzed for future prediction. Similar to Personality context, we could assume preferences are also fixed at some prior constant for all dialogue agents.

Discourse Context. Discourse context here refers to a sequence of speech acts that often appear together under certain patterns to achieve a particular function of social interaction for the dialogue agents. For example, in a discourse context of quarrel, the dialogue agents might fire speech acts as angry, disagreement, scolding, argue, and attack upon each other, whereas in a discourse context of negotiation, there can be speech acts as proposal, counter-offer, acceptance or rejection.

3.2   Computational Model of Context Awareness Reasoning Using DBN

In DBN modeling and implementation [16], we must generally specify the domain sensor model and transition model in terms of conditional probabilities $P(E_t|X_t)$ and $P(X_{t+1}|X_t)$, respectively, where E_t represents the evidence collected from sensors at time t, and X_{t+1} and X_t represent the domain states at time $t+1$ and t. With an assigned initial state $P(X_0)$, we can obtain the states of X at any t :

$$P(X_{0:t}, E_{1:t}) = P(X_0) \prod_{i=1}^{t} P(X_i \mid X_{i-1}) P(E_i \mid X_i)$$

Since each speech act is modeled by the change of dialogue contexts, we could subjectively attach the probability of the possible change of context preconditions and post conditions in the speech act as a transition model. The sensor model gathers evidence from the physical context, which includes the content semantics of the dialogue sentence and other information cues via observations, such as tone of speech, facial expression, gesture, and object location. As shown in Figure 3, we used two DBN models for two participants, agent A and agent B, during conversation. A_t and B_t are unobservable dialogue contexts for their mental state in dialogue step t. The observable data (Ob_t), which include the speech act (SA_t), are the sensor model that reflects states of observable dialogue contexts evidence E_t. The speech act could also affect the dialogue context. The effects of speech act could cause the dialogue context to change with probability P $(X_t \mid X_{t-1}, SA_{t-1})$, in which SA_t is an action model. Using DBN, we can infer context states that we designed, based on the observation of the conversation. With the speech act model, we can obtain the states of X at dialogue step t:

$$P(X_{0:t}, E_{1:t}) = P(X_0) \prod_{i=1}^{t} P(X_i \mid X_{i-1}, SA_{i-1}) P(Ob_i \mid X_i)$$

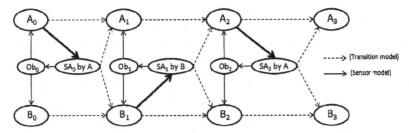

Fig. 3. Two DBN models for both the speaker's and the listener's dialogue contexts. The speech act and other observation information are sensor model in DBN.

Combine CPT with Noise-or Model. To combine the related conditional probability, we use a noisy-or model, under the assumption that all the contexts with conditional probabilities are independent. The idea behind Noisy-OR [5] function is that a speech act SA with n trigger contexts Ci, before there are n probability values pi, where pi is the probability that {SA = true} on {Ci = true} and {Cj = false} for all $j \neq i$.

$$p(SA = true \mid C1_1, ..., C_n) = 1 - \prod_{i:C_i=true}(1 - p_i)$$

The limitation of using the noisy-or model to calculate the CPT is that we can only design triggers for a speech act. We cannot describe the type of condition in which a context might reduce the possibility of inducing a speech act with the noisy-or model. To use the noisy-or model, the assumption that all dialogue contexts are independent can be substantial. However, using the noise-or model, we could simplify the computation complexity of calculating the conditional probabilities table (CPT), by reducing all 2n combinations of true-false possible conditions to only n-item computation.

4   Experiments

We obtained a dialogue sequence from the script of a film called "Doubt" [17], a 2008 film adapted from the Pulitzer Prize winning fictional stage play "Doubt: A Parable" by John Patrick Shanley. In the film, there is a scene in which three characters, Father Flynn, Sister Aloysius, and Sister James, are having an argument dialogue. We illustrated the scene, which has 53 dialogue sentences, in Table 5, and manually annotated the dialogue sentence with observable evidence and possible mental states (such as emotions and other context), as well as correct speech acts, as our test corpus. We modeled and implemented 21 types of speech acts, according to the approaches discussed in Section 3, of which 18 actually appeared in the scene of the selected film script.

Table 5. The dialogue sentences from a scene script from the file Doubt

#1 Aloysius: "The boy's well-being is my responsibility."
#2 Flynn: "His well-being is not a issue."
#3 Aloysius: "I'm not satisfied that that is true."
...
#50 Aloysius: "Intolerance"
#51 Flynn: "That's right. I'm not pleased with how you handled this."
#52 Flynn: "Sister"
#53 Flynn: "Sister"

4.1 Speech Act Model with Multiple Contexts

Speech Act Classification. In the Doubt scenarios, the pragmatic speech acts: ask and interrogations are frequently used in the conversation. Due to the lack of a well-designed domain ontology for the semantic content of the dialogue in the communication language, the two pragmatic speech acts are hard to distinguish. It is because both of them belong to semantic speech act *ask*. However, the pragmatic speech act: ask affects the listener's emotion merely in general sense. In table 6, we defined four kinds of semantic speech act classification and each can be elaborated or interpreted as three to six pragmatic speech acts according to its context. Some of the speech acts can change the emotion context, and some of them need to have special social roles or social relations involved. To distinguish speech acts in such speech act classifications can show that the agent has the ability to identify a proper pragmatic speech act under different context states.

Table 6. Four semantic speech acts and their elaborated pragmatic speech acts in Doubt's scene

Request	*Recount*
. Request	. Recount
. Order	. Censure
. Propose	. Accuse
Ask	*Reply*
. Ask	. Reply
. Interrogate	. Reject
. Interpellate	. Accept
. Threaten	. Controvert
	. Threaten
	. Not-intimidated

Dialogue Context Scheme. We obtained a dialogue sequence from the script of a film called "Doubt" [17], a 2008 film adapted from the Pulitzer Prize winning fictional stage play "Doubt: A Parable" by John Patrick Shanley. In the film, there is a scene in which three characters, Father Flynn, Sister Aloysius, and Sister James, are having an argument dialogue. We illustrated the scene, which has 53 dialogue sentences, in Table 1, and manually annotated the dialogue sentence with observable evidence and possible mental states (such as emotions and other context), as well as correct speech acts, as our test corpus. We modeled and implemented 21 types of speech acts, according to the approaches discussed in Section 3, of which 18 actually appeared in the scene of the selected film script.

In addition to emotion context, we also model several social relation contexts, such as *friendly_with* to model the positive relation, and a set of paired relations {*be_authority_to*, *be_subordinate_to*} to model hierarchical relationship, which is the precondition of the pragmatic speech act: *Order*.

4.2   Experiment 1: Pragmatic Prediction with Dialogue Contexts

In experiment 1, we intend to show that a dialogue agent can predict the correct pragmatic speech act to some extent from its semantic speech act of a dialogue sentence in the agent dialogue conversation given the dialogue contexts of the speech act model.

Table 7. 21 Semantic and pragmatic speech act sequences in Doubt scenario

A.   Semantic speech acts input sequence: (21a)(12b)(21c)(21d)(13e)(31f)(21e)(12e)(21f)(12f)(21e) (12f)(21e)(32e)(23f)(12i)(21j)(12e)(21f)(21e)(12e)(21f) (21e)(12h)(12k)(13k)(21d)(12e)(31f)(21e)(12n)(21h) (31n)(12n)(21h)(12f)(31p)(21e)(12f)(12f)(31t)(13s)(31t) (32e)(23f)(12m)(12e)(21f)(12d)(21u)(12l)(12k)(12k)
B.   Pragmatic speech acts input sequence: (21a)(12b)(21c)(21b)(13e)(31f)(21g)(12e)(21f)(12h)(21g) (12h)(21g)(32e)(23f)(12i)(21j)(12e)(21f)(21g)(12e)(21f) (21g)(12h)(12k)(13k)(21l)(12e)(31m)(21g)(12n)(21h) (31n)(12n)(21h)(12b)(31p)(21q)(12r)(12q)(31t)(13s)(31t) (32e)(23f)(12m)(12e)(21f)(12d)(21u)(12l)(12k)(12k)

In Table 7, we demonstrated that 21 speech acts occurred in the conversation. The 21 semantic and pragmatic speech acts used in the "Doubt" script, from 53 dialogue sentences, are labeled with a symbol from a to u in which: a: *Announce*, b: *Controvert*, c: *Dissatisfied*, d: *Recount*, e: *Ask*, f: *Reply*, g: *Interrogate*, h: *Reject*, i: *Censure*, j: *Rebut*, k: *Say-goodbye*, l: *Accuse*, m: *Agree-with*, n: *Request*, o: *Propose*, p: *Be-glad*, q: *Threaten*; r: *Not-intimidated*, s: *Pride*, t: *Praise*, and u: *Grumble*. The annotations of semantic speech act sequence and pragmatic speech act sequence, corresponding to the 53 dialogue sentences in the dialogue script, are annotated as A and B, respectively. Each dialogue character is labeled with a number: 1. *Father*

Flynn, 2. *Sister Aloysius*, and 3. *Sister James*. Each dialogue sentence can be abbreviated as: (speaker + audience + speech act). For example, Sister Aloysius makes an announcement speech act (a) to Father Flynn, which will be annotated as (21a), in the semantic speech act sequence. The pragmatic speech act is the same as the semantic speech act in this dialogue context, and therefore, it is also annotated as (21a), in the pragmatic speech act sequence.

We assume the correct pragmatic speech acts in the first half of the speech acts in the script are given as known, and then each dialogue sentence is input one by one by continuing the second half of the dialogue. We model two different agents as a test. The first agent will be given the preloaded context information in the first half part of dialogue log. By the pre-loaded context information, we mean all the pragmatic speech acts in the dialogue sequence that has been conducted so far. We observe its prediction ability on the pragmatics on every dialogue sentence in the dialogue sentences at the second half. The second agent will not be given any preloaded context information, so he/she is the third party agent and join in the conversation in the middle.   Intuitively, we expect the second agent to have a lower accuracy for prediction than the first one as a contrast, and the result confirmed this intuition. In the Table 8, the first row is the pragmatic speech act sequence for the second half part in the scenario. The second row is the predicted results of the first agent with pre-loaded context information. The third row is the predicted result from the second agent without pre-loaded context information. The third column in row 2 and 3, we calculated the accuracy ratios of precition of the two agent respectively. All the mismatchs are indicated in grey shade.

Table 8. The accuracy of pragmatic speech act prediction with/without preloaded context

Correct data	lemgnfnnhbpqrqtstefmefdulkk	Accuracy
Results with context info.	lemgnfnnhbpefftstefmefdudkk	15/19
Results w/o context info.	demenfnnffpefftstefmefdudkk	11/19

We only calculate the accuracy with the predicted result for the speech act classification. There are 16 classified speech acts, and 5 speech acts are not classified. It means that if a semantic speech act is not classified, the pragmatic speech act will be equivalent to the semantic speech act. In this experiment, only 19 of 26 sentences have classified semantic speech acts.

The first result in the experiment 1 with preloaded context knowledge has four error predictions with accuracy rate 15/19. The reason of error is due to, in the end of the conversation, emotion intensity is at normal level, so agent can't easily distinguish the pragmatic speech acts using *Emotion* context.

The second result shows a worse performance of an agent without context information. However, it still has an accuracy rate of 11/19. This is due to the *Discourse Act* context used to predict the speech act pair *ask-reply* does not require previous contexts to be identified.

In the experiment 1, we show that the accuracy with preloaded context knowledge (namely, the accumulated context information during dialogue) helps in predicting the pragmatic speech act from a semantic one.

4.3   Experiment 2: The Most Likely Pragmatic Speech Acts Sequence

In experiment 2, we assume only semantics of dialogue sentences are given as known, we attempt to assess if the speech act model could find out the most likely explanation of the dialogue context. Since most dialogue sentences are ask/reply speech acts, but sometimes emotions of dialogue agents can become incompatible with the contexts, the goal of this experiment is to find out to what extent the model could find an explanation of pragmatic context (e.g. *interrogate*) for each dialogue speech act (e.g. *ask*) sentence. With the same reason mentioned in section 4.2, we calculate the accuracy based on the classified speech acts.

Table 9. The probability and accuracy of the most likely pragmatic speech act sequence

Correct data	abcbefgefhghgefijefgefghkk lemgnfnnhbpqrqtstefmefdulkk	Probability Accuracy
Result	adcdefeeffghgefijefeefehkk lgmgnhnnhbpefftstefmefdudkk	6.792e-11 29/40

Using DBN, we calculate a most likely pragmatic speech act sequence from it corresponding semantic sequence whose overall probability is 6.792e-11 with 29 correct pragmatic speech acts matching out of 40 semantic speech acts as shown in Table 9. We reason that the error could be due to the "peaceful" conversation at the beginning of the scenario that provides little emotional context. So the prediction of the pragmatic speech act *interrogate* from semantic speech act *ask* is incorrect at the beginning for about the first one third of conversation.

5   Conclusion

We have established a speech act model to serve as a bridge for virtual agents to reason about multiple sophisticated dialogue contexts that include norms, social relations, emotion, personality, intention or goals among agents in a dialogue scene. We have relaxed the traditional agent communication assumption of ACL that assumes speech acts used by virtual agents be modeled as precisely and as sincerely as possible as suggested by the Grice maxims to avoid ambiguity in communication. By proper modeling the preconditions and post conditions of these contexts in speech acts of various types, and by adopting DBN to conduct the uncertain reasoning and inference among the contexts, it provides a powerful and flexible method to support complicated context awareness reasoning. We experiment our method with a scenario using the dialogue script in a movie as a test bed to show the performance feasibility of this approach. The results show that, with proper model of speech acts in terms of change of dialogue contexts, it could support agent reasoning about pragmatics of other agents in the dialogue. This is important in supporting virtual agents toward more context awareness in various simulated virtual games.

DBN model is adopted and the probabilities are devised based on evidences from the domain and data corpus. We implemented it with customizing subjective conditional probabilities that are reconciled under various constraints to show the feasibilities. It could possibly lead to poor accuracy and some bias in rigorous evaluation. However, after the implementation when an agent detects mass error predictions or encounters misunderstandings of a particular semantic speech act with high frequency, it has a space for incorporating some learning mechanism to automatically refine the parameters in the speech act model.

Therefore, the study has not only shed some light on the context awareness for virtual agents to conduct dialogue, but also pointed out many interesting research directions. The future work includes more elaborated design of the speech acts in various types as well as the automated acquisitions of proper parameters in supporting DBN reasoning. Since we have simplified the semantics of an entire dialogue sentence into a dialogue semantic label (*speaker-audience-speech_act*) by ignoring its actual dialogue content semantic, we are aware that in some situations, context awareness does require the content semantics of a dialogue sentence as well as its background context knowledge to resolve semantic ambiguities. The refined content semantics and background knowledge can not only improve the accuracy of the awareness, but also lead to deeper context awareness in dialogue. To achieve this aim, we need to augment not only the speech act model, but also to augment the domain content ontology and sentence parsing and understanding. Another direction of future research is to integrate with various signal sensor technologies to collect more evidence cues from environment and other agents that can support DBN to achieve a full-fledge context awareness model for the virtual agents to conduct various believable conversations in dialogue.

Acknowledgement. This research is supported by National Science Council of ROC under grant number NSC 99-2221-E-007-090-MY3.

References

1. Ballmer, T., Brennenstuhl, W.: Speech Act Classification. Springer, Heidelberg (1981)
2. Bartneck, C.: Integrating the OCC model of emotions in embodied characters. In: Proceedings of the Workshop on Virtual Conversational Characters: Applications, Methods, and Research Challenges, Melbourne (2002)
3. Bentahar, J., Moulin, B., Chaib-draa, B.: A persuasion dialogue game based on commitments and arguments. In: Proc. of the International Workshop on Argumentation in Multi-Agent Systems (2004)
4. Conati, C.: Probabilistic Assessment of User's Emotions in Educational Games. Applied Artificial Intelligence 16(7-8), 555–575 (2002)
5. Cozman, F.G.: Axiomatizing Noisy-OR. In: 16th European Conference on Artificial Intelligence, pp. 979–980. IOS Press, Valencia (2004)

6. Abowd, G.D., Dey, A.K., Brown, P.J., Davies, N., Smith, M., Steggles, P.: Towards a Better Understanding of Context and Context-Awareness. In: Gellersen, H.-W. (ed.) HUC 1999. LNCS, vol. 1707, pp. 304–307. Springer, Heidelberg (1999)

7. Finin, T., Fritzson, R., McKay, D., McEntire, R.: KQML as an agent communication language. In: Proceedings of the Third International Conference on Information and Knowledge Management, pp. 456–463. ACM, Gaithersburg (1994)

8. Foundation for Intelligent Physical Agents (FIPA). FIPA Communicative Act Library Specification. FIPA00037, http://www.fipa.org/specs/fipa00037/

9. Galley, M., Mckeown, K., Hirschberg, J., Shriberg, E.: Identifying agreement and disagreement in conversational speech: use of Bayesian network to model pragmatic dependencies. Proceedings of the 42nd Annual Meeting on Association for Computational Linguistics, Stroudsburg, article 669, PA, USA (2004)

10. Grice, P.: Studies in the Way of Words, pp. 22–40. Harvard University Press (1989)

11. Inanoglu, Z., Caneel, R.: Emotive alert: HMM-Based emotion detection in voicemail messages. In: Proceedings of the 10th International Conference on Intelligent User Interfaces, pp. 251–253. ACM, San Diego (2005)

12. Kim, S., Georgiou, P.G., Sungbok, L., Narayanan, S.: Real-time emotion detection system using speech: multi-model fusion of different timescale features. In: Proceedings of IEEE 9th Workshop Multimedia Signal Processing (MMSP), Chania, Greece, pp. 48–51 (2007)

13. Murphy, K.P.: Dynamic Bayesian Networks: Representation, Inference and Learning. Ph.D. Thesis, UC Berkley, USA (July 2002)

14. Poesio, M., Traum, D.: Representing conversation acts in unified Semantic/Pragmatic Framework. In: Proceedings of the AAAI Fall Symposium on Communicative Action in Humans and Machines (1997)

15. Pulman, S.G.: Conversation al games, belief revision and Bayesian networks. In: Proceedings of the 7th Computational Linguistics in the Netherlands Meeting (1996)

16. Russell, S., Norvig, P.: Artificial Intelligence: A Modern Approach, 3rd edn., pp. 566–599. Prentice Hall (2009)

17. Schilit, B.N., Adams, N., Want, R.: Context-aware computing applications. In: Proceedings of the Workshop on Mobile Computing System and Applications (1994)

18. Stolcke, A., Ries, K., Coccaro, N., et al.: Dialogue act modeling for automatic tagging and recognition of conversational speech. Computational Linguistics 26(3), 339–373 (2000)

19. The script of the movie: Doubt, http://www.screenplaydb.com/film/scripts/doubt/

Socially-Aware Emergent Narrative

Sergio Alvarez-Napagao, Ignasi Gómez-Sebastià, Sofia Panagiotidi,
Arturo Tejeda-Gómez, Luis Oliva, and Javier Vázquez-Salceda

Universitat Politècnica de Catalunya
{salvarez,igomez,panagiotidi,jatejeda,loliva,jvazquez}@lsi.upc.edu

Abstract. In agent research, *emergent narrative* aims for practical solutions to the *narrative paradox* problem in both drama and interactive
scenarios. At the same time, *organisational frameworks* can be used in
games to provide flexibility, adaptiveness, or social-awareness. In this
paper, we propose an extension of our cONCIENS framework to support emergent narrative in games with two objectives: 1) provide social-
awareness in emergent narrative by means of an organisational model,
and 2) create convincing dynamic and flexible storytelling in games.

1 Introduction

The main objective of the use of Artificial Intelligence (AI) in both fun and serious games is to deliver the illusion of "intelligence" in the non-player characters'
(NPCs) behaviour. While some aspects – e.g., pathfinding – have evolved to a
mature state in both the industry and academic research, it is not the case with
some important ones such as individual behaviour or strategical reasoning.

Current challenges deal with high-level concepts of gaming such as realistic
virtual actors, automatic content and storyline generation, dynamic learning, or
social behavior. Tackling these issues could represent a qualitative improvement
on gaming experience from the player perspective and academic research on AI
has good opportunities to provide solutions to these challenges [9,15].

Solutions taken by the industry are mainly based on domain-dependent low-
level approaches. These solutions arise some obvious issues [3]: lack of flexibility
and adaptation to environmental change, predictable or strange behaviour, low
reusability, or blind specifications of NPCs – i.e. the NPCs always know *how* to
act, few times they know *what* they are doing, but very rarely they know *why*.

One important factor that leads to these problems is the need for a plot or
storyline. NPCs are usually mere enactors of a story previously designed, and
their main use is to help advancing the story rather than *acting on their own*. It
is well known that there is a compromise between narrative control and character
autonomy [18]. This has been a topic of interest from the agent community in
what has usually been called *emergent narrative*: stories can emerge through
simulation of a virtual world inhabited by virtual characters.

As a result of research on *emergent narrative*, some theoretical frameworks
and implementations have appeared, focusing on both plot and characters. In
this paper we add a social aspect to this formula by linking our previous work
on organisational frameworks for games.

M. Beer et al. (Eds.): AEGS 2011, LNAI 7471, pp. 139–150, 2012.

2   Emergent Narrative

Emergent narrative tries to break the common conception of linear narrative being the only possible product of human authorship over a story: human authorship can also be applied to the creation of a more open narrative by balancing character models, event sequences, and narrative landmarks. Furthermore, research on this topic tries to tackle the problem of the *narrative paradox*: virtual environments – such as games – and narratives exist on different ontological levels, and thus there is a fundamental conflict between free-form interactivity provided by the virtual environment and the level of satisfaction produced by a man-made narrative structure [18]. The main hypothesis of emergent narrative is that this problem cannot be solved by treating both issues as separate and combining them, but by treating narrative as a direct result of the actions of the characters [5].

FearNot! [6], is a project based on virtual drama that allows children to explore the consequences of bullying actions. In a virtual environment, a child would act as an *invisible friend* of the victim, influencing his behaviour while treating the victim as a character with an independent inner life by not compromising their autonomy of action. In FAtiMA [10], the architecture *FearNot!* is based on, narrative control is achieved by organising the story in episodes at design-time and sequencing them at run-time. Each episode defines pre- and post-conditions, as well as sets of possible locations, objects, choices, and goals available. However, as discussed in [18], such a strong episodic design is limiting, as a global sense of time – and what happens during scenes, or what happens between them in the "world"– or emotional residue after each scene are not accounted for.

One way to reduce rigidness in narrative control is *distributed drama management*, combined with *double appraisal* [14]. The main idea is that characters take responsibility in managing the drama, including in their plan selection mechanism a bias towards choices that have the greatest impact on the emotions of other characters. This idea of distributed drama management has been adopted by the *Virtual Storyteller* [18], the architecture of which is depicted in Figure 1. Character agents are based on the FAtiMA agent architecture and the world agent is the interface to a simulation layer. The plot agent acts as an intermediary, setting up the simulation and sending perceptions to, and receiving actions from the character agents.

Stories are stored using *Fabula* [18], a formal model based on causal network theory to represent events already occurred with respect to the story. Events are linked to other narrative concepts such as goals, actions, outcomes, or perceptions, via causal relationships which can be, for example, physical, psychological, or motivational. The resultant graph is then used by both the presentation and simulation layers, and can be used for further analysis.

In this framework, characters enact two highly coupled roles: in-character (IC) and out-of-character (OOC) [4]. The former refers to the character behaviour and is driven by individual motivations, as normal agents. The latter, however, constrains the behaviour by trying to increase narrative impact – e.g.,

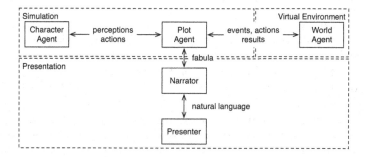

Fig. 1. *Virtual Storyteller* architecture

adopting goals that will probably cause conflict with other characters, looking for a modification on the relationship with them, or making sure that there are always goals to pursue. The action pursued by a story character will then be a function [18] upon believability (IC role), dramatic opportunity and variability (OOC role).

In *Virtual Storyteller*, emergent narrative is achieved by influencing the event sequence in order to *create* choices for the IC role while giving more chances to achieve the OOC role. This can be done in two ways, taken from drama improvisation techniques. *Making events happen* consists in creating an event that will likely enforce an advancement in the plot, e.g., the Princess has been kidnapped by a dragon, thus *forcing* those characters looking for brave actions to go and save her. *Late commitment* is based on the assumption that parts of the initial state of the world do not need to be fixed at authoring time, but dynamically determined at run time when it is purposeful for narrative purposes. In late commitment, OOC roles look for feasible and consistent properties to be added to the initial state and which will provide opportunities to advance the plot towards the storyline objectives, e.g., the story could advance by suddenly discovering that the governor is, in fact, a spy of the enemy.

Although the *Virtual Storyteller* presents a sound architecture for emergent narrative, it is strongly focused on non-interactive storytelling. This has already been noted in [18], stating that games allow for more radical applications of narrative control techniques such as late commitment. Also, from our point of view, the social aspect of multi-agent systems is somehow ignored by keeping character agents as a separate component from the simulation layer.

3   Organizational Frameworks and Games

As discussed on [3], our hypothesis is that it is possible to create elaborate solutions for the issues of both individual behavior control and collective strategy techniques by integrating models based on Organization Theoretical methods to control NPCs' behavior. This theory contributes to the systematic study of how actors behave within organizations. Hence, the actors in a game are described as an organization the behaviour of which is based on specific roles, norms, dependencies, and capabilities.

There are already examples showing that higher levels of abstraction can be successfully used in commercial games' AI. Actually, some recent important commercial games such as *F.E.A.R*[16] or *Fallout 3*, have started to apply more complex cognitive patterns by using *GOAP* (Goal-Oriented Action Planning), a simplified and optimized version of *STRIPS* that allows for real-time planning of actions with pre- and post-conditions, even outperforming *Finite State Machine*-based algorithms in some scenarios[13]. Thus, these games execute complex symbolic reasoning not only about *how* to execute certain actions, but also about *what* to execute at each moment.

In fact, organizational frameworks such as OperA [11] are already being explored for their use in *serious games*. In [19], organizational specifications are used to create a distributed intelligent task selection system that adapts to the player skill level and models the storyline.

cONCIENS [2] advances on this line of work by generalizing the use of organizational models for *fun games*, more focused on the realism of gaming experience, rather than on user modeling and learning. cONCIENS adapts the ALIVE framework [1] to its use in games and allows Game AI developers to think in terms of *why-what-how* when defining the decision-making actions for NPCs. That is, at the Organizational level, the developer defines "why to do something" by describing the elements of the organizational structure in terms of organization objectives, roles, norms, and restrictions. At the Coordination level, the developer defines "what to do" based on possible solutions and tasks to realize in specific situations; finally, at the Game Enacting level, the developer defines "how to do it" in terms of which actual, game-specific actions to perform in order to realize those tasks.

cONCIENS has been part of the research for the European Project ALIVE [1], the objective of which was to combine existing work in coordination and organizational structures with the state-of-the-art in service-oriented computing, allowing system architects to build service-oriented systems based on the definition of organizational structures and on how they interact.

The ALIVE framework adapted for cONCIENS defines three structural levels, which form the cONCIENS environment depicted in Figure 2.

The set of tools and methods of cONCIENS provides inherent support to the development of complex, re-usable Game AI solutions, extending the ALIVE environment by providing:

1. A practical solution to couple agents to the Game Engine, by defining the Game Enactor programming interface.
2. A tool to describe the Organization Ontology, which contains a representation of agent structures.
3. The elements to describe game actors' behavior via social structures based on norms, roles and their enactment, promoting the balance between autonomy and story direction.

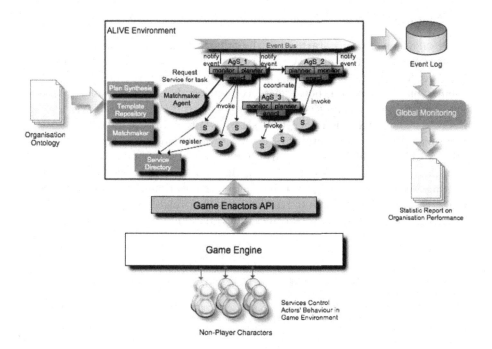

Fig. 2. CONCIENS architecture

The research aim of CONCIENS is to provide solutions to the issues presented in Section 1 by representing the interactions between players and NPCs as compliant to an organisational structure. This approach provides extended flexibility to the elements that imply intelligent behavior, e.g. actors and characters, teams of individuals, and narrative storylines. In addition, it can take advantage of ALIVE's methodology and metrics [17] that can be applied to evaluate the organizational behavior using the games' environments as simulation scenarios. Hence, it would be possible to compare, learn, and improve NPC's behavior with an approach based on organization theoretical solutions for Game AI, contributing to overall flexibility and adaptiveness.

CONCIENS has already been used to implement automatic and flexible team direction in real-time strategy games [2], and to showcase an improved method to detect and enforce traffic violations in free roaming games [3]. The next goal in our research is to test adaptive storytelling in multiplayer games by using narrative emergence, and we will show in Section 4 how we intend to achieve it.

4   Our Proposal

In this section we present our proposal, an extension of CONCIENS to adopt the architecture and some mechanisms of *Virtual Storyteller* to enable emergent narrative in games.

4.1   Mapping *Virtual Storyteller* Components to cOnciens

In cOnciens, everything starts from the organisational description (Figure 3), instanced as OperA documents. OperA consists of two main components, the Social Structure and the Interaction Structure. The Social Structure assigns roles to human players based on their preferences, and can be adapted to meet player's needs, for instance, *Apprentice* role can be removed if there is no player willing to play it. The Interaction Structure shows a set of *scenes* important to the overall plot. Each *scene* contains a set of *landmarks* that are important states of the world regarding the *scene*. Both *scenes* and *landmarks* are connected via *transition arcs* that allow navigating through them. Therefore, agents representing NPCs and players, by using these organisational constructs, become social-aware: they will be able to reason about their relationship with each other in terms of joint objectives, social rules and common interaction patterns.

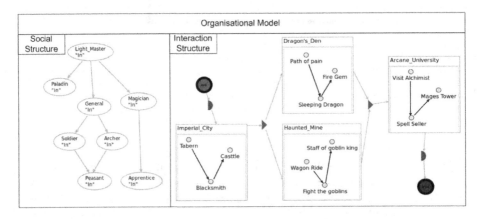

Fig. 3. Organisational Model Example

We intend to incorporate the components of the *Virtual Storyteller* (see Figure 1) as an adaptation of the cOnciens framework as depicted in Figure 4. The components that enable emergent narrative are: the Character Agents, which support both NPCs and players and are represented in cOnciens by the already existing agents of the agent layer; the World Agent, represented by the Global Monitor; the Narrator layer, implemented by the Game Enactor – i.e., converting the world state into generic game concepts such as movement orders or player quests –; and the Presenter layer, in our case the Game Engine. The only new component required is the Plot Agent.

4.2   Constructing the Plot

The Plot Agent will receive a storyline from the story designer. This storyline is implemented as a set of scenes and landmark patterns: the minimal set of states

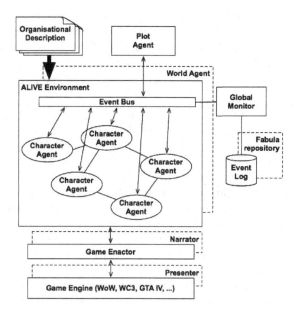

Fig. 4. Adapted cONCIENS architecture

that conform the story and that *have* to be fulfilled in its proper order, from the beginning to the end of the gameplay time. This agent will continuously observe the state of the world and dynamically plan an order of the scenes needed to get to the next storyline landmark. The roles in each scene are assigned to specific Character Agents.

The story designer can decide, in this way, how rigid / flexible the story should be by adding more or less landmarks, and by declaring stronger or weaker conditions as landmarks. The designer will also design the set of possible late commitments and non-causal related events (see Section 2) in the form of framing operators [18], that is, sets of preconditions and a set of effects on these operators that can be done if the change in a specific case is consistent with the history of events – by the use of *Fabula* [18].

4.3 Character Conflicts and Personality

The Character Agent is a BDI agent implemented inside each agent of the cON-CIENS agent level. Every NPC, as well as every player, has a representation as a Character Agent. The IC role (as seen in Section 2) is already implemented at the cONCIENS framework. Egoistic motivations, aims, capabilities, individual behaviour and organisational constraints (social objectives and norms acting as constraints to its behaviour or capabilities) are taken into account by the agent in an autonomous decision making process that produces an appropriate plan. This plan fulfills the agent's personal specifications bringing its own ways into the organisational society as well.

On the other hand, as seen earlier, the agent receives from the Plot Agent a set of landmarks that is processed by the OOC role to help advancing the story. Due to this dual nature of the Character Agents, conflicts between the IC and the OOC can –and probably will– arise. This can be solved by applying negotiation processes, such as argumentation, and will be one of the main focuses of research on this project.

In order to apply personality to the characters –including players–, we will characterise them by using stereotypes or *play styles*. There are two main taxonomies to identify play styles –DGD1 [8]– and interaction between players – Interest Model [7]–. The DGD1 model defines four types of play styles: Conqueror, Manager, Wanderer, and Participant. The Interest Model identifies four types of players: Achievers, Explorers, Socialisers, and Killers. Basically, these taxonomies identify the type of characters by analysing their psychology and behaviour, respectively. NPCs stereotypes will be given by the story designer, but in order to classify players, we will focus on their behavior: every player's action, chat log, and/or evolution will be monitored to identify which stereotype they belong to.

The use of tags on actions or states will be implemented to allow each Character Agent's planner to identify the appropriate actions to fulfill a given landmark: two characters can fulfill the same landmark in different ways, creating the illusion of personality.

4.4   Adding Interactivity to Narrative

Interactivity is achieved by giving enough choices to the player to give an illusion of free will. The actions planned by the Character Agents representing actual players will be enforced in the form of missions or quests offered to the correspondent player taking into account both the IC and the OOC roles. The player, however, will be free to choose; if the player gets too far from the story line, its Character Agent can negotiate (as seen above) changes to the environment to keep the action in the boundaries of the storyline.

However, if the OOC role of a player's Character Agent predicts that the story plans incoming from the Plot Agent are not feasible or too incompatible with the individual plan, framing operators will be checked and studied, and there will be a negotiation process with the Plot Agent to propose and apply them, resulting in applications of *making events happen* or *late commitment*.

In the example shown in Figure 5, the player is supposed to kill the dragon (either with a sword or a bow) in order to obtain the fire gem from it. However, instead of performing the attack, the player decides to cast a spell on the dragon, sending it to another dimension. As the dragon and the player are in different dimensions, the player cannot obtain the fire gem, and thus, the plot cannot advance. The Plot Agent is able to recover the plot from this deviation by: 1) receiving the event that the player has sent the dragon to another dimension, 2) reacting by introducing an event (*make events happen*) on the game via

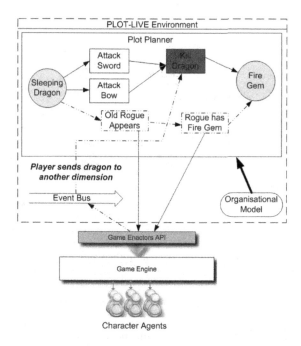

Fig. 5. System Architecture and usage of *late commitment* and *make events happen*

the game enactor, e.g., an old rogue appears, as he *was hiding*[1] in the shadows of the dragon cave, and 3) introducing a *late commitment* in the plot, via the game enactor, e.g. it comes out that the old rogue has the fire gem, as he had stolen it from the dragon before, and decides to give it to the player.

5   Conclusions

In this paper we have proposed an adaptation of an already existing organisational framework for games for its use in scenarios where the *narrative paradox* can be tested. The purpose is two-fold. First, we want to test storyline dynamic adaptation in cONCIENS applied to free-roaming games such as multiplayer role-playing games. Second, we want to explore if emergent narrative can improve with the use of organisational models, strongly focusing on the compromise between character freedom and plot design.

We use cONCIENS as a sandbox for applying the research of our agents group. By combining emergent narrative to the framework, we want to do research not only on narrative in itself but also applied to social aspects, both in-game (NPCs behaving as part of a society), and out-of-game (studying the interaction between players and between a player and the NPCs), from different perspectives:

---

[1] This is only an example of an inferred possible event, assuming it is consistent with the game history.

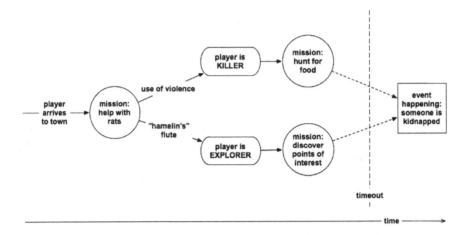

Fig. 6. Example of a simplified plot tree

organisational, normative, emotion representation and detection, user profiling, gamification, and so on.

Our immediate plan is to completely automatise the dynamic generation and parametrisation of missions by using the techniques described in Section 4. For this purpose, we have designed a mechanism for the automatic classification of players into fuzzy stereotyped. This classification is based on the monitoring of the players' actions and will be used to guide the planning of personalised plots. On one hand, we have conducted a survey on almost 300 actual World of Warcraft players based on a personality test with ideas taken from work done in [7] and [20]. On the other hand, we have taken actual player public data from the same volunteers by using Blizzard's API[2]. By using a combination of PCA and clustering techniques, and taking the survey results as training sets, we are currently building and testing an unsupervised learning algorithm capable of classifying World of Warcraft players by monitoring their public data.

In order to provide empirical results, we have already connected cOncienS to an open-source World of Warcraft server, and we have implemented several small plots with its corresponding missions and free actions for double appraisal (see Figures 6 and 7). Although the Plot Agent is still quite simple and the missions are chosen based on basic hardcoded triggers, i.e. specific actions executed by the player, it will allow us to test this small scenario, combined with the automatic classification of players, with a set of actual players and the validation will be driven by using evaluation methods on user experience over time [12].

This paper introduces an approach currently being developed. However, practical results of this research, especially regarding automatic classification of players, are being validated by experts and will be published soon. The source code used for this project is being continuously released as open-source at the

---

[2] http://blizzard.github.com/api-wow-docs/

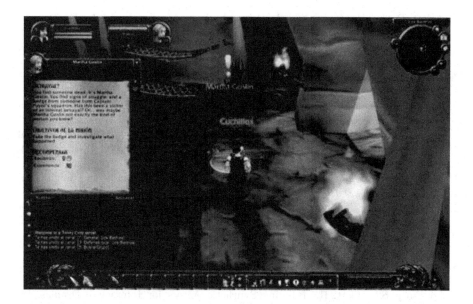

Fig. 7. A mission exemplifying the *making events happen* mechanism

cOnscienS website[3]. Other results, such as anonymised sets of data from the players and documentation on how to test our system, will also be released at the same location.

References

1. Aldewereld, H., Padget, J., Vasconcelos, W., Vázquez-Salceda, J., Sergeant, P., Staikopoulos, A.: Adaptable, Organization-Aware, Service-Oriented Computing. Intelligent Systems 25(4), 80–84 (2010)
2. Alvarez-Napagao, S., Gómez-Sebastià, I., Vázquez-Salceda, J., Koch, F.: cOncienS: Organizational Awareness in Real-Time Strategy Games. In: Proc. of the 13th Int. Conf. of the Catalan Assoc. for Artificial Intelligence, vol. 220, pp. 69–78. IOS Press (2010)
3. Alvarez-Napagao, S., Koch, F., Gómez-Sebastià, I., Vázquez-Salceda, J.: Making Games ALIVE: An Organisational Approach. In: Dignum, F. (ed.) Agents for Games and Simulations II. LNCS (LNAI), vol. 6525, pp. 179–191. Springer, Heidelberg (2011)
4. Arinbjarnar, M., Kudenko, D.: Duality of Actor and Character Goals in Virtual Drama. In: Ruttkay, Z., Kipp, M., Nijholt, A., Vilhjálmsson, H.H. (eds.) IVA 2009. LNCS (LNAI), vol. 5773, pp. 386–392. Springer, Heidelberg (2009)
5. Aylett, R.: Narrative in Virtual Environments - Towards Emergent Narrative. In: AAAI Narrative Intelligence Symposium FS-99-01, pp. 83–86 (1999)

---

[3] http://kemlg.github.com/consciens/

6. Aylett, R., Louchart, S., Dias, J., Paiva, A., Vala, M.: FearNot! - An Experiment in Emergent Narrative. In: Panayiotopoulos, T., Gratch, J., Aylett, R.S., Ballin, D., Olivier, P., Rist, T. (eds.) IVA 2005. LNCS (LNAI), vol. 3661, pp. 305–316. Springer, Heidelberg (2005)
7. Bartle, R.: Designing Virtual Worlds. New Riders Games (2003)
8. Bateman, C., Boon, R.: 21st Century Game Design. Charles River Media (2006)
9. Charles, D.: Enhancing gameplay: Challenges for artificial intelligence in digital games. In: Proceedings of the 1st World Conference on Digital Games (2003)
10. Dias, J., Paiva, A.: Feeling and Reasoning: A Computational Model for Emotional Characters. In: Bento, C., Cardoso, A., Dias, G. (eds.) EPIA 2005. LNCS (LNAI), vol. 3808, pp. 127–140. Springer, Heidelberg (2005)
11. Dignum, V.: A model for organizational interaction: based on agents, founded in logic PhD Thesis, Utrecht University (2004)
12. Karapanos, E., Zimmerman, J., Forlizzi, J., Martens, J.B.: User experience over time: an initial framework. In: CHI 2009: Proceedings of the 27th International Conference on Human Factors in Computing Systems. ACM Request Permissions (2009)
13. Long, E.: Enhanced NPC behaviour using goal oriented action planning. PhD Thesis, University of Abertay-Dundee (2007)
14. Louchart, S., Aylett, R.: Building Synthetic Actors for Interactive Dramas. In: AAAI Fall Symposium on Intelligent Narrative Technologies FS-07-05, pp. 63–71 (2007)
15. Nareyek, A.: Game AI Is Dead. Long Live Game AI. Intelligent Systems (2007)
16. Orkin, J.: Three states and a plan: the AI of FEAR. In: Proc of the 2006 Game Developers Conference (2006)
17. Penserini, L., Dignum, V., Staikopoulos, A., Aldewereld, H., Dignum, F.: Balancing Organizational Regulation and Agent Autonomy: An MDE-based Approach. In: Aldewereld, H., Dignum, V., Picard, G. (eds.) ESAW 2009. LNCS (LNAI), vol. 5881, pp. 197–212. Springer, Heidelberg (2009)
18. Swartjes, I.: Whose story is it anyway? How improv informs agency and authorship of emergent narrative. PhD Thesis, University of Twente (2010)
19. Westra, J., van Hasselt, H., Dignum, V., Dignum, F.: On-line Adapting Games using Agent Organizations. In: IEEE Symposium on Computational Intelligence and Games (CIG 2008), pp. 243–250 (2008)
20. Yee, N.: Motivations for Play in Online Games. CyberPsychology & Behavior 9(6), 772–775 (2006)

Increasing Learners' Motivation through Pedagogical Agents: The Cast of Virtual Characters in the DynaLearn ILE

Michael Wißner[1], Wouter Beek[2], Esther Lozano[3], Gregor Mehlmann[1],
Floris Linnebank[2], Jochem Liem[2], Markus Häring[1], René Bühling[1],
Jorge Gracia[3], Bert Bredeweg[2], and Elisabeth André[1]

[1] Human Centered Multimedia, Augsburg University, Germany
{wissner,mehlmann,haering,buehling,andre}@informatik.uni-augsburg.de
[2] Human-Computer Studies, University of Amsterdam, The Netherlands
{w.g.j.beek,f.e.linnebank,j.liem,b.bredeweg}@uva.nl
[3] Ontology Engineering Group, Universidad Politécnica de Madrid, Spain
{elozano,jgracia}@fi.upm.es

Abstract. Motivation is a critical requirement for successful learning. Previous research has identified that animated pedagogical agents can increase motivation. Following these results, we present the cast of pedagogical agents in the DynaLearn Intelligent Learning Environment. Each of these agents is associated with one of the different support types available in the environment, giving each agent a clearly defined role. We describe the different character roles, how their knowledge is generated and related to the pedagogical purpose at hand, how they interact with the learners and finally how this interaction helps increasing the learners' motivation. To assess this, we conducted a preliminary evaluation with three of the characters and report our findings.

Keywords: Pedagogical Agents, Virtual Characters, Intelligent Learning Environments, Motivation, Engagement.

1 Introduction

Embodied conversational agents are widely used in virtual learning and training environments [1,2,3]. Beside possible negative effects of virtual characters [4], there is evidence that virtual pedagogical agents and learning companions can increase the learners' commitment to the virtual learning experience [5,6]. They can promote the learners' motivation and self-confidence, help to prevent or overcome negative affective states and minimize undesirable associations with the learning task, such as frustration, boredom or fear of failure.

It has been shown that a one-sided coverage of knowledge transfer or the employment of only a single educational role may either lead to satisfying learning success or motivation, but usually not both at the same time [7]. The usage of multiple virtual characters with different but complementing roles can have positive influence on both the learners' learning success and their engagement. Teams

M. Beer et al. (Eds.): AEGS 2011, LNAI 7471, pp. 151–165, 2012.
© Springer-Verlag Berlin Heidelberg 2012

of pedagogical agents can help the learners to better understand the conveyed knowledge [8].

The context of our research is *DynaLearn* [9], an intelligent learning environment (ILE) in which learners learn by expressing their conceptual knowledge through qualitative reasoning models [10]. In this paper, we present DynaLearn's cast of pedagogical agents that were added to the ILE, the educational principles they are built upon and how they interact with each other and the learner. The goal of our research is to increase learners' motivation and learning success when using the learning environment.

The remainder of this paper contains related work (Section 2), a section on the different characters (3), the overall architecture of the system (4), the evaluation we conducted (5) and a critical reflection of our work as well as an outlook (6).

2   Related Work

Kim and Baylor [7,11] reported in their work on virtual learning companions three different aspects like competence, activity and realism. As we did in the DynaLearn project, they adopted human metaphors in their visual designs and focused especially on the three qualities competency, activity and realism. The competency assigned to a virtual character depends for example on the role the character takes. For example instructor-like expertise might weaken the peer-likeness which works against being helpful or motivating. Their experiments show that a high competence avatar decreases self-efficacy belief in tasks but leads to good learning effects and recall-results. Low competence on the other hand may increase self-esteem, confidence and the learner's sense of responsibility, but can be useful for introducing novices to learning and to motivate to explore further fields of the learning objectives. Further research showed that people attribute human properties to computers each time they are using them. Virtual characters may utilize this phenomenon for naturally engagements by adapting and simulating human like behaviors. Nevertheless it was found that too realistic designs leads to unrealistic expectations and therefore to disappointed or irritated feelings for the user. Consequently virtual characters experience a higher acceptance if the user's expectations for the creature's behavior meet the actual experience.

The classical role of an agent in a learning environment is that of a teacher, see for example [12] and [1]. "AutoTutor" [13] allows learners to learn facts from a given domain by having a natural language conversation with a talking head, the virtual tutor. These dialogs are very interactive since both the learner and the virtual tutor work together to improve the learner's answer.

"Betty's Brain" [14] features the virtual character Betty (realized as a talking head) who is a so-called teachable agent. As the name implies, learners can teach Betty by building a concept map (i.e. her brain) and asking questions about it. The goal for the learner is to prepare Betty for a quiz about a given domain. Blair et al. also suggest to have multiple teachable agents compete against each other in a quiz show like application. Questions are asked by a virtual quizmaster and each agent responds according to their concept map.

In [15] another virtual character is mentioned that was added to "Betty's Brain": Mr. Davis, the teacher (also realized as a talking head). Mr. Davis helps the learner to teach Betty by giving guidelines about teaching in general or hints that address specific situations that learners might find themselves in. Since these hints are directed at the learner, there is no real interaction between Mr. Davis and Betty. Moreover, his hints only refer to teaching, not the task or domain at hand.

A closer look at these interactive learning environments shows that all three feature a teacher-like character that interacts with the learner to help or teach. However, how this interaction looks like and what is actually communicated differs widely: One of the systems follows the Learning by Teaching paradigm by introducing a character that is taught by the learner. One system features fully embodied agents, that can also communicate through gestures. Finally, one of the systems features more than one virtual character or rather more than one character role. However, as stated above, these characters only interact with the learner and not with each other.

We hypothesize that a combination of these features, implemented in an integrated set of educational characters may better leverage learning. Hence, in the DynaLearn approach we decided to integrate the following character roles into our learning environment: A *Teacher* who answers specific questions and offers help about the learning environment itself. A *Mechanic* that analyzes a learner's model and offers a diagnosis through an interactive dialog. A *Teachable Agent* who can be taught by the learner. A *Critic* who gives quality feedback and finally a *Quizmaster* who adds a playful and competitive element by asking the learner questions, but who also directly interacts with the teachable agent to form a presentation team as suggested in [8]. Before we start with describing each of the characters in detail in the next section, Figure 1 gives an overview by showing each of the characters with a typical line of dialog with regard to the model depicted in the center.

3   The Characters in DynaLearn

As we delineated in [16], the characters in DynaLearn are cartoonish hamsters. Also, we employ three established teaching methods: *Learning by Teaching* [15], *Scaffolding* [17] and *Educational Quizzes* [18]. The design of our character interactions also incorporates some of the different dialog modes (such as lecture or highlighting) identified for expert tutors by Cade et. al in [19].

During learners' interaction with the software, all virtual characters are available all the time and it is up to the learners which one to consult, depending on the desired type of support. Learners can interact with the characters in two different ways: Buttons above the characters' heads (for starting specific kinds of interactions) and multiple-choice selections in the characters' speech bubbles (for answers and follow-up questions). Figure 2 shows four examples of these interaction possibilities.

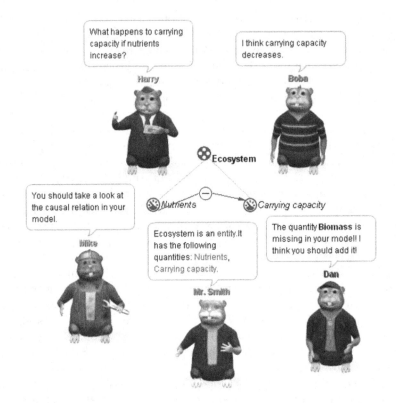

Fig. 1. The DynaLearn Characters (clockwise from top left): Quizmaster, Teachable Agent, Critic, Teacher, Mechanic

3.1 Teachable Agent (TA)

The DynaLearn TA brings the Learning by Teaching paradigm into the ILE. The TA has a knowledge representation that can be created by the learner. From this structured knowledge the TA can extract answers to questions asked by the learner. The TA is also able to explain its reasoning, so the learner can see how causal chains arise in his own model. By testing the TA's understanding of the matter through questioning, the learner can evaluate his own presentation of the knowledge and detect mistakes when the TA does not answer as expected. In DynaLearn, learners can chose between a male and a female TA and also name it. Similar to "Betty's Brain", the interactions learners can perform with their TA are: Ask (TA answers single questions), Explain (TA provides a step-by-step explanation of an answer) and Challenge (TA takes a quiz).

Constant verification of the own understanding is an important part in the learning process that unfortunately often comes short due to the learners' aversion to tests. However, learners are less restrained in confronting an agent several times with the same test than in retaking this test themselves. That's why we allow the learner in our application to take part in a quiz and to send his

Fig. 2. Examples of interaction possibilities with the characters (from left to right): Mechanic offering different ways to proceed, interactions with Teachable Agent trough buttons, multiple-choice answer to question asked by the Quizmaster, hyperlinks in Teacher's answer for follow-up questions

personal teachable agent to this quiz in his place. Since the TA's knowledge mirrors an image of the learner's knowledge, he may serve as a proxy in an educational quiz. We will discuss this learning scenario later in section 3.4.

Though Learning by Teaching aims for learning success the role of the teachable agent is more a motivating one. Following the research of Kim et al. [7] our TA forges a more peer-like relationship to the learner with his low-competent behavior. For example some dialog contents convey an insecure personality of the agent to emphasize his dependence on the learner. There are also dialog parts in which the agent takes a moment to think about a question (either asked by the learner or the quizmaster) so the agent does not seem smarter as the human learner who also needs some time to think in such situations.

3.2   Mechanic

The task of the mechanic is to support learners in analyzing their model. Oftentimes, the simulations results of the model the learner created are not in line with the learner's expected outcome. An automated diagnostic component (based on [20]) detects these discrepancies, and identifies a minimum number of model components that caused this discrepancy. The mechanic is used to communicate these diagnosis results. The learner can then engage with the mechanic character in several ways: First, the learner can alter the model components that the character has suggested and then rerun the simulation to see whether the outcome is now satisfactory. Alternatively, the learner can reaffirm that the model is actually correct, in which case the mechanic points out that under those conditions the fault must be in the learner's expectation regarding the simulation results.

We chose the constructivist approach of Scaffolding as learning principle for this role. Scaffolding emphasizes that the learner should do as much work by himself as possible. The teacher or tutor only provides assistance if the learner does not possess the necessary skills or knowledge to solve the current problem on his own. According to [21], this helps the learner to become more and more independently. While this describes the effect of scaffolding in the long run, in short-term it aims for maximum learning success by keeping the learner motivated and ensuring he makes constant progress in his work.

The work of Lipscomb et al. [17] , Larkin [22] and Cade et al. helped us identify the means for reaching this goal. While Cade et al. mention scaffolding as one of their mutual exclusive dialog modes in one-on-one tutoring sessions, Lipscomb et al. and Larkin describe scaffolding as a more extensive teaching principle. We incorporated both ideas in our mechanic role. The more widespread scaffolding of Lipscomb et al. determines the general behavior of our mechanic, while we use some of the dialog modes of Cade et al. as dialog steps within this behavior.

The aids used by the mechanic during this process are assigned to one of the following three categories: Lecture, Scaffolding, Modeling. These categories are similar to the dialog modes described by Cade et al., although their mode of Highlighting is part of our Scaffolding aid. The agent usually chooses with an equal chance between lecture and scaffolding when providing an aid. These chances are again based on the observations of Cade et al. where lectures and scaffolding were the most present dialog modes with a very similar frequency. As we ideally want the learner to find the solution by himself modeling, the exact correction of the mistake, is only appropriate if the mechanic has exhausted all other means. In this way, we ensure the learner can proceed with the correction of his model even if he can not cope with a particular problem.

3.3   Teacher

In contrast to the mechanic, the teacher offers a more direct kind of help by communicating knowledge pertaining to those aspects of the ILE that are visible to learners and that they can directly interact with. There are three kinds of such directly visible aspects, and each is covered by a different kind of help: Firstly, there is the diagrammatic representation of the learner-created model, consisting of the various modeling ingredients. With respect to any one of these, a "What is X?"-question can be posed. Secondly, there is the visualization of the behavior of the model. This consists of a manifold of changes (each with a cause) in values. With respect to each value a "Why was X derived?"-question can be asked. Thirdly, there are the screens, dialogs and buttons that constitute the interface of the software. A menu of "How to X?"-questions is constantly generated (where X is a task), based on the tasks that are available given the learner-created model and the state of the software. The answers that the teacher character communicates are concise and focused with respect to individual knowledge requests. If the learner wants to know more, the help message contains hyperlinks that pose follow-up questions that allow the exploration of related material. In addition, a glossary of important terms is provided. Whenever a virtual character mentions one of these glossary terms, they are also displayed as hyperlinks. The descriptions in the glossary are interlinked, amounting to a traversable graph of explanatory messages.

3.4   Quizmaster

The quizmaster may be employed in a quiz directly with the human learner or with the learner's TA. The entertaining performance of quizmaster and TA helps to point out flaws and verifies the correct parts of the learner's model. The question generator for the quizmaster is based on the QUAGS question generator [23]. The generation of questions is domain independent and done in four steps: First the given restrictions are analyzed with respect to the simulation and completed with built-in heuristics. Then the resulting criteria lead to the generation of a set of question designs based on the simulation input and a set of templates. Thirdly a selection inference determines the best set of questions given the full set of successful designs. Fourthly this final set of questions is put in a logical order with groups of questions for every state in the simulation.

Knowledge tests are usually perceived as stressful situations having negative effects on concentration or motivation. In observations of quiz forms in several well known television quiz shows we found out that quizmasters sometimes try to loosen up such situations in order to countervail their negative effects and to provide an enjoyable form of test. For that purpose, they start lively conversations with their candidates and discuss topics that are familiar to the participants such as job or leisure activities. We mimic this behavior with our quizmaster character. Beside the quizmaster's general behavior of asking questions and giving feedback, we integrate smalltalk utterances into the dialog. They serve as short, preferable humorous distraction for the participant that actually need no connection to the current topic of the quiz and its questions.

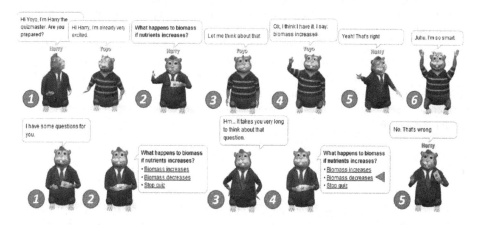

Fig. 3. Different ways of running the quiz: Quizmaster and TA (top), Quizmaster and learner (bottom)

As mentioned in section 3.1 the quizmaster may be employed in a quiz with the human learner or with the learner's teachable agent. The entertaining performance of quizmaster and teachable agents helps to point out flaws in the learner's model and verifies the correct parts of the learner's model. Usually the latter should be the case if the learner follows the suggested order, which means the educational quiz comes after the correction of the model in the instructional scaffolding phase. But this order is not obligatory since the learner can activate the agents whenever he wants. The quiz with the teachable agent as participant might also be used as a test of the model and taken again after the correction phase as a knowledge verification.

Figure 3 shows both ways the quizmaster can be employed: With a learner's TA or directly with a learner.

3.5 Critic

In contrast to the content delivered by the mechanic or teacher characters, the critic's quality feedback about a learner's model is generated through the *semantic repository* in the DynaLearn software. Also, while the others are friendly and helpful, the critic is characterized as more strict and unforgiving. The semantic repository of DynaLearn is intended to store the models created by the users and to provide feedback during the model creation process [24]. These models are semantically grounded, so the terms of the model are linked to semantic descriptions in a common vocabulary (which in our system is DBpedia [25]). The quality feedback is the result of comparing the learner's model with a reference model by using techniques like ontology matching [26], semantic reasoning, and QR specific comparisons between the models.

If two terms are grounded to the same semantic description we infer that they are equivalent terms, even if they are expressed using different lexical information or even in different languages. Then, the set of equivalent terms is enhanced by applying ontology matching techniques. The next step is to analyze each pair of equivalent terms looking for possible differences. These provide the following types of feedback: i)Improvement of terminology (suggest label of reference term if different from current label), ii)Missing and extra ontological elements (point out terms only present in one of the two models), iii)Inconsistencies between hierarchies (point out inconsistencies in entity hierarchies found through semantic reasoning) and iv)Differences between the structures (point put differences in model structure).

4   Architecture

The overall architecture of the Virtual Character Component (VC) and its connection to the Conceptual Modeling Component (CM) can be seen in Figure 4. In DynaLearn, the CM is where learners actually build their models and where the various kinds of conceptual knowledge are generated.

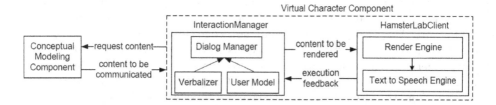

Fig. 4. The Virtual Character Component Architecture

The VC in itself consists of two different components, the InteractionManager (IM) and the HamsterLabClient (HL). The HL is responsible for actually displaying the virtual characters which is handled by a Flash-based render engine. Also, the HL generates the characters' speech using the Mary Text-to-Speech System [27]. The IM's main responsibility is to create the characters' behavior by requesting appropriate content from the CM, arrange it into dialogs between the different characters and create the appropriate scene script that can then be played by the HL. Scene scripts are XML-based and consist of different instructions such as "move", "say" or "animate". A feedback channel informs the IM when a scene script is over. The IM itself consists of three different modules:

- The Dialog Manager governs the overall interaction between the characters and the learner. When necessary, it requests new data from the CM and then decides "What to say". In our implementation, we use SceneMaker [28] as the Dialog Manager.
- The Verbalizer decides "How to say it", i.e. what words to use.
- The User Model keeps track of the learner's knowledge and interactions. The data provided by it can act as a filter or decision criteria for the Dialog Manager.

We will now take a closer look at how these modules interact with each other when creating a dialog for the characters. Figure 5 shows an overview of this process.

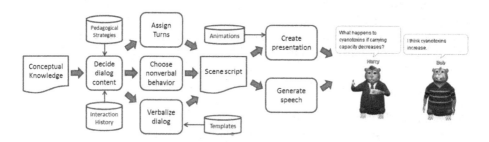

Fig. 5. Character Dialog Generation Process

The process starts with the input from the CM, i.e. a certain kind of conceptual knowledge. As an example let us assume that a learner just sent his TA to take a quiz. As a result the conceptual knowledge submitted in this case will be questions generated by the system, answers to these questions generated from the learner-created-model and finally the correct answers. First the dialog content needs to be decided. This can be based on previous actions by the learner (derived from the User Model) or the characters, as well as certain pedagogical strategies.

Next, the content needs to be assigned to the different characters. In our example, the quizmaster character will ask the questions and present the correct answers, while the TA will present the answers generated by the learner-created-model. Also, the quizmaster will comment on the TA's success and the TA will show a reaction to that.

After that, the dialog turns are verbalized using a collection of templates that are filled in with the appropriate data. If there is more than one matching template, one of them is chosen randomly. For example, the same question could be verbalized as "What happens to cyanotoxins if carrying capacity decreases?" or "Let's suppose carrying capacity decreases, what would then happen to cyanotoxins?", depending on the template selected.

Finally, nonverbal behavior is selected to accompany the dialogs. The characters can move around the screen, perform gestures and facial animations and point out spaces on the screen. In our example, after each question the quizmaster will perform either a thumbs-up gesture or shake his head depending on the TA's success, and the TA will perform a cheering or sulking gesture accordingly.

Based on the decisions made, the scene script XML can then be constructed and sent to the HL. Then, the content of "say"-tags is extracted and the speech is created accordingly. Together with the appropriate data from the animation library, the dialog can finally be presented by the render engine.

5   Evaluation

We conducted an evaluation to investigate the learners' attitude towards and interactions with three of the characters (teacher, quizmaster, teachable agent) and the employed learning principles (instructional scaffolding, learning by teaching, educational quiz). In addition, we compared the learners' level of engagement when they participated in a quiz as opposed to sending their TA. It should be noted that the interaction with the teacher was based on a mock-up version rather than a fully functional one.

5.1   Method

We recruited 20 subjects (10 male and 10 female, aged between 25 and 33, mostly computer scientists) who interacted with the three characters in the following situations: First, the subjects had a look at a faulty model and could ask the teacher for help in order to correct the model. After that, they participated in a quiz where they had to answer questions posed by the quizmaster. Finally, the subjects were requested to train their own TA and test its performance in another quiz with the quizmaster. Since it did not make sense to confront the subjects with the TA before they got acquainted with the learning scenario, we decided not to present the subjects with the single characters in a randomized order, but in a didactically appropriate one. Each subject's interaction with the characters lasted 30 minutes, 10 for each of the three situations. After each interaction with a character, subjects were asked to fill in a questionnaire, judging features of the interaction on a 5-point Likert scale (1 to 5, where 5 meant full agreement).

5.2   Results

Attitude towards the Different Agents and the Educational Setting.
Overall, the subjects considered the agents' behaviors as quite natural. A t-test for one sample revealed that the ratings given to the agents were significantly above the neutral value of 3.0. The learners rated the naturalness of the teacher with a mean value of 3.65 ($t(19)=2.459$, $p \leq 0.03$), the naturalness of the quizmaster with a mean value of 4.2 ($t(19)=8.718$, $p \leq 0.001$) and the naturalness of the TA with a mean value of 4.0 ($t(19)=6.164$, $p \leq 0.001$). Furthermore, we were interested in the question of whether the agents' role was properly conveyed. Our subjects attributed to the teacher the highest level of competence with a mean value of 4.45 followed by the quizmaster with a mean value of 3.70. The teachable agent was attributed the least level of competence with a mean value of 3.25. Applying the Bonferroni post hoc test showed that the differences between TA and teacher ($p \leq 0.001$), as well as teacher and quizmaster ($p \leq 0.05$) were significant.

We also investigated the motivational effect of the agent roles. The learners found the interaction with the teacher less enjoyable with a mean value of 3.55 than the interaction with the TA with a mean value of 4.15 and the interaction with the quizmaster with a mean value of 4.3. Employing the Bonferroni post hoc test showed that the difference between the ratings for teacher and TA were significant ($p \leq 0.04$).

Furthermore, we investigated whether the learners thought the employed learning principle contributed to their learning process. The subjects found the teacher helpful with a mean value of 4.30 ($t(19)=8.850$, $p \leq 0.001$), they had the feeling that the quiz contributed to their understanding with a mean value of 4.60 ($t(19)=11.961$, $p \leq 0.001$) and they thought that they learned something themselves by teaching their own agent with a mean value of 4.20 ($t(19)=6.0$, $p\leq 0.001$). In all cases, the mean values were significantly above the neutral value of 3.0. In addition, the learners thought it made sense to employ a virtual teacher with a mean value of 3.7 ($t(19)=2.774$, $p \leq 0.02$), to employ a quizmaster with a mean value of 4.65 ($t(19)=15.079$, $p \leq 0.001$) and to employ a teachable agent with a mean value of 4.05 ($t(19)=4.098$, $p \leq 0.001$).

Finally, we evaluated whether the learners understood the employed metaphor when interacting with each character. In particular, we were interested in the question of whether the learners would be able to see the connection between the creation of a model and instructing an agent. We applied t-tests for one sample to evaluate whether the ratings given by the learners were significantly above the neutral value of 3.0. The learners had the feeling to ask a teacher a question with a mean value of 3.7 ($t(19)=2.774$, $p \leq 0.02$), to participate in a quiz with a mean value of 4.65 ($t(19)=15.079$, $p \leq 0.001$) and to teach somebody with a mean value of 4.25 ($t(19)=5.0$, $p \leq 0.001$). The results are shown in Figure 6.

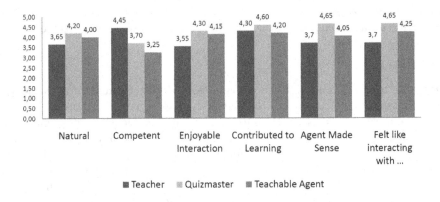

Fig. 6. Attitude towards the different agents and the educational setting

Comparison of Direct and Indirect Participation. We also compared the two versions of the educational quiz, i.e. learner as participant vs. TA as participant. The learners showed more engagement when their TA participated in the quiz than when participating themselves. In particular, they were more interested in a good performance with a mean value of 4.25 as opposed to a mean value of 3.85, more pleased about a good performance with a mean value of 4.55 as opposed to a mean value of 4.15 and more curious about the results with a mean value of 4.20 as opposed to a mean value of 3.60. However, the difference was not significant. The difference between the averaged ratings for the engagement items was weakly significant ($t(38)=-1936$, $p \leq 0.061$) with mean values of 3.86 for participating themselves and 4.33 for participating via the agent. An overview of the results is given in Figure 7.

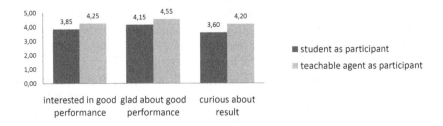

Fig. 7. Learner as quiz participant vs. TA as quiz participant

6   Conclusion

In this document, we presented our approach to a cast of pedagogical agents, whose interaction with the learner offer a variety of services that help learners to verify and correct their models and conceptual knowledge, while motivating and engaging them at the same time. We showed how presenting different kinds of knowledge through different character roles and teams of characters can result in an improvement in the use of virtual characters in ILEs. We also explained how our approach to the virtual characters' architecture supports this as it allows us transform conceptual knowledge into multimodal dialog scripts for multiple characters. We believe that our approach of an entire cast of pedagogical agents is a viable option for ILEs that aim at conveying knowledge trough multiple means: First, because each of these means can be linked to and associated with a specific character for easier identification. Second, because providing characters of different competence levels will positively affect both learners motivation and learning success.

To a certain degree, this was confirmed by the findings of our preliminary evaluation: Learners enjoyed the interaction with our pedagogical agents and perceived the virtual classroom setting as engaging and motivating. They understood the employed metaphor with its different learning scenarios and the justification of each of the three characters. They felt that the pedagogical agents, respectively their educational roles successfully helped learning.

However, since this is only a subjective measure of learning success, we plan to conduct further evaluations with regard to this topic. Other pointers to future work include evaluations of all character roles and learners' attitude towards them, as well as a measuring learners' motivation and engagement while interacting with the characters.

Acknowledgments. The work presented in this paper is co-funded by the EC within the 7th FP, Project no. 231526, and Website: http://www.DynaLearn.eu.

References

1. Johnson, W.L., Rickel, J.W., Lester, J.C.: Animated pedagogical agents: Face-to-face interaction in interactive learning environments. International Journal of Artificial Intelligence in Education 11, 47–78 (2000)
2. Ndiaye, A., Gebhard, P., Kipp, M., Klesen, M., Schneider, M., Wahlster, W.: Ambient Intelligence in Edutainment: Tangible Interaction with Life-Like Exhibit Guides. In: Maybury, M., Stock, O., Wahlster, W. (eds.) INTETAIN 2005. LNCS (LNAI), vol. 3814, pp. 104–113. Springer, Heidelberg (2005)
3. Kenny, P., Hartholt, A., Gratch, J., Swartout, W., Traum, D., Marsella, S., Piepol, D.: Building interactive virtual humans for training environments. In: Proceedings of IITSEC, pp. 1–16 (2007)
4. Rickenberg, R., Reeves, B.: The effects of animated characters on anxiety, task performance, and evaluations of user interfaces. In: Proceedings of the SIGCHI Conference on Human Factors in Computing Systems, pp. 49–56. ACM (2000)

5. Lester, J.C., Converse, S.A., Kahler, S.E., Barlow, S.T., Stone, B.A., Bhogal, R.S.: The persona effect: affective impact of animated pedagogical agents. In: CHI 1997: Proceedings of the SIGCHI Conference on Human Factors in Computing Systems, pp. 359–366. ACM, New York (1997)

6. van Mulken, S., André, E., Müller, J.: The persona effect: How substantial is it? In: Proc. of HCI 1998, pp. 53–66 (1998)

7. Kim, Y., Baylor, A.L.: PALS Group: Pedagogical agents as learning companions: The role of agent competency and type of interaction. Educational Technology Research and Development 54, 223–243 (2006)

8. André, E., Rist, T., van Mulken, S., Klesen, M., Baldes, S.: The automated design of believable dialogues for animated presentation teams. In: Embodied Conversational Agents. The MIT Press (2000)

9. Bredeweg, B., Liem, J., Linnebank, F., Bühling, R., Wißner, M., del Río, J.G., Salles, P., Beek, W., Gómez Pérez, A.: DynaLearn: Architecture and Approach for Investigating Conceptual System Knowledge Acquisition. In: Aleven, V., Kay, J., Mostow, J. (eds.) ITS 2010. LNCS, vol. 6095, pp. 272–274. Springer, Heidelberg (2010)

10. Bredeweg, B., Linnebank, F., Bouwer, A., Liem, J.: Garp3 – workbench for qualitative modelling and simulation. Ecological Informatics 4, 263–281 (2009); Special Issue: Qualitative models of ecological systems

11. Baylor, A.L., Kim, Y.: Pedagogical Agent Design: The Impact of Agent Realism, Gender, Ethnicity, and Instructional Role. In: Lester, J.C., Vicari, R.M., Paraguaçu, F. (eds.) ITS 2004. LNCS, vol. 3220, pp. 592–603. Springer, Heidelberg (2004)

12. Conati, C., Zhao, X.: Building and evaluating an intelligent pedagogical agent to improve the effectiveness of an educational game. In: Proceedings of the 9th International Conference on Intelligent User Interfaces, pp. 6–13. ACM (2004)

13. Graesser, A.C., Person, N.K., Harter, D.: The Tutoring Research Group: Teaching tactics and dialog in autotutor. International Journal of Artificial Intelligence in Education 12, 257–279 (2001)

14. Blair, K., Schwartz, D., Biswas, G., Leelawong, K.: Pedagogical agents for learning by teaching: Teachable agents. Special Issue of Educational Technology on Pedagogical Agents 47, 56–61 (2007)

15. Biswas, G., Roscoe, R., Jeong, H., Sulcer, B.: Promoting self-regulated learning skills in agent-based learning environments. In: Proceedings of the 17th International Conference on Computers in Education (2009)

16. Mehlmann, G., Häring, M., Bühling, R., Wißner, M., André, E.: Multiple agent roles in an adaptive virtual classroom environment. In: Safonova, A. (ed.) IVA 2010. LNCS, vol. 6356, pp. 250–256. Springer, Heidelberg (2010)

17. Lipscomb, L., Swanson, J., West, A.: Scaffolding - emerging perspectives on learning, teaching and technology. The University of Georgia (2008), http://projects.coe.uga.edu/epltt/index.php?title=Scaffolding

18. Randel, J.M., Morris, B.A., Wetzel, C.D., Whitehill, B.V.: The effectiveness of games for educational purposes: a review of recent research. Simulation and Gaming 23, 261–276 (1992)

19. Cade, W.L., Copeland, J.L., Person, N.K., D'Mello, S.K.: Dialogue Modes in Expert Tutoring. In: Woolf, B.P., Aïmeur, E., Nkambou, R., Lajoie, S. (eds.) ITS 2008. LNCS, vol. 5091, pp. 470–479. Springer, Heidelberg (2008)

20. de Koning, K., Breuker, J., Wielinga, B., Bredeweg, B.: Model-based reasoning about learner behaviour. Artificial Intelligence 117, 173–229 (2000)

21. Vygotsky, L., Cole, M., John-Steiner, V., Scribner, S., Souberman, E. (eds.): Mind in Society: Development of Higher Psychological Processes. Havard University Press (1978)
22. Larkin, M.: Using scaffolded instruction to optimize learning. eric digest. ERIC Development Team (2002)
23. Goddijn, F., Bouwer, A., Bredeweg, B.: Automatically generating tutoring questions for qualitative simulations. In: Proceedings of the 17th International Workshop on Qualitative Reasoning, pp. 87–94 (2003)
24. Gracia, J., Liem, J., Lozano, E., Corcho, O., Trna, M., Gómez-Pérez, A., Bredeweg, B.: Semantic Techniques for Enabling Knowledge Reuse in Conceptual Modelling. In: Patel-Schneider, P.F., Pan, Y., Hitzler, P., Mika, P., Zhang, L., Pan, J.Z., Horrocks, I., Glimm, B. (eds.) ISWC 2010, Part II. LNCS, vol. 6497, pp. 82–97. Springer, Heidelberg (2010)
25. Bizer, C., Lehmann, J., Kobilarov, G., Auer, S., Becker, C., Cyganiak, R., Hellmann, S.: DBpedia - a crystallization point for the web of data. Web Semantics: Science, Services and Agents on the World Wide Web 7, 154–165 (2009)
26. Euzenat, J., Shvaiko, P.: Ontology matching. Springer (2007)
27. Schröder, M., Trouvain, J.: The german text-to-speech synthesis system mary: A tool for research, development and teaching. International Journal of Speech Technology 6, 365–377 (2003)
28. Gebhard, P., Kipp, M., Klesen, M., Rist, T.: Authoring scenes for adaptive, interactive performances. In: Proc. of the 2nd Int. Joint Conf. on Autonomous Agents and Multiagent Systems, pp. 725–732. ACM (2003)

ADAPT: Abstraction Hierarchies to Better Simulate Teamwork under Dynamics[*]

Meirav Hadad[1] and Avi Rosenfeld[2]

[1] Research Division, Elbit Systems Ltd, Rosh Ha'Ayin 48091, Israel
[2] Jerusalem College of Technology, Jerusalem 91160, Israel
Meirav.Hadad@elbitsystems.com, rosenfa@jct.ac.il

Abstract. In this paper we present a lightweight teamwork implementation by using abstraction hierarchies. The basis of this implementation is ADAPT, which supports **A**utonomous **D**ynamic **A**gent **P**lanning for **T**eamwork. ADAPT's novelty stems from how it succinctly decomposes teamwork problems into two separate planners: a **task** network for the set of activities to be performed by a specific agent and a separate **group** network for addressing team organization factors. Because abstract search techniques are the basis for creating these two components, ADAPT agents are able to effectively address teamwork in dynamic environments without explicitly enumerating the entire set of possible team states. During run-time, ADAPT agents then expand the teamwork states that are necessary for task completion through an association algorithm to dynamically link its task and group planners. As a result, ADAPT uses far fewer team states than existing teamwork models. We describe how ADAPT was implemented within a commercial training and simulation application, and present evidence detailing its success in concisely and effectively modeling teamwork.

1 Introduction

Effectively quantifying teamwork problems is critical in many environments [5,12]. However, one of the key challenges in creating teamwork models is how inter-agent rules can be encoded such that the team can still effectively behave in complex and dynamic environments [2,12]. In particular, when multiple agents operate in these types of environments, their different mental states must be resolved so that a unified behavior can be formed for the team. One key research challenge for distributed artificial intelligence researchers is how these models can be created and implemented [12].

One leading solution is to decompose the group's actions into a set of rules which must be solved [12]. Following this approach, the group's actions can be represented as a hierarchical structure of joint intentions and individual intentions and beliefs about others' intentions. However, this approach has two major drawbacks. First, the size of the model might be too large to realistically solve. Previous research found that many classes of teamwork problems exist for which finding the optimal sequence of actions is of intractable computational complexity [11]. Second, the structure of the tree must be flexible to dynamically changing conditions, such as changes in the environment, goal changes, and local or general constraints. Thus, even if a solution could be found

---

[*] This research is based on work supported in part by Israel's Ministry of Science and Technology grant # 44115.

M. Beer et al. (Eds.): AEGS 2011, LNAI 7471, pp. 166–182, 2012.

for a given time period, that solution might quickly become irrelevant. Hence, solutions must be found that reduce the size and structure of the team model such that it may be tractably and quickly solved, even in dynamic environments.

In this paper we present ADAPT, a novel approach for **A**utonomous **D**ynamic **A**gent **P**lanning for **T**eamwork. The key difference between ADAPT and other teamwork hierarchical approaches [2,5,6,12,13] stems from how teamwork is modeled. Previous approaches attempted to exhaustively depict all possible teamwork states. However, as has been previously demonstrated [11], the number of possible interactions between team members grows exponentially for many real-world domains, making these approaches difficult to implement, even in small to medium-sized groups.

Instead, ADAPT uses hierarchical abstraction as its basis in order to reduce the number of states which need to be considered. While abstraction has previously been used in planning and other problems [1], to the best of our knowledge it has never been previously been used in teamwork problems. Specifically, a given teamwork problem is converted into two hierarchical networks: a **task** network to model the set of activities a given agent can perform and a separate **group** network for addressing organization factors. Within both hierarchical networks, behaviors are decomposed such that the general task and group problems are progressively redivided into partial plans involving smaller sets of subtasks and subgroups. ADAPT contains two novel elements designed to further reduce the size of these hierarchies. First, as hierarchical abstraction is used, agents incrementally add only relevant task and group information during task execution. Second, ADAPT uses an association algorithm to effectively perform task allocation. Agents only check those constraints which it may possibly perform, further adding to ADAPT's concise nature. The net result is that ADAPT can effectively simulate teamwork problems, even in dynamic environments, yet uses far fewer states than existing approaches.

While the ADAPT framework is general and is likely applicable to a variety of teamwork problems, in this paper we focus on how ADAPT was critical in implementing a multi-agent simulation. In Section 2 we present related teamwork models and compare those approaches to ADAPT, while Section 3 formally defines ADAPT and its algorithms. Sections 4 and 5 detail how ADAPT was implemented. Specifically, Section 4 focuses on describing the existing commercial multi-agent simulation into which ADAPT added. In Section 5 we discuss how ADAPT was successfully implemented into this framework, detail results which demonstrate the effectiveness of this framework in dynamic environments and show that the number of teamwork states that must be considered within ADAPT is significantly less than in other state-of-the-art approaches. This allowed the existing simulation to more effectively handle complex multi-agent tasks. Section 6 provides our conclusions.

2 Background and Motivation

Because of the importance of coordination problems, a variety of teamwork frameworks and formalizations have been proposed by the multi-agent research community [5,2,12]. The SharedPlans approach [2] consists of creating teamwork recipes based on modeling agents' beliefs and intentions. Tambe's STEAM teamwork engine [12] provides a set of generalized teamwork rules. The TAEMS framework [5] consists of hierarchical rule based approach where coordination relationships are quantified into groups, tasks, and methods.

ADAPT decomposes teamwork in a novel fashion by creating two hierarchical networks: a **task** network which addresses how the agent must plan its actions, and a **group** network that addresses how inter-agent assignments must be set. Previous work of multi-agent planning (e.g., [3]) and teamwork structures [5,2,12] suggested addressing the team's **task** planning as one multi-agent network which needs to be decomposed. Other works from social sciences [14] address how people within a team should be organized in order to facilitate the best planning of the activity. This approach parallels our creating a **group** network based on the agents in the team. However, ADAPT's novelty stems from applying abstract search techniques [9] to address multi-agent planning in its task and group network.

Previous approaches also separate team behavior into different components. Most similar to our approach, BITE is a behavior based teamwork architecture that separates task behaviors from behaviors between a single agent and its organization [6]. Similarly, ADAPT compartmentalizes teamwork between the task and the group. More generally, the TEAMCORE architecture uses a decision-theoretic structure to select different hierarchical team behaviors [13]. TAEMS separates team activities into tasks that are performed by the team with methods that can be performed by the agent [5]. However, in previous approaches, teamwork models were completely defined before task execution. They are required to explicitly define how every agent interacts with every other agent, and even how dynamics may affect these relationships, a process that can potentially lead to an exponential number of inter-agent states. When implementing these models, this state explosion can be prohibitively difficult as the number of team members grows.

In ADAPT, the task and group abstractions are incrementally built and dynamically changed during task execution. This difference allows us to significantly reduce the number of inter-agent states even when addressing dynamics. Additionally, ADAPT enables replanning for specific subproblems, allowing for more effective teamwork. Consequently, ADAPT allows for a more concise model which, in turn, facilitates easier simulation of complex, real-world tasks. We detail this approach in the next section.

3   Technique Description

ADAPT's model is based on taking a teamwork problem and then decomposing it into both task and group elaboration processes. As such, each of the task and group problems are decomposed in a top-down manner from a higher level, into progressively lower levels. The planning strategies of the elaboration processes in ADAPT are based on abstract search techniques [9]. Accordingly, the planning procedures of each elaboration process involves three major steps: (1) A *branching* step identifies possible candidates for expanding a partial plan; (2) A *refinement* step for adding constraint information to the partial plan; (3) a *pruning* step for removing unpromising candidates based on these constraints in order to avoid failure. While abstract-search is a well known technique for automated task planning [9], ADAPT's contribution stems from applying these techniques to teamwork modeling.

3.1   A Dynamic Planning Teamwork Example

To clarify how we intend to use these concepts, consider the following general example. Assume that a group must work as a team on a joint mission, say to capture a flag. A group of blue agents must plan how they will infiltrate the territory of the opposing team of red agents who are defending the flag. This type of scenario is typified in many real-world scenarios, such as military missions involving destroying an enemy target. In dynamic environments it is almost impossible to predict all possible event permutations that may occur while the blue agents complete their task.

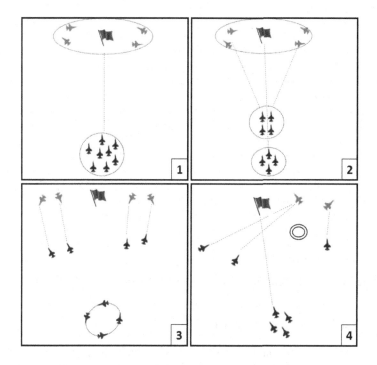

Fig. 1. Four Stages in a Mission Storyboard

Figure 1 depicts one series of group states during the execution of the "Capture the Flag mission". At the start, a group of 4 red agents are divided into 2 subgroups of pairs located on either side of the flag to defend it (see the top left corner). At the same time, a group of 8 blue agents approach the flag area. In the second stage (see top right corner), the blue group splits into two subgroups of 4 agents according to their capabilities. One subgroup splits again into two subgroups of 2 agents and each subgroup approaches and engages the 2 red subgroups. In the next stage (bottom left) the blue agents engage the red ones to attempt to capture the flag. However, during this stage an unplanned event occurs, and one of the blue agents is incapacitated by a member of the opposing red team. The result of this change is that the group must replan their mission with only 7 of the 8 agents. In the final stage (bottom right), we see the group of 7 remaining blue agents still completing the task and capturing the flag.

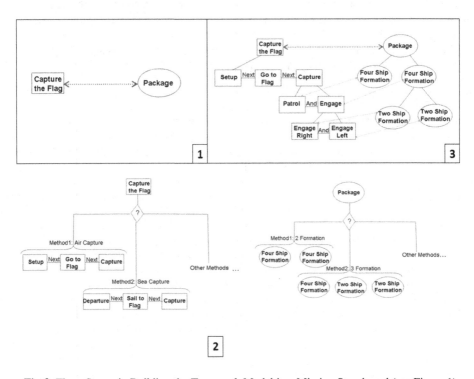

Fig. 2. Three Stages in Building the Teamwork Model in a Mission Storyboard (see Figure 1)

3.2   High Level Overview of ADAPT

While the ADAPT agents plan their task, they use the branching, refinement and pruning stages of abstract search techniques to limit the size of the teamwork model. We depict the stages of the teamwork model formation for the blue team in Figure 2. As previously described, ADAPT decomposes teamwork into both task and group networks. In the first stage (Stage 1 in Figure 2) each of these components are described only generally in the form of one abstract node. To graphically differentiate between the two task and group abstractions, we present the task hierarchy in rectangles, and the group hierarchy in ovals. At the beginning of execution, one rectangular task node describes the high level "Capture the Flag" task, and the group hierarchy "Package" describes the blue agents' attributes and capabilities which can be used to perform this task. In order for the blue agents to perform the team task, "Capture the Flag", their group and task planners must decide exactly how they will properly connect these two hierarchies. To make this decision, the agents' planners must apply their *branching* step to expand their abstract components of all applicable group and task options, which we refer to as *methods*. This is graphically represented in Stage 2 of Figure 2. However, unique to ADAPT and beyond similar previous teamwork approaches such as BITE and TEAMCORE [6,12,13], we then apply a *refinement* step where each agent generates the best applicable option based on its locally available information and the set of constraints associated with each option. We model each distributed agent as having a planner which uses a Distributed Constraint Optimization Problem (DCOP) solver to help create teamwork plans. In our implementation, the DCOP solver is based on the existing OptAPO algorithm [7]. As per the OptAPO algorithm, a mediator agent is elected which collects each of the distributed agents' constraints. In the next *punning* step, the mediator agent selects the best option given the choices each distributed agent presents. The mediator agent then informs each distributed agent about the option chosen, which is then selected by the local agent and executed.

Referring again to the example in Figure 2, the distributed planner decides that the best sequence for the blue agents to execute the team task, "Capture the Flag", is to first select the "Setup" subtask, then "Go to Flag", and lastly the "Capture" subtask. Within each subtask a further decomposition may occur into additional subtasks and subgroups. For example, the "Capture" subtask is decomposed into two subtasks which are assigned to 2 subgroups. One subgroup of four agents performs the "Patrol" subtask, while the second subgroup of four agents perform the "Engage" activity, where they engage the red agents defending the flag. The allocation step, where each agent is assigned to a given subtask, is also performed by the *refinement* step (Stage 3 of Figure 2). The best assignment is decided by the OptAPO mediator agent. As only a subset of all agents can perform certain activities, we can then apply the *pruning* step by which we reduce the teamwork model to only those states which are theoretically feasible. The mediator is also responsible for checking, or associating, between the task and group networks in order to ensure that the solution is feasible. Combining the *refinement* and *pruning* steps allows for a significantly smaller teamwork model than previous approaches [6,12,13] as their approaches stop model construction at the *branching* step. Thus, our work searches for a teamwork solution in a much smaller state space than in previous approaches.

In the following sections we formally describe and further detail the exact process by which these group and task networks are built. We also describe how these networks are associated such that teamwork problems can be solved in real-time and yet address dynamic changes from within the problem.

3.3   Modeling ADAPT's Constraint Networks

We model each task and group network as having a hierarchical structure which must be solved as a type of distributed constraint optimization problem (DCOP). Following previous DCOP work we define a DCOP problem as a set of variables where each variable is assigned to an agent who has control of its value. Cooperative agents must then coordinate their choice of values so that a global utility function is optimized. Formally, this process has previously been described as [7]:

- A set of N agents A = $A_1, A_2 \ldots, A_N$
- A set of n variables V = $X_1, X_2 \ldots, X_n$

- A set of domains D = $D_1, D_2 \ldots, D_n$ where the value of X_i is taken from D_i. Each D_i is assumed finite and discrete.
- A set of cost functions f = $f_1, f_2 \ldots, f_m$ where each f_i is a function $f_i : D_{i,1} \times \ldots \times D_{i,j} \to N \cup \infty$. Cost functions are also called *constraints*.
- A distribution mapping Q : V $\to$ A assigning each variable to an agent. $Q(X_i) = A_i$ denotes that A_i is responsible for choosing a value for X_i. A_i is given knowledge of X_i, D_i and all f_i involving X_i.
- An objective function F defined as an aggregation over the set of cost functions. Summation is typically used.

In the following sections we describe how we have implemented DCOP to create team-work behavior in ADAPT's task and group network.

Modeling ADAPT's Task Network. As our goal is to succinctly implement the simula-tion of group behavior, ADAPT contains many similarities to previous Hierarchical Task Network (HTN) planning approaches [5,10,9,4,8] but includes extensions for dynamic multi-agent environments. Formally, we define an *atomic task* (or primitive task) as an action $act(\vec{v})$ that can be directly executed by the agents (e.g., $FlyTo(origin, dest)$). A (higher-level) *complex task* $c(\vec{v})$ is one that cannot be executed directly and is de-composed into subtasks (e.g., $Defend(v_1, v_2, v_3, v_4)$. Each task may be associated with two kinds of boolean formulas – a *precondition rule* and *postcondition rule* – to indi-cate the required situations for starting and ending the task execution (e.g., $(IsFuel > 200.lib) \wedge (IsTime = $ 5:00PM). We define tasks as being either a *single-agent task* or a *multi-agent task*. A single-agent task can be executed by one agent by itself and multi-agent tasks require 2 or more cooperative agents to complete the task.

To execute a high-level complex task $c(\vec{v})$, agents must identify a *method* that encodes all constraints for how this task may be performed, including key in-formation about which agent can perform this task and constraints as to how it can be performed. Specifically, we define a method, m, as a 5-tuple contain-ing: $\langle name(m), task(m), constr(m), subtasks(m), relation(m) \rangle$, where $name(m)$ is the name of the method and $task(m)$ is the name of the complex task. We define $subtasks(m)$ as the sequence of tasks and $constr(m)$ as the set of constraints $\{\rho_1 \ldots \rho_p\}$ that may apply when using the method m. Each constraint ρ_k involves a subset of variables and specifies all combinations of values for these variables. We de-fine these variables as the set of $\{X_1 \ldots X_n\}$ where each value X_i is taken from a set of D_i possible values for a given problem. Constraints may include specific required capabilities that a certain number of agents perform specific $subtasks(m)$. For exam-ple, there may be a constraint stating that the number of agents required to perform a subtask must be between 2 and 5 (formally, $2 \geq X_{agentNun} \leq 5$). Alternatively, these constraints may specify the type of agent that can perform a certain subtask, for example that the type of agent must be a fighter plane. In our implementation, we assumed these constraints were boolean. The relationship, $relation(m)$, contains constraints on the execution of the $subtasks(m)$ and may be one of the following: (i) AND denotes that the task(m) is accomplished iff all the $subtasks(m)$ are accomplished; (ii) OR denotes that the task(m) is accomplished iff at least one of the $subtasks(m)$ is accomplished; and (iii) NEXT orders constraints between $subtasks(m)$ such that one subtask must be performed before another. These constraints contain similarities to the QAF and NLE constraints within the TAEMS teamwork framework [5].

We define a *task network* $d_{task} = [G_{task}, \rho]$ as a collection of tasks that have to be accomplished under constraints ρ. The task network is represented by an acyclic digraph $G_{task} = (V_{task}, E_{task})$ in which V_{task} is node set, E_{task} is the edge set, and each node $v \in V_{task}$ contains a task. The *task planning domain* $\mathcal{D}_{task} = (\mathcal{M}_{task}, \mathcal{A})$ consists of a library task methods $\mathcal{M}_{task}$ of methods and library $\mathcal{A}$ of atomic tasks. A *task planning problem* is defined as a triple $P_{task} = \langle d_{task}, \mathcal{B}, \mathcal{D}_{task} \rangle$ where d_{task} is the task network to be executed, $\mathcal{B}$ is the initial state and $\mathcal{D}_{task}$ is the planning domain. A *task plan* is a sequence $act_1 \ldots act_n$ of atomic actions.

Given a task planning problem instance, the planning process involves the *branching*, *refinement* and *pruning* steps. The *branching* step is defined by retrieving the entire set of methods in $\mathcal{M}_{task}$ which may be applied to the required task. *Refinement* then has each local agent check its $constr(m)$ and send what it considers to be its best option to the mediator agent within the DCOP solver. More formally, given a set of possible applicable methods $\{m_1, \ldots, m_t\}$ each method contains constraints $constr(m_j)$ that contain sets of variables $\{X_1^{m_j} \ldots X_n^{m_j}\}$ where each value $X_i^{m_j}$ is taken from a set of $D_i^{m_j}$. Consistent to the general DCOP formalization, the ADAPT agent must minimize the cost functions $f = \{f_1, \ldots, f_m\}$ where each $f_i(d_{i,1}^{m_j}, \ldots, d_{i,k}^{m_j})$ is a function of $f_i : D_{i,1}^{m_j} \times \ldots \times D_{i,k}^{m_j} \rightarrow N \cup \infty$. The teamwork problem is considered solved if an assignment $A^* = \{d_1^{m_j}, \ldots, d_n^{m_j} | d_i^{m_j} \in D_i^{m_j}\}$ is found such that the global cost, F^{m_j}, is minimized. As DCOP problems have been proven to be NP-complete [7], keeping the search space as small as possible is critical for implementing a working application, especially one capable of running in real-time even as it handles dynamics.

In ADAPT's *pruning* stage, the mediator uses the OptAPO algorithm to search for this teamwork solution. If a solution for $\mathcal{M}_{task}$ cannot be constructed, the mediator agent asks each agent to iteratively select its next possible method until a solution is found. This process can either result with a plan being found, or a NULL plan in failure. Assuming dynamics change the environment, the entire planning process is repeated from the *branching* step.

For example, referring back to Figure 2, a complex task by the name of "Capture the Flag" is to be performed (Stage 1). The complex task may be decomposed according to a set of methods from $\mathcal{M}_{CapturetheFlag}$ which can be used to indicate different ways to plan this task (Stage 2). In this example, the selected method includes the subtask Setup which is an atomic task, while the subtask Capture is a complex subtask which must then continue to be decomposed by additional methods. Stage 3 in Figure 2 depicts the last stage in task network for $G_{CapturetheFlag}$.

Modeling ADAPT's Group Network. In parallel to the task hierarchy, ADAPT also deconstructs teamwork into a group component to model constraints about which agents can perform given tasks. We refer to the hierarchy about the entities combined capabilities as the **group**. Parallel to our task definitions, we decompose the hierarchy as per the **group decomposition** into higher levels of **complex entities** and **atomic entities** which cannot be divided into further levels.

More formally, an *atomic entity* indicates a single agent and its basic capabilities $agent(\vec{v})$ (e.g., $Airplane(Engine, Fuel, \ldots)$). A (high-level) *complex entity* $c(\vec{v})$ indicates a multi-agent group that can be decomposed into subgroups. The decomposition of the *complex entity* into subgroups is done according to group decomposition *method*. Specifically, method m is defined as a 4-tuple: $\langle name(m), entity(m), constr(m), subgroups(m) \rangle$, where $name(m)$ is the name of the *method* and $entity(m)$ is the name of the *complex entity*. The $subgroups(m)$ indicates either atomic or complex entities. Similar to task method the $constr(m)$ indicates set of constraints $\{\phi_1 \ldots \phi_r\}$ that may apply when using the method m. These constraints indicate the required capabilities from agents to be assigned to the $subgroups(m)$ and the different constraints on the group (e.g, maximum group members). A *group network* $d_{group} = [G_{group}, \phi]$ is a collection of groups that have been organized in a hierarchical manner under constraints ϕ. The group network is represented by $G_{group} = (V_{group}, E_{group})$ in which V_{group} is a node set, E_{group} is the edge set, and each node $v \in V_{group}$ contains group information.

The *group planning domain* $\mathcal{D}_{group} = (\mathcal{M}_{group}, \mathcal{E})$ consists of a library $\mathcal{M}_{group}$ of methods and a library $\mathcal{E}$ of atomic entities. A *group planning problem* is defined as a triple containing P_{group}, which is defined as $\langle d_{group}, \mathcal{B}, \mathcal{D}_{group} \rangle$ where d_{group} is the group network to be executed, $\mathcal{B}$ is a set of agents with their concrete capabilities and $\mathcal{D}_{group}$ is the planning domain. A *group plan* assigns agents to the appropriate nodes in the group network based on their capabilities in such a way that all the constraints are satisfied.

Similar to the task planning process, given a group planning problem instance, the planning process again involves the *branching*, *refinement* and *pruning* steps as well. The *branching* step is defined by retrieving the entire set of methods in $\mathcal{M}_{group}$ which may be applied to the *complex entity*. The *refinement* stage then has each local agent check its $constr(m)$ and send what it considers to be its best option to the mediator node within the DCOP solver. In the *pruning* stage the mediator node then checks all received constraints and checks if a solution for $\mathcal{M}_{group}$ can be constructed. If several solutions are possible, it selects the solution with the highest expected utility (or the lowest cost). If no plan can be formed based on these constraints, each agent iteratively selects its next possible method until a solution is found. This process can either result with a plan being found, or a NULL plan in failure. Assuming dynamics change the environment, the entire planning process is repeated from the *branching* step.

For example, referring back to Figure 2, a *complex entity*, "Package" contains all possible group configurations. The *complex entity* may be decomposed according to a set of methods from $\mathcal{M}_{Package}$ which can be used to indicate different group compositions to plan this group organization. In this example, the selected method "FourShip Formation" includes that a group decomposition of two groups of four agents to be formed from the *complex entity* "Package".

3.4   Association to Create Teamwork

It is important to stress that after the *pruning* stages described above in both the task and group networks, the mediator agent must check the consistency, or what we refer to as the *association*, between these two sets of constraints to see what teamwork action should be selected. The association process serves as an intermediary between the DCOP mediators for both the task and group planners within the two abstract networks. The association process may connect one or more vertices of the task and group networks. Thus, the association enables loose coupling between the planners by allowing each of them to modify the corresponding plan independently.

Algorithm 1. *The major steps for dynamic association*
Input: *Initial vertices $v_t \in V_{task}$ and $v_g \in V_{group}$*
Output: *Teamwork plan for current world state W*
01   Create initial links between v_t and v_g;
*02   **while** the task plan is not completed:*
*03   **if** request from task planner is received **then:***
04   Send planning request to group planner
05   Receive the set of the vertices V'_{task} and V'_{group}
*06   **if** Can-Associate (V'_{task}, V'_{group}) **then:***
07   Generate-links (V'_{task}, V'_{group})
08   Apply partial teamwork plan if possible;
*09   **else***
10   Send request for replanning (task or group)
11   Receive perceptions from the world:
*12   **if** the new data causes to conflicts between links*
13   Send request for replanning (task or group)

The major steps of solving a teamwork problem are given in Algorithm 1. The teamwork problem is divided into a two separate networks, d_{task} and d_{group}. An initial network is represented as a single vertex of the highest level task or group. The group planner is responsible to assign the initial agent(s) to the vertex of the initial network and the association process creates a link between these initial networks (line 1). Then the task planner creates a partial plan by expanding its task network as much as possible based on the constraint's world state W currently available to the agents' mediator (line 2). These constraints will typically include data such as the current states of the environment (e.g. weather) or the informational status of the agent (e.g. fuel level or position). During the task planning process, the mediator is responsible to assign an agent (or agents) to subtasks in the task network. The mediator then sends a request with the proposed assignment to the association process so possible group constraints can be checked. The association process connects to the group mediator (line 3) which checks all possible ways a given task can be allocated by expanding its group network under the constraints of the task planner (line 4). This is our implementation of the branching step. The association process is then responsible for linking the new vertices that were added to the group network to the corresponding vertices in the task network (lines 6-7). ADAPT then applies the partial solution on the environment through interleaving planning with execution (line 8). In this way, plans are built incrementally during real-time. Note that steps 6–8 correspond to the *refinement* and *pruning* stages of abstract search techniques. Next, if it is impossible to generate a partial plan because of information obtained from the *refinement* step, the association sends a replanning request to either the task planner or group planner (lines 9-10), and each local agent sends additional constraints and the plan is expanded as described in the former section. Finally, the association algorithm checks if the changes to the available data cause conflicts with the existing assignments (lines 11-13). If any conflict with the existing plan is detected due to the dynamic changes to the environment, the entire process is repeated.

4   Implementation Issues

We have implemented ADAPT within a commercial training and simulation system at Elbit Systems LTD. Elbit specializes in large-scale defense solutions in the areas of aviation, land and naval military systems with ten of thousands of workers worldwide. One division within Elbit has been developing sophisticated simulation systems such that personnel can be trained without the cost and potential risk of using actual equipment. Towards this goal, Elbit has already developed realistic simulators for airplane cockpits, naval stations and ground forces. We propose a new application that builds upon Elbit's existing simulators to simulate more complex team training missions through using ADAPT to help reduce the teamwork model size so it may be effectively implemented.

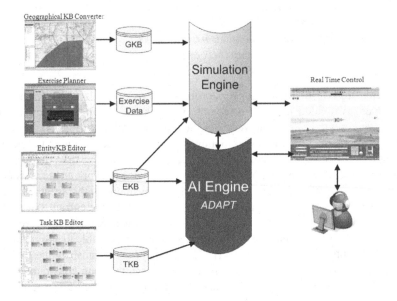

Fig. 3. A high level overview of the simulation system

Towards this goal, we created a working system at Elbit by integrating ADAPT within existing single-workstation simulation systems. Figure 3 depicts a high level description of the system's four major components. Elbit's previously developed simulation engine is still responsible for creating the base simulation environment. As part of this component, a Geographical Knowledge Base (GKB) contains geographical data about the training scenario and an exercise planner (EP) database is created with initial data of the training exercise (e.g., agents types, agents' forces, their initial location, their initial mission). Special to the ADAPT project, a Entity Knowledge Base (EKB) is created containing properties on each agent (e.g. aircraft type, max, min velocity). In addition, it includes various types of entities, including complex entities (e.g., platoon, battalion), and their decomposition methods that describes possible ways of decomposing the groups into subgroups. Thus, this database contains all relevant information about ADAPT's group network. Also, a Task Knowledge Base (TKB) is created containing a set of tasks that the agent can perform and their appropriate methods. Within military applications, this database represents a **doctrine**, or the key task that must be performed, or ADAPT's task network. Agents' decisions are based on the dynamic and static knowledge that the agents gather from the simulation engine as well as the constraint information in the EKB and the TKB. The Real Time (RT) control component enables the human trainer to interact with the simulated arena. Additionally, it provides the human interface to the simulation system.

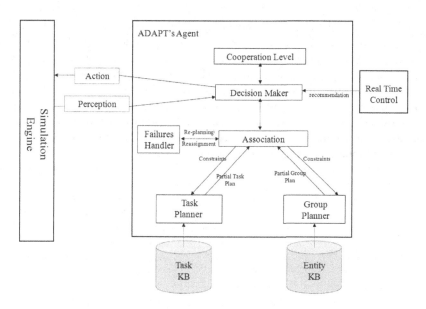

Fig. 4. General description of an ADAPT agent

Figure 4 provides a detailed description of how ADAPT and the algorithms presented in section 3, are integrated as the basis for creating this behavior. Moving from top to bottom within the Figure, each simulated entity is comprised of: a decision making process; a cooperation level; a failure handling process; and two types of planners (connected through the association process). Note that the Task Planner in Figure 2 is used to solve ADAPT's task network, and the Group Planner is used to solve ADAPT's group network. The decision maker is responsible for receiving the agent's perceptions and deciding on the agent's next steps accordingly.

5 ADAPT's Usefulness in a Simulation System

In studying ADAPT's usefulness in Elbit's simulation system, we focused on three key issues: 1. Can content experts easily work with the application to effectively impart their knowledge? 2. Does ADAPT indeed succinctly model teamwork, and how does it compare with other state of the art models? 3. Does the system perform effectively, and can it deal with system dynamics?

Specifically, we applied the general technique in Section 3 regarding the Capture the Flag problem, and applied this technique to scenarios involving fighter jets attempting to destroy an enemy target. Each scenario involved a target that needed to be destroyed, as well as groups of attacking and defending planes. The attacking planes form the blue group and are constructed from bomber and fighter planes (e.g. F16 fighters and Stealth bombers), and the defending group consist exclusively of red fighter planes (F16). The goal of the blue fighters is to disable the enemy's red fighters after which the blue bombers are able to destroy the target. The scenarios focused on different group sizes for the blue and red teams. Dynamics focus on unknown issues including the number of planes on each team that were disabled. In order to create the task and group networks, we consulted with a group of professional fighter pilots whose expert knowledge was then directly encoded. We relied on these experts to provide details about how they would perform theoretical missions. We then successfully encapsulated this information as the Task and Entity databases to form ADAPT's task and group methods. In creating the task's methods we utilized the existing predicates 241 predicates) and the atomic actions (135 actions) of the simulation engine. To demonstrate the above scenario we created 103 task methods and 9 group methods. The number of complex tasks were 79 and the number of complex groups were 4 A pictorial description of one scenario involving seven blue and six red planes is given in Figure 5.

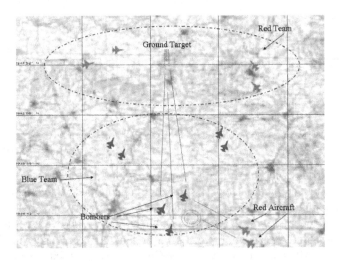

Fig. 5. Attack a ground target - simulation view snapshot

To study the savings in the number of states within ADAPT versus other previous static approaches [6,12,13], we focused on missions with groups of 5, 8 and 12 blue planes which needed to destroy one target on the red team guarded by a fixed number of 5 jets. We recorded the number of task and group nodes required to encode teamwork within ADAPT throughout the task's execution. We then compared how many states would be needed in these same problems by BITE [6]. We decided to compare the number of states needed by BITE as it too divides teamwork into Task and Group hierarchies and thus is the closest comparable model to ADAPT. However, as ADAPT uses abstract search as well, we would expect BITE to use a fixed number of possible task and group permutations, while ADAPT would only store those states actually needed to deal with problem execution. Furthermore, one would expect that the number of states in ADAPT can and will change during task execution, especially as problem dynamics are addressed. To study this point, we assumed 2 blue agents were disabled during task execution.

Table 1. Comparing the number of task and group teamwork states in ADAPT versus BITE teamwork models

	BITE		ADAPT max		ADAPT average	
Number of Agents	Task States	Group States	Task States	Group States	Task States	Group States
5	561	18	44	5	37.1	3.67
8	624	146	53	8	39.65	6.29
12	829	400	68	8	56.86	6.17

As Table 1 demonstrates, we found that ADAPT's use of abstraction yielded an enormous savings in the number of teamwork states needing to be stored. In columns 2 and 3, we present the size of BITE's task and group network within the problems we implemented. Compare these values to the **maximal** size of ADAPT's task and group networks in columns 4 and 5. The average state size is even smaller, and is presented in columns 6 and 7. These very significant savings are because ADAPT only stores task and group network nodes that are found to be relevant based on the current conditions as dictated by *branching*, *refinement*, and *pruning* stages. In contrast, static approaches such as BITE must preplan for all possible contingencies. This difference becomes more pronounced as ADAPT uses real-time planning based on the agent's current state. ADAPT interleaves planning and execution and thus applies partial group and task networks. This is why ADAPT has no need to create complete plans for all contingencies in advance. The net result is that ADAPT's group and task networks are initially defined abstractly and incompletely and built incrementally only as needed, based on the specific environment settings that the agents encounter during task execution based on ADAPT's associative algorithm. Thus, the maximum number of task and group nodes within ADAPT is far larger than its average. This difference can be observed by comparing the differences in the maximal model size and the average size for task states (columns 4 and 6) and group states (columns 5 and 7).

In addition to studying the size of ADAPT's teamwork model, we also evaluated the ease by which ADAPT could be implemented to verify that in fact it did facilitate tractably computing the team's optimal behavior even when faced with dynamics.

Recall that the task and group planners are based on a state-of-the-art DCOP algorithm [7] to solve these constraints. However, as these problems are NP-complete, no DCOP algorithm can yield definite performance guarantees for all theoretical problems. As our production simulation must be able to run without noticeable lags, even when simulating complicated scenarios with high levels of dynamics, we believe that having a smaller teamwork model is critical towards achieving this goal. To evaluate this point, we implemented 3 variations of scenarios involving a team of 8 blue agents attempting to achieve their joint mission, i.e. *attack ground target*, versus a group of 5 red agents. To study the impact of dynamics on ADAPT, three levels of dynamic changes were tested: low-change, middle-change and high-change. In the low-change scenario the red force tried to defend the ground target but could not eliminate any of the blue force members and the group planner did not need to replan due to dynamics. This case represents the baseline of the study, as it allowed the blue force to complete its task with no changes in its force and with little need to change its mission plans. In the middle-change scenario, the red force succeeded in eliminating one or two of the blue fighters from the arena (based on non-deterministic effects), triggering some changes in the group hierarchy of fighters and requiring a moderate degree of mission and group replanning. In the high-change scenario the red force succeeded in eliminating three or more planes from both the fighter and bomber planes, causing more changes in the group hierarchy. This necessitated significant replanning efforts in both the task and group networks.

We measured the total planning time needed by the blue team agents using ADAPT to plan successful joint missions. We defined mission success as the elimination of the ground target and the blue team returning home. To examine ADAPT's performance, we compared the time needed by its problem solvers in 30 trials for each of the 3 different levels of dynamic changes (90 total trials) from sets of 5 minute simulations. We ran the ADAPT simulation on a 2.8 GHz Pentium D computer with 2 GHz of memory.

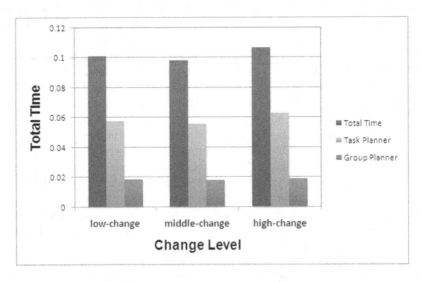

Fig. 6. The influence of dynamics on the total time needed by ADAPT's teamwork planners

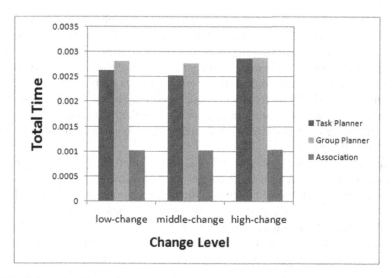

Fig. 7. The influence of dynamics on the average time per simulation cycle needed by ADAPT's teamwork planners

Figure 6 shows the total time utilized by the task planner, group planner and the decision maker to completely plan the joint mission. The total time represents the overall time used by the ADAPT engine to solve the teamwork problem. This time includes the component needed by the task planner, the group planner and the association process. In all cases, the task and group planners operated within fractions of seconds. Similarly, the total time used by ADAPT was under 0.12 seconds in even the most dynamic scenarios.

Figure 7 shows the breakdown of the average time utilized by the task planner, the group planner and the association processsduring the decision maker cycle. In Elbit's simulator, each cycle lasts for 0.1 seconds (10 Hertz). Within this cycle, we measured the length of time required by the task and team planners as well as by the association process. Please note that any given cycle may have had need for planning, but often did not. Similarly, it is possible that there was need for planning within the task planner and not the group planner, or vice versa. For this reason, in Figure 7 is seems that the Group planner required more time per cycle, while in Figure 6 the total time used by the Task planner was greater. While the Task planner in the scenarios we considered had to replan for dynamics less often than the Group planner, once one of these events occurred it took slightly more time on average for the Group planner to generate a new plan. Nonetheless, the average time required by both of these planners was minimal – of the 0.1 seconds per cycle, averages were consistently less than 0.003 or 3% of the cycle length within all scenarios. Thus, we found that ADAPT facilitated real-time teamwork simulation, even in highly dynamic environments.

6   Conclusions

In this paper, we present ADAPT, a framework to decompose teamwork into abstract task and group networks. As ADAPT is the first teamwork model to use abstract search methods, it represents a radical departure over previous models which need to exhaustively describe all possible interactions prior to task completion [6,12,13]. As these models can be of exponential size, the problem of finding the optimal teamwork behavior can be of intractable complexity [11]. In contrast, ADAPT builds teamwork models incrementally during task execution, thus allowing agents to apply *refinement* and *pruning* steps to limit the size of the teamwork model needing to be stored. This fundamental difference not only yields teamwork models that are smaller by several orders of magnitude, but allows agents to quickly find their optimal behavior within this smaller model as described in this paper.

This paper also described how ADAPT was implemented within a challenging military simulation domain. We present results pertaining to how ADAPT formed the basis of a commercial system. We detail the specific task and group networks ADAPT created, how ADAPT can handle domain dynamics, and the time required by ADAPT to identify the optimal team behavior. While we have only implemented ADAPT to date in one series of planning problems, we are confident that this approach can be equally successful in other planning and scheduling problems due to ADAPT's generality.

References

1. Bergmann, R., Wilke, W.: Building and refining abstract planning cases by change of representation language. JAIR 3, 53–118 (1995)
2. Grosz, B.J., Kraus, S.: Collaborative plans for complex group action. AIJ 86(2), 269–357 (1996)
3. Hadad, M., Kraus, S., Gal, Y., Lin, R.: Time reasoning for a collaborative planning agent in a dynamic environment. Annals of Math. and AI 37(4), 331–380 (2003)
4. Hoang, H., Lee-Urban, S., Muoz-Avila, H.: Hierarchical plan representations for encoding strategic game AI. In: AIIDE 2005. AAAI Press (2005)
5. Horling, B., Lesser, V., Vincent, R., Wagner, T., Raja, A., Zhang, S., Decker, K., Garvey, A.: The TAEMS White Paper (January 1999)
6. Kaminka, G.A., Frenkel, I.: Integration of coordination mechanisms in the BITE multi-robot architecture. In: ICRA 2007, pp. 2859–2866 (2007)
7. Mailler, R., Lesser, V.: Using Cooperative Mediation to Solve Distributed Constraint Satisfaction Problems. In: AAMAS 2004, pp. 446–453 (2004)
8. Muñoz-Ávila, H., McFarlane, D.C., Aha, D.W., Breslow, L., Ballas, J.A., Nau, D.S.: Using Guidelines to Constrain Interactive Case-Based HTN Planning. In: Althoff, K.-D., Bergmann, R., Branting, L.K. (eds.) ICCBR 1999. LNCS (LNAI), vol. 1650, pp. 288–302. Springer, Heidelberg (1999)
9. Nau, D., Ghallab, M., Traverso, P.: Automated Planning: Theory & Practice. Morgan Kaufmann Publishers Inc. (2004)
10. Nau, D.S., Au, T.-C., Ilghami, O., Kuter, U., Murdock, J.W., Wu, D., Yaman, F.: Shop2: An HTN planning system. J. Artif. Intell. Res (JAIR) 20, 379–404 (2003)
11. Pynadath, D.V., Tambe, M.: The communicative multiagent team decision problem: Analyzing teamwork theories and models. JAIR 16, 389–423 (2002)
12. Tambe, M.: Toward flexible teamwork. JAIR 7, 83–124 (1997)
13. Tambe, M., Pynadath, D.V., Chauvat, N., Das, A., Kaminka, G.A.: Adaptive agent integration architectures for heterogeneous team members, pp. 301–308 (2000)
14. Toseland, R.W., Rivas, R.F.: An Introduction to Group Work Practice. Allyn and Bacon (2001)

An Architecture for Affective Behaviour Based on the Conservation of Resources

Sabrina Campano, Etienne de Sevin, Vincent Corruble,
and Nicolas Sabouret

Université Pierre et Marie Curie, Laboratoire d'Informatique de Paris 6
4, place Jussieu, 75005 Paris, France
{sabrina.campano,etienne.de-sevin,vincent.corruble,
nicolas.sabouret}@lip6.fr

Abstract. The display of emotions in virtual agents' behaviours is usually recognized as an important element to enhance their believability. Therefore, applications aimed at realistic simulations or entertainment have to consider this aspect. This paper presents a model for autonomous virtual agents that enables them to adopt behaviours that can be perceived by human observers as emotional. Our goal is to obtain believable behaviours for several simulation scenari like a waiting line where conflicts can emerge between agents. The proposed architecture is based on a principle of conservation and acquisition of resources.

Keywords: affect, emotion, virtual agent, simulation, behaviour.

1 Introduction

Modelling believable behaviours is required to design human-like agents that can be used for credible simulations in domains such as security, urban planning, or video games. In particular, emotions have been considered as necessary components for lifelike virtual agents [1]. They are used to display natural gestures or facial expressions, and also to drive the reactions of an agent to its environment or to other agents' behaviours. However, the link between emotions and behaviour remains insufficiently detailed to use them easily for simulation purposes. The difficulties concerning the association of emotions with behaviours have already been mentioned [4]. In this paper we present an architecture without emotion categories, that enables autonomous virtual agents to display behaviours describable with affective terms, i.e. affective behaviours. This model aims at several simulation contexts, as a realistic virtual city, with waiting lines as locations where conflicts can emerge between agents, and where danger like fire or riots can arise in the environment. Besides, we want it to be applicable to basic physical actions like "run away", but also to verbal communication acts between agents like "threaten". Our objective is to define a model able to produce lifelike affective behaviours compatible with these situations and behaviour types.

M. Beer et al. (Eds.): AEGS 2011, LNAI 7471, pp. 183–194, 2012.

Several computational models have been already proposed in this direction. Most of them rely on cognitive appraisal processes, inspired by psychological theories [2], in which a category of emotion is triggered by a specific context, and favours a set of cognitive strategies or behaviours [4,6]. However, neither psychology nor computational science have come to an agreement on a basic set of emotions necessary and sufficient to cover the range of human behaviours : some claim for only two affective variables [7], others for six basic emotions [8], or even for twenty-two emotion variables [4], and their choice is justified by different criteria that all seem valid. This emotional parsing does not solve the issue of behaviour in computational models, since the same emotion is associated with multiple behaviours, and a behaviour can be associated with several emotions.

Considering these observations, and relying on the work of psychologist L.F. Barrett [11], we propose to view emotions as concepts independent from the core architecture that generate behaviours. Our hypothesis is that emotions are categorizations that are useful for reasoning and communication purpose, but are not components at the origin of most affective behaviours. Hence, we aim at an architecture that should be able to generate behaviours describable with a lexicon of emotions by a human observer, without using emotion categories as components of the model. In this paper we present a generic model for affective behaviours based on the theory of conservation of resources formulated by psychologist S.E. Hobfoll [13]. The central tenant of this theory is that humans try to protect their acquired resources, and seek to gain new ones.

After having considered related work, we present the core architecture of our model. The description of resources and how they fulfill an agent's needs will be explained, along with the selection process for resource-oriented behaviours. Finally we discuss the proposed evaluation of our model, based on observation and human rating of the resulting behaviours.

2   Related Work

Common sense lets one think that everyone knows what an emotion is, and that they are identifiable components of our brain system. "Fear", "anger", "joy", "sadness" are words often used in our everyday vocabulary. However, a close look at the litterature shows that emotions are all but *natural kinds* [11], and that there is currently no consensus on the number of existing emotions, neither on their role or consequences on cognition and behaviour [5,15].

J. A. Russell [7] identifies only two types of *core affect* dimensions which are valence, i.e. how good or bad a feeling is, and arousal. He points out that any additional differenciation is based on contextual differences made upon various non-emotional processes. In a study on culture and categorization of emotions, Russell lists emotion words for which there is no equivalence from a language to another, revealing that emotion categories are culture specific, and that even the categories of *fear* and *anger* are not universal [9]. P. Ekman distinguishes among six basic emotions, grounded on the hypothesis of universal facial expressions, and on distinctive patterns of physiological changes during emotional episodes.

These distinctions are still under debate, because even if autonomic specificity has solid support, it is difficult to match these patterns with definite emotion categories [3]. Besides, it is worthy of note that, according to R. W. Levenson, these studies do not prove the existence of emotions, but the existence of a correlation between an autonomic response and an emotional interpretation of this response by the subject.

Psychological theories of emotion are numerous and propose different emotion sets based on different valid criterias. S. S. Tomkins enumerates nine affects and three valences [17], adopting a functional approach of emotions, and Ortony, Clore and Collins (OCC model) account for twenty-six emotions [4]. The OCC model has been widely used in computational science. It aims at predicting which emotion category could be associated to a situation. However, it was not originally intended to the simulation of behaviours. In this model categories are issued from a cognitive appraisal of contextual variables. A difficulty in linking emotions with behaviours is that it is not possible to match a unique behaviour with each emotion. For example fear and anger could both lead to agressive behaviours. Furthermore, Lazarus' original model of cognitive appraisal [2] is centered around the question of how individuals interpret a situation to cope with it, not at how universal emotion categories could trigger behaviours.

Some work show that emotions are culture specific [9], and that they are also individual specific [10]. According to psychologist L.F. Barret, if no set of clearly defined emotion patterns has been found, it is because emotions are concepts instead of being distinct entities in our affective system [11]. Human beings experience emotions the same manner as they experience colors, they use their kwnowledge to label their perceptions with categories. Hence if emotions are concepts, it is possible to parse our affective space with a infinite number of emotion sets.

From this conclusion, a question arises : which components are required for an affective architecture producing behaviours labelled as "emotional" ? Our hypothesis is that the theory of conservation of resources by psychologist S.E. Hobfoll [13] offers an interesting lead. In this theory, the drive for the acquisition and protection of resources is at the core of the dynamics which explains the stress or well-being of an individual, and is even able to predict it. The notion of resource refers to many types of objects : social ones such as self esteem or caring for others, material ones such as a car, or physiological ones such as energy. The main principle is that individuals strive to protect their resources, and to acquire new ones. This model has been developped originally for the domain of psychology, but we think that it can be adapted to the simulation of credible agents. This framework is generic to every computational environment where a description of available resources is provided, along with the behaviours associated with the acquisition or protection of these resources.

3   Proposed Model

In the current section we propose a model for providing autonomous agents with affective behaviours based on the theory of conservation of resources (COR)

[13]. This model considers that behaviours are intended to acquire or protect resources, with well-being as a consequence of these successfull or failed attempts. The COR theory was not conceived in order to be implemented, since the initial goal was to predict or explain an individual's stress level. The original theory focused only on critical resources involved in the psychological health of an individual. We extended it to all other kind of resources, like a rank in a waiting line, because we think that the principles of this theory are generic enough to be used for simulation purposes.

3.1 Principle of the Model

The model is based on the following principles : (a) an agent strives to acquire resources that it desires (b) once a resource is acquired, an agent tries to protect it (c) an agent's well-being depends on its capacity to acquire or protect resources (d) an agent's well-being regulates the tendency for acquisition or protection of resources.

A desired resource triggers acquisition behaviours, and a threatened resource triggers protective behaviours. Each resource type is associated with a particular set of acquisition and protective behaviours. For example an acquisition behaviour for a resource "Rank" in a waiting line is "move forward", and an acquisition behaviour for a resource "Social Interaction" is "talk to somebody". A protective behaviour for an acquired "Rank" is "stay close to next agent", and a protective behaviour for an ongoing "Social Interaction" is "speak loud" in order to be not interrupted by other agents.

The intensity with which a resource is desired by an agent is dynamic and can change over time as a consequence of agents' behaviour or events in the environment. For example a fire will trigger a high need level for security, and a long waiting time in a front of a ticket counter before a train departure will increase the need for the "Train Ticket" resource.

3.2 Architecture

Our agent affective architecture is composed of five affective sets which constitute the basis of the model. The presence of a resource in one of these sets is a key factor influencing an agent's behaviour. A distinction is made between a *type* of resource and an *instance* of resource. For example a "Ticket Counter" type could have several instances in the simulation environment, e.g. ticket counters located on the map and effectively usable by an agent.

Let A the set of agents and R the set of resources in a simulated world S, with $A \subset R$. $\forall i \in A$ at time t, we denote the four following affective sets :

- $N_i(t)$, the resource types that agent i needs;
- $DR_i(t)$, the resource instances desired by agent i;
- $AR_i(t)$, the acquired resource instances for agent i;
- $TR_i(t)$, the threatened resource instances for agent i;
- $LR_i(t)$, the resource instances that agent i has lost.

Let $V \in \mathbb{N}$ be a finite set of values. $\forall r \in DR_i(t)$, we denote $\mu_i^r(t) \in V$ the level of desire that i has for a resource instance r at time t. This value is defined by the need value for the resource type of r denoted as $\mu_i^{type(r)}(t)$. For example if an agent i needs a resource of type "Ticket Counter" in order to buy a resource of type "Train Ticket", its desire for two instances tc_1 and tc_2 with $type(tc_1) = type(tc_2) = TicketCounter$ is given by $\mu_i^{TicketCounter}(t)$.

Affective sets are initialized before the start of a simulation. It is possible to set them empty, to generate random desired resources, or to set them with specific resources in order to run a given scenario. Some needs for resource types like "Food", "Drink", "Social Reputation" or "Safety" should always be added for a realistic behaviour, unless no resource and no behaviour in the simulation environment allow to acquire or protect these resources. An example for a default setting could be : $\forall i \in A$, $N_i(t) = \{Food, Drink\}$, with $\mu_i^{Food}(0) = \mu_i^{Drink}(0) = x$, where x corresponds to a need value. The setting for a scenario where an agent $i \in A$ has to buy a train ticket could be : $N_i(t) = N_i(t) \cup \{TrainTicket\}$, with $\mu_i^{TrainTicket}(0) = f(TrainDepartureTime)$, where the closer one gets to the train departure time, the more the need for a train ticket is increased. The dynamics of this process is detailed in 4.1.

$\forall r \in R$, there is compensation degree $C_i^r \in [-MAX_V, MAX_V]$ which is the level to which a resource r can decrease or increase $\mu_i^{type(r)}(t)$ when it is acquired or lost by i. For example, two instances of type "Food" may not compensate agent's need for food at the same level. Given two instances of type "Food" in the simulation environment which are *hamburger* and *carrot*, it is possible to set $C_i^{hamburger} > C_i^{carrot} > 0$. This means that the instance hamburger decreases μ_i^{Food} with a higher degree than the instance carrot. We assume that a resource instance compensates a unique need type for simplification purpose.

During the simulation, addition and removal of resources in affective sets, as well as behaviour selection, are handled by the Affective Controller. This module takes into account resources available in agent's environment, behaviours executed by other agents, and agent's needs level. Each behaviour selected by this module has the purpose to acquire or protect a resource.

3.3   Behaviour Realization

The set of behaviours that can be performed by an agent i is composed of the acquisition behaviours corresponding to the agent's desired resources, and the protective behaviours corresponding to the agent's threatened resources. Let $B_i(t)$ the set of behaviours that can be performed by an agent i at time t. A behaviour $b \in B_i(t)$ has effects over resources during and after its realization for a given set of agents denoted as $ptnt(b)$. For example, if an agent i performs the "insult" behaviour towards an agent j during a verbal confrontation in a waiting line, the consequences of this behaviour is that j's "Reputation" resource will be threatened, and this will trigger protective behaviours from j in order to protect this resource.

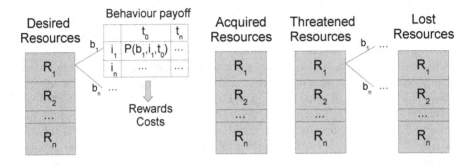

Fig. 1. General Architecture

$\forall b \in B_i(t), \forall j \in ptnt(b)$, we denote :

- $R_b^+(j,t)$: resource instances acquired by j at time t;
- $R_b^\sim(j,t)$: resource instances of j threatened at time t;
- $R_b^o(j,t)$: resource instances of j protected at time t;
- $R_b^-(j,t)$: resource instances lost by j at time t;

These effects represent agents' understanding of the consequences of their behaviours. However these effects are not guaranteed, because the behaviour is not
always successful, the behaviour can be interrupted, or it can trigger unexpected
reactions from other agents. For instance, if an agent j engages a protective behaviour, this may lead to an over aggressive physical reaction from the other
agent. Our model does not consider such long term effects.

To perform behaviour selection, an utility value is computed for each behaviour $b \in B_i(t)$, taking into account the behaviour's effects described above.
This value is computed with the compensation value of a resource upon an
agent's need level : a decrease of a need level is considered as a reward, and an
increase is considered as a cost. Hence the loss of a resource like "Reputation'
is a cost, since it causes an increase in agent's need level for "Reputation" : the
agent no longer possesses the resource satisfying its need. The behaviour selected
by an agent i corresponds to the behaviour with the maximum positive utility
for i.

See figure 1 for an overwiew of the general architecture of the model.

3.4   Personalization

An agent knows its needs, the behaviours it could trigger in its environment on perceived resources, and the a priori effects of these behaviours. It can therefore anticipate immediate gains and costs. These raw values can be modified by individual factors which are agent's well-being, optimism/pessimism, and egoism/altruism. We develop these parameters in section 4.4.

4   Needs, Rewards, and Costs

The need value for a resource type determines the utility value of resource instances in the environment for an agent. If there is a strong need for i to obtain a resource of type "Social Interaction", then the utility of instances of social interactions in the environment will be high for i.

Reminder :

- $N_i(t)$: resource types that an agent i needs at time t;
- $\mu_i^{type}(t) \in V$: need value of i for a *type* at time t;
- $C_i^r \in [-MAX_V; MAX_V]$: compensation degree of r on $\mu_i^{type(r)}(t)$.

4.1   Computation of Needs

Some need values vary spontaneously as a function of time, whereas others vary as a function of environment events. Events are agent's behaviours, or physical events like a fire in an enclosed space, or a storm. Variations as a function of time are called *intrinsic*, and they relate to resource types like "Food" or "Drink". These needs increase over time until a resource satisfying the need is acquired. Need variations as a function of events are called *extrinsic*, and occurs when a resource instance corresponding to a need type is gained or lost. This variation is determined by the compensation value of the resource.

Intrinsic Variation. Let RI a set of resource types whose value need level x depends on an intrisic variation. We define a function $f_{type}(x, I(x))$ which actualizes a need value for a type *type* taking into account $I(x)$, the time interval in hours since the need value has not been actualized. $\forall type \in RI, \forall i \in A$, $\mu_i^{type}(t+1) \leftarrow f_r(\mu_i^{type}(t), I(\mu_i^{type}(t)))$.

Example: given the type "Food" $\in RI$, $f_{Food}(x, I(x))$ is the intrisic variation function associated to this type, and $max(V)$ the maximum value of $V \in \mathbb{N}$.

$$f_{Food}(x, I(x)) = \begin{cases} MAX_V, & \text{if } x = MAX_V \\ x+1, & \text{if } I(x) > \Delta_i \\ x, & \text{otherwise} \end{cases}$$

This means that if $MAX_V = 5$, $\mu_i^{Food}(t) = 3$, $\Delta_i = 4$ (in hours), and five hours has passed since the last modification of this need value, then $\mu_i^{Food}(t+1) = 4$, and $I(\mu_i^{Food}(t+1))$ is initialized with 0. The need for the resource type "Food" has increased from 3 to 4 after 5 hours. It is possible to refine this variation function to make it closer to a biological model, but it is not in the scope of this paper.

Extrinsic Variation. Each resource instance $r \in R$ has a compensation value for an agent i denoted as $C_i^r \in [-MAX_V, MAX_V]$. A positive compensation of r decreases the need of i for the type $type(r)$, and a negative compensation increases it. When an agent acquires a resource r, its need for $type(r)$ is computed as :

$$\mu_i^{type(r)}(t+1) = \mu_i^{type(r)}(t) - C_i^r \tag{1}$$

with $\mu_i^{type(r)}(t+1)$ bounded by 0 and MAX_V.

Example: let i be an agent for which $\mu_i^{Reputation}(t) = 4$, and $MAX_V = 5$, that means i is very interested in acquiring reputation. We define a resource instance r with $type(r) = Reputation$, and $C_i^r = 3$. If r is acquired by i, then $\mu_i^{Reputation}(t+1) = \mu_i^{Reputation}(t) - C_i^r = 4 - 3 = 1$. The agent's need for type "Reputation" has decreased, i is gives less importance to reputation.

For each resource type, each agent has a default need level μDef_i^{type}. When an agent looses a resource instance r, if no other resource of $type(r)$ exists in agent's acquired resources $AR_i(t)$, then $\mu_i^{type(r)}(t)$ is set to its default level μDef_i^{type}. If other resources of $type(r)$ exist in $AR_i(t)$, then $\mu_i^{type(r)}(t)$ is computed with the resource of this type that has the maximum compensation value.

4.2   Activation of Behaviours

Each resource r is associated with a set of behaviours which contains acquisition or protective behaviours. If r is desired, then acquisition behaviours for r are activated, and if r is threatened, then protective behaviours for r are activated. A behaviour originally aimed at acquiring a resource can also threatens other agents'resources, since behaviours have multiple effects. Let $B_i(t)$ the set of behaviours that can be performed by an agent i at time t, B_r^+ the set of acquisition behaviours for r, and B_r^o the set of protective behaviours for r. The behaviours activated for an agent i at time t is computed as :

$$B_i(t) = \left(\bigcup_{r \in DR_i(t)} B_r^+ \right) \cup \left(\bigcup_{r \in TR_i(t)} B_r^o \right) \tag{2}$$

Activated behaviours are concurrent and selected by an utility value computed for each behaviour (see 4.5).

4.3   Computation of Behaviour's Payoff

The execution of a behaviour may change the state of a resource for an agent. A resource can be desired, acquired, threatened, or lost. If a resource instance that can decrease an agent's need type is acquired or protected for this agent towards a behaviour b, it entails a reward that is a positive value. On the contrary, if such a resource is threatened or lost for this agent, it entails a cost that is a negative value. These values computed before the possible execution of a behaviour b represent the impact of this behaviour on an agent's need level. The predicted payoff at time $t+1$ of a behaviour b for an agent j allows us to proceed behaviour selection (explained in section 4.5). It is computed as :

$$
P(b,j,t+1) = \sum_{r \in R_b^+(j) \cup R_b^o(j)} (1 + \mu_j^{type(r)}(t)) * C_j^r
$$
$$
- \sum_{r \in R_b^-(j) \cup R_b^\sim(j)} (1 + \mu_j^{type(r)}(t)) * C_j^r
\tag{3}
$$

4.4   Individual Parameters Influencing Behaviours' Payoff

Some parameters influence rewards and costs perceived by an agent, either dynamically, or as a fixed characteristic of the agent. *Well-being* parameter is directly linked to the architecture of conservation of resources, while *optimism/pessism* and *altruism/egoism* are parameters that has been introduced to make agents act differently in the same situation.

Well-Being. The well-being of an agent acts as a sensor that guides an agent towards appropriate behaviours to readjust the state of its affectives sets. For example an agent that has endured too many losses has a low well-being that pushes it to acquire new resources. That means that if an agent has lost an important resource as its job, it may try to readjust its well-being with easy resource acquisitions like resource instances of "Food" type.

The state of well-being of an agent $\alpha_i^{WB}(t) \in [0,1]$ influences its sensitivity to reward. Concretely, on our model, a value $\alpha_i^{WB}(t)$ is computed based on $LR_i(t)$, $DR_i(t)$, $TR_i(t)$, $AR_i(t)$, and the more this value is low, the more it increases the positive payoffs that i anticipate for itself before executing a behaviour. The computation of $\alpha_i^{WB}(t)$ is not detailed in this paper. The predicted payoff $P_i(b,i,t+1)$ of an agent i from its own point of view for behaviour b executable at time $t+1$ taking into account well-being is given by equation 4.

$$
P_i(b,i,t+1) = \begin{cases} P_i(b,i,t+1) * (1 + (1 - \alpha_i^{WB}(t))), & \text{if } P_i(b,i,t+1) > 0 \\ P_i(b,i,t+1), & \text{otherwise} \end{cases}
\tag{4}
$$

Optimism and Pessimism. An optimistic agent gives more importance to rewards, and a pessimistic agent gives more importance to costs. Let i be an agent,

$\alpha_i^{rew} \in [0,1]$ a variable representing the importance of rewards, and $\alpha_i^{cos} \in [0,1]$ a variable representing the importance of costs. The predicted payoff $P_i(b,j,t+1)$ of an agent j from i's point of view for behaviour b executable at time $t+1$ taking into account optimism and pessimism is given by equation 5.

$$P_i(b,j,t+1) = \begin{cases} P_i(b,j,t+1) * (1 + \alpha_i^{rew}), & \text{if } P_i(b,j,t+1) > 0 \\ P_i(b,j,t+1) * (1 + \alpha_i^{cos}), & \text{if } P_i(b,j,t+1) < 0 \end{cases} \quad (5)$$

Egoism and Altruism. Egoistic agents give more importance to their own payoff, and altruistic agents give more importance to other agents' payoff. Let $\alpha_i^{alt} \in [0,1]$ be the altruistic tendency of an agent, and $\alpha_i^{ego} \in [0,1]$ be the egoistic tendency of an agent. For a given behaviour $b \in B_i(t)$ executable by an agent i at time t, the behaviour's payoff foreach agent j concerned by the behaviour, as i considers it, is modified as below :

$$P_i(b,j,t+1) = \begin{cases} P_i(b,j,t+1) * \alpha_i^{alt}, & \text{if } j \neq i \\ P_i(b,j,t+1) * \alpha_i^{ego}, & \text{else} \end{cases} \quad (6)$$

4.5   Behaviour Selection

The behaviour selection consists in selecting a behaviour with the maximum positive utility among all activated behaviours of an agent i. Let $ptnt(b)$ be the set of agents concerned by the effects of a behaviour b. Given $B_i(t)$ the set of activated behaviours for agent i at time t, $\forall b \in B_i(t)$, $\forall j \in ptnt(b)$, $P_i(b,j,t+1)$ is the payoff that j will receive from behaviour b at $t+1$ according to i's point of view. Behaviours' utility for agent i at time t are computed as :

$$\forall b \in B_i(t), U_i(b,t) = \sum_{j \in ptnt(b)} P_i(b,j,t+1) \quad (7)$$

The selected behaviour $b_i^*(t)$ is :

$$b_i^*(t) = \max_{b \in B_i(t)} \{b : U_i(b,t) > 0\} \quad (8)$$

If no behaviour with a positive utility value exists, then no behaviour is executed. Since our model does not include planification, we assume that it is better for an agent to do nothing than to execute a behaviour which is costly, even if this behaviour could prevent in the future behaviours executed by other agents with worse consequences. If there are more than one behaviour with a maximum positive utility, a behaviour is randomly chosen among them.

5   Example

We consider a scenario where agents have to buy train tickets provided by ticket counters in the simulation environment. The provided resources are "Ticket Counters", "Ranks" in the waiting line, and each agent has a "Reputation" resource.

When agents are in a waiting line, they each possess a "Rank" corresponding to their position in the waiting line. If an agent i starts to pass another agent j in the waiting line, the resource "Rank" of j is threatened. Then j may choose to execute a protective behaviour in order to protect its resource "Rank", like telling b to go away, which threatens the "Reputation" resource of i. If the "Reputation" resource of i is more valuable than the "Rank" it tries to acquire, then i goes back. The acquisition of ranks in waiting lines in real life, as well as many other resources, are regulated by FIFO rule (First In, First Out)[12]. When an agent i ignores this rule so as to gain ranks, it is costly for all agents between the current and previous rank of i. If agent's i need for a train ticket is very strong and if b is egoistic, it gives a great importance to the reward brought by the acquisition of a better "Rank", and a small importance to the "Ranks" lost for other agents. So i can choose the behaviour of ignoring waiting line's rule.

6   Discussion and Future Work

We presented in this paper an architecture aimed at providing virtual agents with affective behaviours in various environments as urban simulation. Our hypothesis is that simulating behaviours that can be labelled as "emotional" do not necessarily requires an architecture grounded on emotion categories. Behaviours in a waiting line are assumed to be driven by emotions [14], and a waiting line is also considered as a small social system regulated by the principles of property [12]. Our hypothesis is that the processes of resource acquisition and protection can be used as the basis of affective behaviours. Actually, this idea could be applied to various contexts : in case we run from a fire, we try to protect our primary resource which is our health, in case we become friends with someone, it is because we find useful resources in this friendship (see the "social exchange theory" by Thibaut and Kelley [16]), and so on. We believe that the architecture presented in this paper can account for several principles in social science and psychology theory, and is adaptable to various simulation scenari.

On another hand, an emotion vocabulary is used in human langage, and it would be useful to derive emotion concepts from our architecture in order that agents can use them to communicate. Thus, we plan to work on how the model of conservation of resources can be associated with such emotion concepts for verbal communication. To do so, we could derive emotion categories from the current state of an agent's affective sets and behaviours, following the approach of cognitive evaluation already used in the OCC model [4]. For instance, if an agent's resources are threatened, and the agent cannot engage in a behaviour to protect them, then this agent could be labelled as *afraid*. It could then verbally communicate to other agents that it is *afraid*.

The model has been implemented and the evaluation of the model is part of another work. Our evaluation relies on rating the credibility of agents' behaviours based on simulation video clips. We implemented two different scenarii (one involving social communication, one considering only individual actions) and we asked human observers to describe the scenes and to rate both the believability and the emotional aspect of the agents' behaviours. Our first results show that human observers identify affective behaviours and that the model positively influences both realism and emotion perception. However, further studies need to be conducted. In particular, we would like to compare the agents' behaviours in the simulation with behaviours described in psychological and sociological studies.

Finally once the evaluation protocol is completed, we plan to extend our model to groups and crowds, in order to use it for simulations with a large amount of agents.

References

1. Bates, J.: The role of emotion in believable agents. Communications of the ACM 37, 122–125 (1994)
2. Lazarus, R.S., Folkman, S.: Stress, Appraisal and Coping. Springer, New York (1984)
3. Levenson, R.W.: Autonomic specificity and emotion. In: Davidson, R.J., Scherer, K.R., Goldsmith, H.H. (eds.) Handbook of Affective Sciences, pp. 212–224. Oxford University Press, New York (2003)
4. Ortony, A., Clore, G.L., Collins, A.: The cognitive structure of emotions. Cambridge University Press, New York (1988)
5. Ortony, A., Turner, T.J.: What's basic about basic emotions? Psychological Review 97, 315–331 (1992)
6. Elliott, C.: The affective reasoner: A process model of emotions in a multi-agent system. Northwestern University Institute for the Learning Sciences, Chicago (1992)
7. Russell, J.A.: Core affect and the psychological construction of emotion. Psychol Rev. 110(1), 145–172 (2003)
8. Ekman, P.: Basic Emotions. In: Dalgleish, T., Power, T. (eds.) The Handbook of Cognition and Emotion, pp. 45–60. John Wiley & Sons, Ltd., Sussex (1999)
9. Russell, J.A.: Culture and the categorization of emotions. Psychological Bulletin 110(3), 426–450 (1991)
10. Barrett, L.F., Gross, J., Christensen, T.C., Benvenuto, M.: Knowing what you're feeling and knowing what to do about it: Mapping the relation between emotion differentiation and emotion regulation. Cognition & Emotion 15(6), 713–724 (2001)
11. Barrett, L.F.: Solving the emotion paradox: Categorization and the experience of emotion. Personality and Social Psychology Review 10, 20–46 (2006)
12. Gray, K.: The legal order of the queue. University of Cambridge (2007) (unpublished paper)
13. Hobfoll, S.E.: Conservation of resources: A new attempt at conceptualizing stress. American Psychologist 44(3), 513–524 (1989)
14. Norman, D.A.: The Psychology of Waiting Lines (2008)
15. Scherer, K.R.: Appraisal theory. In: Dalgleish, T., Power, M. (eds.) Handbook of Cognition and Emotion, pp. 637–663. Wiley, Chichester (1999)
16. Thibaut, J.W., Kelley, H.H.: The social psychology of groups. Wiley, New York (1959)
17. Tomkins, S.S.: Affect Imagery Consciousness: The Complete Edition, vol. 1-4. Springer (2008)

Author Index